On the Chilean Social Explosion

On the Chilean Social Explosion uses the methods of literary, cultural, and subaltern studies to examine what cultural foundations and practices gave rise to this political uprising.

On 18 October 2019, Chile exploded into a series of nationwide protests that placed the socio-political order of neoliberalism, settler colonialism, and patriarchy under structural crisis. In March 2020, however, the quarantining measures taken in response to the COVID-19 pandemic put this grassroots rebellion on pause. The author explores and analyzes these five months which have come to be known as the Chilean social explosion [*estallido social*].

This book will be of value to researchers of cultural studies, cultural and radical politics, resistance and protest, subaltern studies, and Chilean and Latin American politics. It will also interest a broader audience concerned with social movements, grassroots organizing, and expressions of dissent across the world.

Maxwell Woods is Assistant Professor in the Department of Literature in the Faculty of Liberal Arts at Universidad Adolfo Ibáñez, Chile.

Routledge Studies in Radical History and Politics

Series editors: Thomas Linehan, ***University of Ulster, and*** **John Roberts,** ***Brunel University***

The series *Routledge Studies in Radical History and Politics* has two areas of interest. Firstly, this series aims to publish books which focus on the history of movements of the radical left. 'Movement of the radical left' is here interpreted in its broadest sense as encompassing those past movements for radical change which operated in the mainstream political arena as with political parties, and past movements for change which operated more outside the mainstream as with millenarian movements, anarchist groups, utopian socialist communities, and trade unions. Secondly, this series aims to publish books which focus on more contemporary expressions of radical left-wing politics. Recent years have been witness to the emergence of a multitude of new radical movements adept at getting their voices in the public sphere. From those participating in the Arab Spring, the Occupy movement, community unionism, social media forums, independent media outlets, local voluntary organisations campaigning for progressive change, and so on, it seems to be the case that innovative networks of radicalism are being constructed in civil society that operate in different public forms.

The series very much welcomes titles with a British focus, but is not limited to any particular national context or region. The series will encourage scholars who contribute to this series to draw on perspectives and insights from other disciplines.

On the Chilean Social Explosion
Maxwell Woods

I Saw Democracy Murdered
The Memoir of Sam Russell, Journalist
Colin Chambers and Sam Russell

For more information about this series, please visit www.routledge.com/Routledge-Studies-in-Radical-History-and-Politics/book-series/RSRHP

On the Chilean Social Explosion

Maxwell Woods

Routledge
Taylor & Francis Group
LONDON AND NEW YORK

First published 2022
by Routledge
4 Park Square, Milton Park, Abingdon, Oxon OX14 4RN

and by Routledge
605 Third Avenue, New York, NY 10158

Routledge is an imprint of the Taylor & Francis Group, an informa business

British Library Cataloguing-in-Publication Data
A catalogue record for this book is available from the British Library

Library of Congress Cataloging-in-Publication Data
Names: Woods, Maxwell, author. Title: On the Chilean social explosion / Maxwell Woods.
Description: Abingdon, Oxon ; New York, NY : Routledge, 2022. | Series: Routledge studies in radical history and politics | Includes bibliographical references and index.
Identifiers: LCCN 2021049708 (print) | LCCN 2021049709 (ebook) | ISBN 9781032123547 (hardback) | ISBN 9781032124520 (paperback) | ISBN 9781003224594 (ebook)
Subjects: LCSH: Protest movements—Chile—History—21st century. | Social movements—Chile—History—21st century. | Demonstrations—Chile—History—21st century. | Chile—Social conditions—21st century.
Classification: LCC HM883 .W66 2022 (print) | LCC HM883 (ebook) | DDC 303.48/40983—dc23/eng/20211222
LC record available at https://lccn.loc.gov/2021049708
LC ebook record available at https://lccn.loc.gov/2021049709

ISBN: 978-1-032-12354-7 (hbk)
ISBN: 978-1-032-12452-0 (pbk)
ISBN: 978-1-003-22459-4 (ebk)

DOI: 10.4324/9781003224594

Typeset in Times New Roman
by codeMantra

For Leslie.

For all those who faced and face political persecution in Chile as a result of the social explosion.

Contents

Acknowledgments

First and foremost, I would like to thank each and every person with whom I interacted in the streets, in assemblies and *cabildos*, in artistic interventions, in marches, and at *ollas comunes*. Without you, without our dialogues, without our affective connections—even if ephemeral—this book does not exist. I insist that this book is a co-generated work among the relations we developed during 2019–2020. I'd also like to thank friends who marched alongside me and gave me places to sleep, including (but not limited to) Bruno Marambio, Carolina Mulvey, Francisco Rojas, and Esteban Barraza. Additionally, thanks go to Catalina Yazigi with whom I had conversations about the social explosion while in Leipzig. I would like to specifically thank all participants of the Coordinadora Acción Cultural Valparaíso (CAC). It was that space that largely transformed my thinking about what politics could be and what cultural work could do in moments of uprisings. This book is rooted in our conversations, interventions, actions, and organizing. All praise for this work should be given to the CAC and social explosion participants, all faults are entirely my own. Unless otherwise stated or cited, all translations in this book are done by myself.

Danny Reveco, the FáBRiKA workshop, and Manuel Sanfuentes were instrumental in the realization of this work, permitting the reproduction of their works within its pages. Thank you for your support, response, and conversation.

Early research for chapters one and two was initially presented at the Center for Twenty-First-Century Studies at the University of Wisconsin, Milwaukee in February 2020. My deepest gratitude goes to Maureen Ryan and Richard Grusin for organizing that talk. I would also like to thank everyone who participated in the wonderful dialogues during that visit. Their insight was immensely helpful in the development of ideas about this work.

I'd also like to acknowledge the Institute for Regional Geography (IfL), in Leipzig, Germany. In January 2020, I had the honor of being a visiting fellow as part of the PUTSPACE project ("Public transport as public space in European cities: Narrating, experiencing, contesting") which I carried out at the Institute. It is during that time that I developed chapter two of this book and received initial feedback on this research. Beyond the immediate aid provided by this research stay, however, the very framing of

PUTSPACE—that public transport serves as a public space—was the theoretical foundation of chapter two. Without the existence of PUTSPACE, that chapter would not have come to be. Special appreciation is due especially to Laura Kemmer (my co-fellow during my time in Leipzig), Tonio Weicker, and Wladimir Sgibnev. Our conversations and writing over the course of January 2020 and afterwards have been formative to my thinking. Further thanks is due to the Institute for Regional Geography in general, to whom I presented this early research and whose feedback ended up forming the basis for chapter six, as well as the PUTSPACE project in general, to whom I also presented this early research. Thanks is also owed to Jason Finch who introduced me to the PUTSPACE project. Without your advice, this intellectual connection would have been impossible.

Individual thanks must be given to Jessica Budds and Magalí Rabasa who were kind enough to have shared research with me and tolerated email correspondence from a stranger. Their work on water justice in Chile and autonomous small presses proved vital for the thinking of this book.

The faculty, staff, and administration of Universidad Adolfo Ibáñez was central in the development of *On the Chilean Social Explosion*. Without their institutional and intellectual support, the daunting task of putting together this text would have been impossible. It is difficult to express the benefits of this institutional home for the overall advancement of my research.

Everyone at Routledge has been crucial to the publication of *On the Chilean Social Explosion*. Specific thanks is owed to Craig Fowlie and Hannah Rich of Routledge as well as John Roberts and Thomas Linehan, the editors of the *Routledge Studies in Radical History and Politics* book series. Without their support, trust, criticism, and encouragement, this book would not have come to fruition.

The thinking of this book has appeared in other venues. In addition to the lectures given at the Center for Twenty-First-Century Studies and as a PUTSPACE visiting fellow, I published an analysis of another one of CAC's interventions with *Cultural Geographies* ("Narrative, the Chilean Social Explosion, and Affective Geography: On the Catharsis of the 'Artistic Candlelight Vigil' of Valparaíso," *Cultural Geographies,* forthcoming) and a book review of Magalí Rabasa's monograph with *A Contracorriente* ("Review of *The Book in Movement: Autonomous Politics and the Lettered City Underground* by Magalí Rabasa," *A Contracorriente* 19, no. 1: 260–269). Although the research in *On the Chilean Social Explosion* is unique, the thinking developed in that writing is reflected at various points in this text (especially the introduction and chapter three). Some of the facts I gathered about water use in Chile mentioned in chapter three were used to support the video, "¿Y a dónde se fue la lluvia?", by CAC. All translations are mine unless mentioned otherwise in the bibliography, in the text itself, or in a footnote.

Lastly, I would like to thank my patient and loving partner, Leslie Alfaro. During the social explosion we were separated as she was living in the United States while I was in Chile. Our long-distance conversations about what I was witnessing are what motivated me to continue this draining work. Your kindness, fortitude, and patience are at the heart of this book.

Introduction
On Autonomy

For five months, the neoliberal, patriarchal, and settler-colonial social order of the Chilean State was under structural crisis. For five months, the nation's oppressed—women sick of gender violence and inequality, Indigenous communities demanding land repatriation and recognition as autonomous peoples, the laboring classes pressing for a dignified living, sexual dissidents openly claiming space in the public sphere, and so on—were struggling to reconstitute Chilean society based on *their* terms, on *their* ways of living in common. For five months, the world turned upside down seemed to be setting itself right again in this narrow strip of land on the Pacific Coast of Latin America. These five months—from 18 October 2019 until mid-March 2020—are what have come to be known as the Chilean social explosion [*estallido social*].

To describe the social explosion in broad strokes[1]: in early October 2019 the Chilean government raised the Santiago subway fare 30 Chilean pesos (approximately four cents USD). What often goes unmentioned, however, was that there had been multiple fare hikes in the previous years and that the fare had risen about 80 percent since 2007 (Garrido 2019). In response, students organized massive collective subway fare evasions—holding open exit doors, hopping turnstiles, and so on—transforming public transport into a public space of insurrection. During the week of October 14, the evasions spread across the entirety of the metropolitan area and students eventually began occupying entire subway stations, destroying turnstiles, and confronting police forces deployed to repress the movement. On October 18, State repression escalated when the police shot a student with pellet, leading to protestors increasing their confrontations with police forces and damaging various subway stations across the city.[2] That night, the Chilean president, Sebastián Piñera, declared a state of emergency in Santiago. This date, October 18, is frequently cited as the official start of the social explosion.

The following day, October 19, protests exploded not just in the streets of Santiago but across the entire nation of Chile. By that night Piñera had declared states of emergency in various regions across the country, deployed the military in the streets of Chile to defend 'public order,' and instituted a government-mandated curfew which would stay in place until October 28.

DOI: 10.4324/9781003224594-1

Additionally, the Chilean social explosion had quickly expanded beyond its initial protest of the subway fare hike in order to challenge the very social, political, and economic foundations of the nation. By November 15, the Chilean government had agreed to hold a referendum in April 2020 (later postponed to 25 October 2020 due to the COVID-19 pandemic) to determine if Chile would write an entirely new constitution. In less than a month, protestors moved from critiquing a 4-cent raise in subway fare to placing the very constitution of the nation in question.

This grassroots rebellion, however, was put on pause in mid-March 2020 due to the nationwide quarantining measures taken in response to the COVID-19 pandemic. As such, we are now in a position to retrospectively examine this phenomenon. Taking this as its starting point, this book seeks to answer the following question: What were the cultural foundations and practices of the social explosion? In response, this book outlines a basic thesis in regard to this bursting forth of popular political mobilization: the social explosion represents the subaltern of Chile attempting to reconstitute Chilean society in a way that recognizes as legitimate and autonomous their modes of coordinating social relations. As such, I suggest, these five months of 2019–2020 were not only about leveraging for material gains (though this is without a doubt an element of the protests), but about the subaltern seeking to be recognized as *institutionally validated agents*[3] within Chilean society. The social explosion is not only about increasing the minimum wage, reforming the pension system, reconfiguring the health care system, and so on, but also about who has the right to determine said political questions. In this way, the social explosion is just as much a *cultural* struggle as it is a *political* struggle.

This book is therefore highly skeptical of many emerging narratives in which the social explosion has been explained exclusively in terms of discontent rooted in economic inequality created under a neoliberal governance structure that was introduced during the Chilean dictatorship and then continued in the post-dictatorship era. In this narrative, the question posed by the social explosion is one of policy and economics. *On the Chilean Social Explosion* argues that this is not the whole story: central to the social explosion is a cultural struggle over which voices hold agency within Chile. Indeed, the common narrative focused on economic inequality and neoliberal policy often misses that feminist organizing against patriarchal violence as well as Indigenous struggles for decolonization and the recognition of plurinationality were two key driving forces of social mobilizations. The social explosion is not only about the economic inequality and ineffective policy of neoliberalism (though it is about this too!); it is also a challenge to hegemonic Chilean sociality founded on modernity, coloniality, patriarchy, and environmental exploitation.

This book argues that the Chilean social explosion is addressing questions of culture, which can be operationally defined as "the actual, grounded terrain of practices, representations, languages and customs of any specific historical society" (Hall 1986: 26). In more critical terms, as Edward Said (1983) argues, culture is an

> instrument for identifying, selecting, and affirming certain 'good' things, forms, practices, or ideas over others and in so doing culture transmits, diffuses, partitions, teaches, presents, propagates, persuades, and above all it creates and recreates itself as specialized apparatus for doing all those things.
>
> (176)

Moreover, this affirmative side of culture—the 'good' practices, representations, languages, and customs of a given community—implies its negative: the categorization of 'other' practices, representations, languages, and customs in terms of "anarchy, disorder, irrationality, inferiority, bad taste, and immorality" (11). A culture is a self-reproducing "system of evaluations" (11) that determines whose voice is legitimate and whose voice represents 'anarchy, disorder, irrationality, inferiority, bad taste, and immorality.'

In this way, each and every culture, *independent of its position with regard to specific legislation or social issues*, is inherently political and each and every politics is inherently cultural insofar as a culture empowers certain voices as legitimate—and therefore trusted to determine the ordering of social relations—and disempowers others as illegitimate. Through a critical reading of Matthew Arnold, Said (1983) concludes by identifying "a triumphant culture with the State, insofar as culture is man's best self and the State its realization in material reality. Thus the power of culture is potentially nothing less than the power of the State" (10). In short, "To be for and in culture is to be in and for a State in a compellingly loyal way" (11). A culture legitimizes the voices of a select few. When that culture has "extend[ed] its sway" (10) over a given territory, the State becomes its institutional manifestation and is tasked with disciplining all subjects within that territory according to its script, a *political* domination that is based on "setting the valorized culture over" all others (12). The political function of culture is how it enables the maintenance of State control in the hands of those select few (the elite) while denying the participation of others as illegitimate (the subaltern).

This distinction between elite and subaltern, between those who do and do not have an institutionally validated voice, this book argues, lies at the core of the social explosion's discontent. In this sense, the Chilean social explosion is a cultural struggle by the subaltern to creatively activate new modes of expression in order to be heard within a social landscape constructed for the purposes of denying them a voice. If the subaltern cannot speak because a neoliberal, patriarchal, and modernist cultural hegemony reigns in Chile in which dominant elites cannot hear what the subaltern says (Rivera Cusicanqui 2010b: 67–68; Spivak 1999), then the social explosion represents the subaltern's reconfiguration of cultural expression in a manner that forces the elite to hear that subaltern. More precisely, *On the*

Chilean Social Explosion argues that the social explosion represents the attempt to generate a cultural environment in which no subject (collective or individual) is elite or subaltern. The challenge posed by the social explosion is the following: What is culture when it is no longer a self-reproducing system of evaluations serving to enforce the power of the State, and what is its attendant political form?

This introduction serves to introduce the theoretical framework of this book as well as connect the Chilean social explosion to other radical social movements. Primarily, I introduce the concept of the *politics of autonomy* and the theoretical stakes at the heart of discussions of radical autonomous movements. This serves two ends. First, it will be the consistent argument of this book that the social explosion represents the attempt to resolve various dilemmas of the politics of autonomy. More precisely, this book is concerned with the role of cultural workers in radical autonomous social movements. Second, this introduction will functionally connect the social explosion to other autonomous movements like the 2001 Argentinian protests, Occupy, the Bolivian water and gas wars, and so on. I then close with an outline of the book and a discussion of my methodology.

Beyond the Pink Wave: Or, Towards a Critical Autonomy

What I am pointing to is that the social explosion requires us to think through the relationship between culture and what has been called *the politics of autonomy*. The reader will note that *On the Chilean Social Explosion* avoids a detailed discussion of what has constituted a central focus of much postmillennial discussion of radical politics in Latin America: the so-called Pink Tide, a series of leftist governments across the continent that introduced sweeping progressive reforms in the 2000s and early 2010s. Although the most famous representatives of this political trend were the farther left Hugo Chávez in Venezuela, Lula da Silva in Brazil, and Evo Morales in Bolivia, a 'softer' Pink Tide affected other countries including Chile with the presidencies of Michelle Bachelet and Ricardo Lagos. By the mid-2010s, it appeared that this wave was receding with a new right-wing group of politicians rising into power including Jair Bolsonaro in Brazil and Mauricio Macri in Argentina. Latin America was ostensibly participating in what Ivan Krastev and Stephen Holmes (2019) have called a right-wing "worldwide anti-liberal revolt" (13).

Many have subsequently asked why the Pink Tide apparently failed, if failure is defined as the capacity to maintain a long-lasting presence in positions of State power. On the right, a general narrative has focused on how the left was unable to fulfill their promises, leading to broad disillusionment among their constituency. According to this narrative, the mission of the Pink Tide was a fantasy that lacked any pragmatic means of implementation. On the left, many pointed out that the Pink Tide was fundamentally structured on a contradiction: political movements based on grassroots mobilizations were constrained by the limits of capitalism, thereby forcing them to make disappointing concessions to various elites. As George Ciccariello-Maher (2020) succinctly summarizes, the Pink Tide did not seek to "confront global capital as individual nations," but instead sought "regional diplomatic, economic, and lending alliances to help buffer capitalism's tides" (353). The issue is not that the left went too far, it's that they did not go far enough. When Tomás Moulian in 1997 defined revolution as "the destruction of State apparatuses, through which [a political group's enemies had] established their law, their order, their mode of coercion" (159), he also noted that part of the reason why Salvador Allende's 1970s socialist government in Chile failed was that they simply tried to occupy the already existing State without trying to transform it for their needs. It appears as though the Pink Tide suffered the same fate. As Moulian might put it, they had not prepared themselves for a revolution, "they had prepared themselves to negotiate" (160).

Macarena Gómez-Barris (2018) has put forward an alternative thesis: in the midst of and prior to the Pink Tide, artists and activists throughout the Americas were "reinvent[ing] politics by reaching deeper into historical and structural inequalities and by imagining beyond the traditional affairs of the state" (2). She demonstrates, for instance, that various leftist artists and activists in the 2010s were already highly critical of Pink Tide governments and were seeking new ways of envisioning liberatory social relations that went beyond the "confining, normative, and often stifling politics of the nation-state" (2). Gómez-Barris even has a particular focus on art, music, literature, and cinema in Chile, examining how artists like Ana Tijoux—"a mestiza rapper and singer" who became "the sound of the [2011] student movement" (22) and whose single, "Cacerolazo," went viral during the 2019–2020 social explosion—Cecilia Vicuña, and Pedro Lemebel (whose work I will discuss in Chapter 2) were generating a socio-cultural paradigm that could enable a novel autonomous politics, a paradigm, I argue in *On the Chilean Social Explosion*, that formed the foundation for Chilean mobilizations during 2019–2020. A new autonomous cultural-political imaginary was growing in Chile in the new millennium.

This dedication to autonomy should be unsurprising especially in the case of Chile. Although much radical historiography has focused on the rise of the Salvador Allende socialist administration in the 1960s and early 1970s, new research has focused on the significance of anarchist organizing in the early twentieth century. According to these histories, the implementation of capitalist social relations during the nineteenth century led to the formation of the proletariat as a collective subject. Anarchists in the late nineteenth century and early twentieth century autonomously organized this working class outside the confines of the State in order to directly confront capitalists and to imagine new forms of coordinating social relations from the bottom-up. Within this revised history, the rise of socialism was largely a suppressive measure that sought to incorporate into the State, and thereby neutralize, the proletariat without granting power directly to their novel autonomous political bodies. Indeed, it was socialist-leaning administrations that largely enforced laws that prohibited non-State-sanctioned union activity. While the dichotomy between anarchism and socialism/communism has been rightfully critiqued in theorizations of autonomous politics (Albertani 2011; Modonesi 2011), the history of anarchy within Chile demonstrates two things. First, there is a long history of radical autonomous political organizing in Chile. Second, the hyper-focus on State-based politics—whether that be the Salvador Allende regime or Pink Tide administrations—serves to erase this alternative history.[4]

Beyond Chile, the politics of autonomy in Latin America has been garnering more and more critical attention since at least the early 2000s. More than simply referring to political organizing outside of the State and capitalism—a naïve understanding that has been critiqued by autonomist theorists themselves insofar as such a pure positioning outside of the State and capitalism is nearly impossible (Dinerstein 2015)—autonomous politics refers to grassroots movements that seek to "recuperate their possibility of deciding in a non-delegative manner issues of public concern…starting from the reappropriation by people freely associated for their autonomous ends" (Gutiérrez Aguilar 2008: 23). Autonomy "supposes the organization of oppressed classes independently of dominant state structures, that is, not subordinated to the dynamic imposed by those institutions" (Thwaites Rey 2011: 152). In autonomous politics, "one proceeds as if the State does not exist" (Graeber 2009: 203). As such, autonomy is a "change of being" that is exercised "in the deliberation and execution of that which is decided, in the confrontation with instituted power, and in the fight for the legitimacy of oneself [*lo propio*]" (Gutiérrez Aguilar 2008: 14). Autonomy, derived from the Greek words of 'auto' (self) and 'nomos' (law or norm), refers to the struggle "*to rule oneself by one's own laws*" (López y Rivas 2011: 110). Drawing from the thinkers cited in this paragraph, autonomy can be operationally defined as the prefigurative politics of imagining and actualizing alternative horizontalist modes of coordinating social relations in which there is no distinction between ruler and ruled, governor and governed, those with power and those subjected to power.

The basic goal of autonomous politics is, to use John Holloway's (2005) turn of phrase, *to change the world without taking power*, or, more precisely, to imagine a revolution that does not include seizing State power. Holloway's argument—one mirrored by many theories of autonomy—is that the modern State is founded on a logic of subordination insofar as it requires the formation of powers "splintered off from society" that subsequently become "a separate elite that makes decisions or leads struggles or resolves internal conflicts" (Zibechi 2010: 7). If the State is dependent upon *the sovereign*, "elected in order to carry out the will of the people by exerting power in the territory" (Holloway 2005: 13), then State-based politics is structured around disciplining a given society by "subordinating the myriad" struggles of that society to "a hierarchy of struggles...usually expressed in the form of the party programme" (Holloway 2005: 17). The modern State, following Pierre Clastres's (1989) conception, is "the instrument that allows the ruling class to bring its violent domination to bear on the dominated classes" (203)—that is, the State is founded on the command/obedience relationship—but in so doing, *law*—the control of social relations enforced through the threat or realization of violence—generates a comprehensible social order (Graeber 2004). Within many autonomist theorizations, the State serves to define social relations.

Within this understanding, political organizing based around the State implies a hierarchical relation between the definers and the defined, sovereign and subject, leaders and the led, those who determine the party programme and those who obey it or, at the very most, can only put pressure on leaders to change it. Recognizing this reality, traditional revolutionary theory has focused on winning State power with the idea that such a gain allows the revolutionary party to redefine social relations in a more egalitarian manner. As Marx and Engels categorize the beginning of the communist revolution,

> the first step in the revolution by the working class is to raise the proletariat to the position of ruling class to win the battle of democracy. The proletariat will use its political supremacy to wrest, by degree, all capital from the bourgeoisie, to centralise all instruments of production in the hands of the State, *i.e.*, of the proletariat organised as the ruling class.
>
> (26)

Holloway argues that this theorization is inherently flawed since any seizure of the State will reproduce the State's hierarchical relations of power. Upon seizing the State, there will continue being the distinction between those who define social relations and those who are subjected to and resist those definitions, those who lead and those who are led and "struggle against the State" (Clastres 1989: 218). In seeking a revolution that refuses to take State power, then, one is seeking other forms of coordinating social relations that "preven[t] the concentration of power or, similarly, preven[t] the emergence of a separate power from that of the community gathered in assembly" (Zibechi 2010: 16). The question posed by autonomous politics is the following: What political and insurgent forms allow for everyone to participate in defining social relations, never permitting the establishment of the distinction between definer/defined, governor/governed, leader/led?

In other words, the successes of autonomous politics present an implicit rejoinder to the Statist focus of the Pink Tide: against the State-based politics of the progressive regimes throughout Latin America, a postmillennial strain of radical autonomist politics has been spreading across Latin America. This thesis—a focus on autonomous politics forces us to reconsider the Pink Tide—is put forth by both Raúl Zibechi (2010, 2012) and Raquel Gutiérrez Aguilar (2008). For both authors, the Pink Tide was in fact the institutionalization and neutralization of various radical autonomous social movements that had arisen in Latin America during the 1990s and early 2000s. For instance, Gutiérrez Aguilar argues that the rise of Evo Morales in Bolivia was largely a consequence of the autonomous organizing of coca leaf farmers, and the Bolivian Pink Tide functionally neutralized these movements by subordinating them to the institutional demands of the State. If we accept Zibechi's and Gutiérrez Aguilar's argument that these autonomous movements sought to imagine a new political form in which all participate in the definition of social relations, then the rise to power of these movements within the State ironically undermined their political foundations by forcing them to once again accept the distinction between sovereign/subject, definer/defined, governor/governed, leader/led. Quite simply, the State imposes an institutional distinction between, for instance, Morales—who is the sovereign of Bolivia and therefore "the sole source of legitimate speech…for it goes by the name *command* and wants nothing save the *obedience* of the executant" (Clastres 1989: 151)—and the participants in the *cocalero* social movement that had fueled his rise to power. Regardless of the egalitarian objectives of the Morales administration, the very institutional form of the State annihilates the political foundations of autonomous social movements.

Recent critiques of autonomous politics have focused on how theories of autonomy ignore that any social movement will eventually need to engage with the State, whether that be willingly or whether that be the State co-opting or suppressing (violently or otherwise) their efforts (Beverley 2011; Harrison 2018; McNaughton 2008). That is, these critiques call on us to address a fairly basic reality. Regardless of the attractiveness, viability, and robustness of autonomous politics, the State is a hostile force that coercively imposes its imagined social order onto its subjects. Given the history of States' brutal use of violence to suppress autonomous social movements—the War of Canudos (Campos Johnson 2010), the long history of settler-colonial administrations violently dissolving movements for Indigenous autonomy (Dunbar-Ortiz 2014; Rivera Cusicanqui 2010b), bloody Sunday following the Paris Commune in which the French government massacred 10,000 and imprisoned 40,000 more (Tombs 1999), the use of witch-hunts to suppress autonomous working-class women organizing (Federici 2004), and so on—to expect that autonomous social movements will be able to freely develop without State interference is naïve at best (Graeber 2009; Notes from Nowhere 2003; Sitrin and Azzellini 2014).

The critiques of autonomous politics referenced above posit that social movements need to voluntarily engage and reconfigure the State. Agreeing with autonomous theorizations' challenges to the limitations of revolutionary praxis founded on taking State power, such critiques instead recommend critically occupying the State in order to radically transform it (Beverley 2011). The failures of the Pink Tide, however, have now given us ample evidence that such a hope is largely misplaced. As Zibechi and Gutiérrez Aguilar note, the Pink Wave's institutionalization of social movements did not open up opportunities to transform the State, it merely neutralized the radical politics of those very social movements by exposing them to the institutional mechanisms of State apparatuses. As such, we can hypothesize that autonomous social movements cannot flourish without eventually calling for the end of the State itself (Gluckstein 2011).

The apparent conclusion is that autonomous politics will have to instrumentalize violence to their advantage in one of two ways. First: use violence to smash the State. That is, Raúl Zibechi's (2010) call to "disperse power" will at some point require coercion: autonomous political bodies will need to forcefully require the State's dissolution. This response proves to be theoretically contradictory. Autonomy's drive to form an *anti-power* that "dissolves" capitalism and the State rather than a *counter-power* that seizes hold of the State (Holloway 2005: 14–15), never discusses how such an anti-power will actually go about dissolving them. As a result, this theorization never adequately distinguishes a counter-power from the anti-power use of force to dissolve capitalism and the State. Why is dissolving capitalism and the State any different than the State dissolving autonomous social movements? Why is the autonomous *command* to smash the State and institute an alternative autonomous political configuration (i.e., a new law) qualitatively different than the State's use of violence and the law to command its subjects?

Second, there is the drive to use defensive violence in the tradition of the "autonomous zone" (Bey 1991). In this understanding, an autonomous political body occupies a given territory and then uses violence to impede invasions and disruptions of their internal organization. One of the more memorable instances of such use of defensive violence is the "You Are Now Entering Free Derry" mural in Northern Ireland painted during 'The Troubles' by Irish anti-colonialists that functionally marked off a decolonized autonomous zone. Irish anti-colonialists erected barricades that were then patrolled by their own security forces, effectively constructing "spaces of exclusion" from invading British forces as well as generating "chronic violence" (Feldman 1991: 31). Although this example is extreme, it is exemplary of the logic of defending autonomous zones against hostile dominant forces such as a colonial army. When Zibechi (2012) claims that, "Autonomy rests upon the control of territory" (129), he does not mention the corollary consequence: the need to defend that territory against hostile enemies (crow 2018).

Judith Butler (2019) has criticized this defense of defensive violence. They outline the basic rationale of violence in the service of self-defense in this way:

> I am willing to defend those who are *like* me, or who might be understood as part of the generalized regime of myself, but not to defend those who are unlike me, which converts rather easily into the claim: I

> will defend only those who are like me, or recognizable to me, but will defend *against* those who are not recognizable to me and with whom no ties of belonging seem to exist
>
> (Ch. 1, "Violence and Nonviolence," par. 7).

The result is that such a "defensive rationale" becomes "imbued with paranoia and hatred" (Introduction, par. 25), regarding certain lives as *grievable*—i.e., those worth defending—and others as *disposable*. The very act of defending the autonomous zone reproduces the very logic of the State that autonomous politics is trying to overcome: those participating in the autonomous political body have the power to define who is grievable and who is disposable (Mbembe 2003).

To put it another way, we can turn to Butler's reading of Walter Benjamin's (1996a) distinction between mythic and divine violence. For Benjamin, mythic violence serves to institute or preserve the law, the State's ordering of social reality. If autonomy means, to return to Gilberto López y Rivas's definition, "*to rule oneself by one's own laws*," then it would appear that no violence would be necessary since autonomy dispenses with such a top-down conception of the law. Yet their use of 'oneself' [*uno mismo*] evades a central problematic of the autonomous zone: Who belongs? Who is defined as a citizen of this territory? This theorization of the politics of autonomy has not sufficiently attended to the question of citizenship.

Although Holloway (2005) repeatedly attempts to avoid this problem by imagining a political formation in which the power to define is distributed to everyone, he also implicitly defines those who do not belong: capitalists and representatives of the State (the police, the army, and so on). When he argues that self-determination is not "first we destroy capitalism, then we create a self-determining society" but rather "a moving forward of self-determination against a society which negates it" (218), he does not sufficiently respond to the question: What happens to someone who not only refuses to abide by the rules of the politics of autonomy—for instance, refuses to acknowledge the rules organizing an assembly—but is hostile to its functioning, especially when that someone is in fact a well-funded collective with a standing army to support its hostility? Indeed, *establishing boundaries*—an element of the territorial aspect of the politics of autonomy that is rarely acknowledged—is seen as a prime example by Benjamin (1996a: 249) of law-establishing and law-preserving mythic violence. Such defense of an autonomous zone does not take power, but it does institute law.

This is where Benjamin's (1996a) second form of violence, *divine violence*, becomes so important. For Benjamin, divine violence puts a halt to all mythic violence, "If mythic violence is lawmaking, divine violence is law-destroying; if the former sets boundaries, the latter boundlessly destroys them" (249). The consequence of divine violence, then, is "the absence of all lawmaking" (250). Butler (2019) reads this theorization against the grain as a call to an aggressive and forceful nonviolence. Benjamin (1996a) himself argues that whereas mythic violence "is blood," divine violence "is lethal without spilling blood" (249–250), and, as Butler notes, he writes in his discussion of mythic violence that, "a totally nonviolent resolution of conflicts can never lead to a legal contract" (Benjamin 1996a: 243) and that "there is a sphere of human agreement that is nonviolent to the extent that it is wholly inaccessible to violence: the proper sphere of 'understanding,' language" (245). What Butler (2019) suggests is the following,

> If such techniques of nonviolence suspend the legal frameworks that govern our understanding of violence, then perhaps that 'suspension' of legal violence is precisely what is meant by 'divine violence.' It is a violence done to the violence of the law, exposing its lethal operation and establishing within civil society an alternative, ongoing technique that has no need of the law.
>
> (Ch. 3, "Law's Violence: Benjamin, Cover, Balibar," par. 9)

In other words, any politics of autonomy must by definition be a nonviolent movement that is perceived by the State as violent insofar as it annihilates all law. More precisely: *the politics of autonomy confounds the violence/non-violence distinction.*

Concretely, what is this paradoxical nonviolent divine violence? For Butler (2019), it is *radical interdependency* founded on the "enduring dependency" that is constitutive of our very existence. What Butler is recommending is that each and every subject is not an autonomous 'self,' but is constructed by a web of dependencies that constitute their self-hood. As they write, "The dependency that constitutes what I am prior to the emergence of any pronoun"—i.e., the parent/child relationship—"underscores the fact that I depend on the ones whose definition of me gives me form" (Ch. 2, par. 48). I am I because of my relationships with and dependence upon others, my 'self' is in fact a knot formed by weaving together these relationships and interdependencies. Autonomy, then, is not founded on self-determining (and self-policing) autonomous zones, but rather on a universal recognition of our multiplicitous interdependency, *regardless of our feelings about one another.* As Butler concludes, "We do not have to love one another to be obligated to build a world in which all lives are sustainable" (Ch. 1, "Violence and Nonviolence," par. 21). Here is the challenge for autonomous politics. While Butler (perhaps unintentionally) repeats the basic thesis of autonomy—"The institutional life of violence will not be brought down by a prohibition, but only by a counter-institutional ethos and practice" (Ch. 1, "Violence and Nonviolence," par. 17)—their thesis reframes the task of autonomy as imagining social relations based on a new subjectivity founded on a constitutive interdependency. Social relations within a given territory would no longer be defined by the sovereign State, but instead by the dynamic, unstable, and ever-shifting relations between multiple interdependent individuals, collectives, and communities.[5]

Nonetheless, Butler deftly avoids a simple question in her critique of self-defense: What does one do when a knife is at their throat? Is shoving away the assailant—an act of violence to be sure—a betrayal of interdependency?[6] Priyamvada Gopal (2019), for instance, argues that decolonial violence frequently forced and forces many colonizers to recognize their interdependence with the colonized. To use Franz Fanon's (1986) phrasing, such violence allows the colonized to "make myself known" when "the other hesitate[s] to recognize me" (115) (we will return to this in Chapter 1 via the concept of dignity). Implied in this thesis is that this mode of decolonial violence is not a means to a political end. Decolonial violence is not instrumentalized in order to coercively institute new laws as defined by the colonized, but becomes a means for the colonized to claim their existence within an interdependent universal humanity. As Gopal (2019) insists, the decolonial texts she examines are founded on reclaiming universal "human commonality and equality," with "claims to radical alterity...rarely to be heard in the language of resistance, even as there is often a fierce insistence on cultural specificities" (24–26). In short, this violence paradoxically makes possible the recognition of interdependency among subjects as called for by Butler's nonviolence. This form of decolonial violence serves to reinforce interdependency, not to make distinctions between grievable and disposable life.

Gopal's analysis calls on us to can ask: What form of force illuminates our interdependence? Can we conceptualize shoving the assailant not as self-defense, but rather as the forceful call to recognize our interdependence? Rather than defending spaces of autonomy or smashing the State, might we reconsider such force as a call for representatives of the State and capitalism to acknowledge their interdependence with others and to reconfigure their way of engaging the world in a way that recognizes this interdependence? Might this shove precisely be the law-annihilating violence hypothesized by Benjamin insofar as it is founded on the desire for a recognition of interdependency, rather than the imposition of law? And if that's the case, what does such a shove look like on a collective scale? What does such a rebellion constitutive of radical autonomous politics look like?[7]

(Post-)Hegemony

The reader may likely be put off by what is perceived as an overly simplified definition of the State in the previous section—the institution that defines, institutes, and enforces a social order within a bounded territory by monopolizing violence. Within this definition there appears to be no difference between, for instance, a dictator and a democratic parliamentary republic. Yet when Carl Schmitt (2005) wrote, "Sovereign is he who decides on the exception" (5), he made precisely just such a point insofar as the dictator appears in moments of emergency in order to protect constitutional order against a perceived threat (an invasion, a rebellion, a pandemic, etc.). As McCormick (1998) notes, although the dictator may be "unrestrained by norm or law," they are "severely limited beyond the specific task in that [they cannot] change or perpetually suspend the regular order" (218). A parliamentary democracy requires the selective use of a dictator—whether that be a "personal dictator" or a "collective one" (220)—in order to protect its basic functioning during a perceived emergency. More abstractly, the sovereign is whoever has monopolized the power to use violence to protect a given ordering of social relations when faced with an emergency. A horizontalist politics based around "power-sharing and egalitarian principles" that nonetheless instrumentalizes "temporary but organized" "community armed self-defense" (crow 2018: "Some Important Distinctions," para. 1) functionally reflects this Schmittian politics of protecting friends against enemies during an emergency.[8]

One might say that the politics of autonomy is trying to imagine a horizontalist mode of coordinating social relations without sovereignty. Recognizing the critiques that autonomist theories have not adequately thought about their relation to the State (i.e., the existing sovereign), the problematic I posed at the end of the previous section is effectively: What act annihilates sovereignty without the agent (collective or personal) of that act implicitly installing themself as the sovereign?[9] What act destroys the sovereign without the agent perceiving themself as deciding on the exception as to when violence can be used? Without perceiving themself as having the power to use violence to protect their autonomous ordering of social relations? For the use of defensive violence to protect the autonomous assembly in a moment of emergency—e.g., when the existing State attempts to violently disperse the assembly—is still nonetheless following the very logic of Schmitt.[10]

Such an analysis tacitly assumes that the role of the State is always one of domination and coercion, never of leadership and consent.[11] Antonio Gramsci's idea of the "extended State" (Liguori 2015b) is precisely a rejoinder to this idea. As Gramsci claimed in a 1931 letter from prison, although the State "is usually thought of as political society—i.e., a dictatorship or some other coercive apparatus used to control the masses in conformity with a given type of production and economy," he redefined it as "a balance between political society and civil society, by which I mean the hegemony of one social group over the entire nation, exercised through so-called private organizations like the Church, trade unions, or schools" (Gramsci 1979: 204). For Gramsci, the State is not merely the sovereign exercise of violence over a social body in order to guarantee the installation and preservation of a given social order. Instead, as he writes elsewhere, the "task and duty" of the State is to disseminate "its own conception of life" (Gramsci 1992a: 187), and it does this through the generation of those "so-called private organizations." Rather than merely coercing a society into abiding a given social order, the State's task is to foster an institutional structure within civil society that upholds and guarantees popular support for the ruling social order.[12]

As such (and as already briefly expressed in the opening salvo of this introduction), culture, ideology, theory, language, and so on are not mere cultural ornaments on the hard foundation of the extended State, but instead constitute the "intimate cement" that guarantees the institutional integrity of that State (Liguori 2015b: 79). As Gramsci writes,

> Culture...unifies in a series of strata, to the extent that they come into contact with each other, a greater or less number of individuals who understand each other's mode of expression in differing degrees, etc... From this one can deduce the importance of the 'cultural aspect,' even in practical (collective) activity. An historical act can only be performed by 'collective man,' and this presupposes the attainment of a 'cultural-social' unity through which a multiplicity of dispersed wills, with heterogeneous aims, are welded together with a single aim, on the basis of an equal and common conception of the world.
>
> (Gramsci 1992a: 349)

For Gramsci, there is a direct relationship between culture and politics: a given culture glues a social body together, this social body generates a "'material structure' articulated in 'apparatuses'" (Liguori 2015b: 79)—i.e., a structure of civil society organizations that can disseminate and actualize that social body's "common conception of the world"—and then the functioning of this civil society is protected by political society which has monopolized the use of violence. The State is not the locus of all power, but is instead simultaneously the ultimate synthesis as well as the disseminator of the social order exercised within so-called civil society; and the political artist is not the propagandist aestheticizing the party programme, but is instead the actor that glues together a social body by conceptualizing their coherent "conception of the world."

There are two important things to note of Gramsci's theorization. First, Gramsci posits "the necessary existence of governing elites or minorities over governed majorities" (Fontana 2015: 69). Culture is formed by the dialectical interaction between the spontaneity of the grassroots and "conscious leadership" that can mold dispersed spontaneity into a common conception of the world (Liguori 2015a: 124). Although Gramsci insists that this leadership must be rooted in the communities that they are to lead—what he famously termed the *organic intellectual*—and that there must be a "philosophy of praxis" through which the grassroots themselves autonomously educate themselves (Thomas 2015), his theorization requires a hierarchy between leader (intellectual, political, social, etc.) and led (student, citizen, member, etc.).

Second, Gramsci develops a concept to refer to those who have no "institutionally validated action" (Spivak 2012: 110): the subaltern. The subaltern refers to all those who cannot represent themselves within the cultural contours of a dominant conception of the world and, additionally, have not developed an alternative unified conception of the world, meaning that they have neither the capacity to develop a counter-institutional framework nor a place of belonging within the existing hegemonic extended State—they are neither citizens nor capable of offering a coherent counter-form of citizenship. For this reason, despite the valid critiques of her reading of Gramsci (Liguori 2015a; McNally 2015), Spivak (2014) insists that "one of the most important themes" of Gramsci's writing is "the fact that the subaltern is not the proletariat" (193) insofar as the subaltern is defined by their "distance from the state" (193), not their level of exploitation. The subaltern are the leftovers, those "without part" (Rancière 2010: 36) within a hegemonic ordering of a historical society. When Susan Stryker (2006) announced her experience as a trans woman as "between the pains of two violations, the mark of gender and the unlivability of its absence" (250)—i.e., "one's personhood" is "cognizable" only when they accept the compulsory "gender attribution" assigned at birth, meaning that trans personhood is defined either by being unrecognizable within the hegemonic gender order (claiming one's trans identity) or by denying one's gender identity (accepting the "gendering violence" at the foundation of the "human condition of human subjectivity" by affirming "that short sentence in the delivery room: 'It's a girl'")—she implicitly described the subaltern experience. In her article, Stryker is not oppressed as a trans woman, she is engaged in "the struggle to exist" (238).[13]

As Marcus Green (2015: 166) argues, subaltern groups are *subjected to* the extended State of the ruling class insofar as they are not only coerced by political society's apparatuses of force but are obliged to develop as individuals within the civil society organizations that uphold the extended State. *This* is the sense of Spivak's claim that the subaltern is the subject without institutionally validated action: the subaltern, by definition, has no cultural unity, therefore no civil institutional manifestation of that unity, therefore no capacity to become the State, and therefore no power to exercise hegemony. The subaltern is not an oppressed social identity or position that is nonetheless recognized by the State and can therefore mobilize for material gains and recognition, it is "a position without identity" (Spivak 2012: 431). There is a difference between, for instance, the proletariat in conflict with the bourgeoisie—"conflict in the restricted sense of an unequal relationship between two individuals, groups, or ensembles that compete, within the same space, with the aim or purpose not of liquidating an adversary, and the relationship itself, but of modifying the relationship, or at least strengthening their relative positions" (Wieviorka 2009: 9–10)—and the subaltern struggle to exist.

For Gramsci, revolutionary political and cultural action has a very specific and concrete task: to culturally unify the subaltern, generate a counter-institutional framework in civil society in order to disseminate their coherent conception of the world, and then attempt to gain power within political society. Through *popular unity* the subaltern binds together to construct "a collective, popular based, will" (Briziarelli and Martínez Guillem 2016: 55). Though what this means remains under debate—whether it is the formation of a coherent singular collective identity that vies for hegemonic institution (Mouffe 2005) or "a process of unification (never totally achieved), founded on strategic alliances between different sectors, not on their pre-given identity" (Hall 1986: 25)—what persists is that the subaltern is an intrinsic product of Gramsci's extended State. There will always be "a position without identity" within the hegemonic civil institutional network, and therefore there will always be the need for subaltern groups to organize against that hegemony.

In this way, one can hypothesize three distinct subject positions within Gramsci's view of the extended State: elite, citizen, and subaltern. The elite is whoever has the power to define social relations; the citizen is whoever finds their voice—and therefore becomes a recognizable subject and agent—within the civil society proper to a given extended State; and the subaltern is whoever's action remains illegitimate and unidentifiable within that extended State, they are the leftovers of that system. Of course, no subject is purely situated in one position (see Chapter 6). For instance, a local city-council member in the United States has the power to define certain social relations but is severely limited by those above them in the hierarchy. These serve as operational descriptions and should be used fluidly.

The politics of autonomy, then, is working towards a novel solution: not only the annihilation of political society, but the reconfiguration of civil society in a way that no longer seeks to unify a social body through the voice of a cultural leader and through the organizing activity of a community leader. The politics of autonomy prefiguratively imagines and actualizes a horizontalist social ordering in which no entity is elite and no entity is subaltern, begging the following question: What is culture when a coherent understanding of the world is no longer *disseminated* within a social body but is *co-generated* amongst all of its members? What is a culture and its attendant social order that no longer permits the differentiation of the social body into elite/citizen/subaltern? What is the role of the artist and the activist if it is no longer to mold popular 'spontaneity' into a coherent social body with an identifiable conception of the world and a concrete counter-institutional manifestation?

I am arguing that the politics of autonomy not only prefiguratively imagines a world without political society, but additionally a world without hegemony exercised via civil society. The politics of autonomy is inherently a *post-hegemonic* politics. Although critics have noted that the details of his critique of hegemony are limited insofar as he does not adequately account for the depth and nuance of Gramsci's thought (Thomas 2020), Jon Beasley-Murray's *Post-Hegemony* (2010) offers a coherent theorization of this political vision that aims to reconceive collective subjectivities around "resonance rather than identity, expansive inclusion rather than demarcated difference" (188), thereby displacing a politics founded on molding a hegemonic conception of life. As such, post-hegemonic sociality is reconfigured around a *co-generated relationality* or *interdependency* rather than *shared hegemonic meaning* (206–207), and post-hegemonic revolution is dedicated to "dissolv[ing] all structures of command and control" (225). Against contractual meanings shared among "defined entities" (248), post-hegemony is constituted by "complex networks that depend upon connections and contacts rather than contracts regulated by a higher power" (269). Post-hegemony attempts to imagine the coordination of social relations without the extended State, a coordination of social relations that can be understood in terms of relationality, networks, contacts, resonance, and interdependency rather than identity, meaning, contracts, hegemony, and so on.

What, then, is the culture proper to post-hegemony and, with it, to the politics of autonomy?[14] Magalí Rabasa (2019) has identified one concrete example: "the production and distribution practices of underground political publishing networks" (4) in Argentina, Mexico, Bolivia, and Chile. Rabasa's work detailing the continental-scale networks of independent book publishers "creat[ing] and disseminat[ing] a new body of political theory" (4) that "reject[s] the form of the state and capitalism" (35) illuminates that there is a growing popular cultural movement that enables autonomous social coordination structured around "self-organization, horizontalism, cooperativism, and mutual aid" (5). She reveals how autonomous organizing is actively producing an attendant relational culture that offers an alternative to the hegemonic process described by Gramsci.

Yet, as I have discussed in more detail elsewhere, Rabasa's work avoids the question of hegemony and with it the problem of moving from the "underground" networks of small presses to a world in which such a culture fostered by this autonomous cultural practice might become the principal way through which our everyday social relations are coordinated (Woods 2021c). Although she demonstrates that an egalitarian, horizontalist, autonomous, post-hegemonic culture is concretely possible, the question of revolution and rebellion is outside the scope of her analysis. That is, although the cultural worker's role in a revolution tied to hegemonic culture is quite clear—the unification of a social body through cultural practices that enable the subsequent attempt by that social body to seize power—Rabasa's intervention calls on us to consider what revolution tied to post-hegemonic culture might look like. Although there have now been dozens of diverse rebellions or social movements understood in a post-hegemonic lens to which we will return throughout this book—Occupy, Zapatismo, the 2001 protests in Argentina, and so on—it remains unclear how to theorize culture in relationship to these rebellions.

This is particularly important given the implicit critique by Walter Mignolo (2009) of post-hegemonic theorizations of social change. As Benjamin Arditi (2007: 215) has argued, the post-hegemonic project of Beasley-Murray is organized around the dynamic and always unsettled unification of "singularities" brought together as a multitude within the commons. As Mignolo notes, this idea of the commons and the multitude "is part of the imaginary of European history" and runs in conflict, for instance, with the Indigenous Aymara concept of *the communal*, which is organized around the *ayllu*. Traditionally translated as 'community' or 'communal system,' the *ayllu* is

> a kind of extended familial community, with a common (real or imaginary) ascendancy that collectively works a common territory...Each *ayllu* is defined by a territory that includes not just a piece of land, but the eco-system of which that land is one component.
>
> (Mignolo 2009)

Mignolo takes this definition from Felix Patzi Paco's (2009) theorization of *ayllu* communality, which, as I have argued elsewhere (Woods 2020a), is explicitly *against* the Western conception of subjectivity in terms of an independent singularity in communal relation with other singularities. To insist on the post-hegemonic commons is functionally a *colonial hegemonic project* that will replace *the communal* proper to Aymara existence.

What is needed, Mignolo (2009) argues, is a *plurinational* interlinking of communal systems in which the Latin American left,

> with its European genealogy of thought, cannot have the monopoly over the right to imagine what a non-capitalist future shall be. There are many non-capitalist pasts that can be drawn from, many experiences and memories that perhaps do not wish to be civilized—neither by the right nor by the left.

In other words, a decolonial post-hegemonic project would recognize not only a socio-political and cultural system structured on the relations between singularities, but between *communities* and *communal systems* as well. Returning to Butler, to recognize our autonomous interdependency is to recognize that the social forms of such interdependency are not always equivalent—the communal system, for example, is not equal to the commons—and that such interdependency requires an interlinking among *communities* and *collectivities* and not just singularities linked together as a multitude.[15]

As such, autonomous political projects need to resolve two dilemmas. First, how to imagine a horizontalist political formation in which there is no subaltern, in which every entity has an *institutionally recognized voice*. Second, how to imagine a political formation in which no collective imaginary (e.g., the post-hegemonic commons) becomes hegemonic.[16]

Book Outline

This theoretical discussion has therefore led us to a set of four questions. First, what is the divine force proper to autonomous politics? In other words, what is rebellion for the politics of autonomy? Second, what is the culture of such an autonomous politics that recognizes interdependency?

That is, how can a radical autonomous politics attempt to "change the world," to return to Holloway's phrasing, without seeing itself as a potentially hegemonic project? Third, what is the relationship between the artist and the autonomist rebellion? Fourth, what does an autonomous interdependency—instead of the formation of an insurgent collective will that can attempt to impose its hegemony over the nation—look like on a concrete level? The thesis of this book is therefore rather simple: elements of the Chilean social explosion substantially respond to these lingering questions with regard to autonomous politics.

Chapter 1 argues that *the barricade* during the social explosion was imagined as the 'shove' that annihilates the law and illuminates autonomous interdependency. More precisely, this chapter first discusses the current common understandings of the barricade during the social explosion—that it was a meaningless criminal act (the response by the Chilean government), that it was a cry of anger but without adequate political expression (the liberal and leftist response in the US media), and that it was a valid protest tactic to be instrumentalized for material gains (the institutionalized social-movement position in Chile)—and counterposes them with the perception of the barricade in a popular street-art mural by Danny Reveco in Valparaíso. What I argue is that the barricade does not serve to institute a collective will, to mark off a temporary autonomous zone, or to effect change within the State by coercively putting civil-society pressure on politicians. Instead, the barricade illuminates an underlying autonomous interdependency and how the State works as an anti-social force to disrupt it.

Chapter 2 argues that the subaltern culture generated in *public transport as a public space* can serve as an example of an insurrectionary autonomous culture. More precisely, I look at Pedro Lembel's representations of the public space of public transport in peripheral neighborhoods of Santiago to argue that the opening salvo of the social explosion—the massive evasions of public transit fares—were in fact an autonomous rebellion by a subaltern collective formed in the cultural crucible of public transport that sought to insist on the interdependency between its cultural practices and the neoliberal hegemony on which Santiago's public transit system is based. A reading of Lemebel in dialogue with the evasion movement thereby responds to the second question stated above.

As such, Chapters 1 and 2 are dedicated to a discussion of the pre-history of the social explosion: Chapter 1 extensively discusses the social movements that gave rise to the social explosion, and Chapter 2 discusses the long history of the use of public transport as a public space that produced the cultural foundation for the evasion movement. Chapters 3–6 shift focus and examine how cultural actors actively intervened during the social explosion, thereby exploring how they were aiding in the social explosion. More precisely, these chapters examine the collectivities being imagined by those in the streets and how that cultural imaginary was translated into a revolutionary vision.

Chapter 3 examines how artists' interventions sought to enable the autonomous political formations of the social explosion. More precisely, this chapter argues that artists during the social explosion were forced to reconsider what *cultural intervention* signifies in the midst of rebellion. To analyze this question, this chapter examines how various performance artists in the Valparaíso region assembled interventions with regard to water justice, questioning what it means to be an artist committed not only to the social explosion but to environmental justice. The central argument of this chapter is that the post-hegemonic autonomous artist stops attempting to glue together a social body or intervene in a social body's 'common sense,' but instead illuminates that a given collectivity has the autonomous power to collectively define their relationship with the environment and take control of water-society relations.

Chapter 4 examines how the social explosion attempted to link together three different threads of revolt that were feeding mobilizations in the street: anti-neoliberal, decolonial, and feminist. The central argument of this chapter is that significant elements of the social explosion did not attempt to cohere these threads into a united front with a collective will that could seize power of the State. Instead, the social explosion was largely concerned with how to weave together these different threads in a way that took into account the differing and multiplicitous social positions of each participant—a white feminist activist reflecting on how to weave together decolonial, anti-neoliberal, and feminist perspectives would do so differently than Indigenous youths of an urban area. This chapter argues that this woven collectivity sought to undermine sovereignty itself and reconsider collective and individual subjectivities within an autonomous framework.

Chapter 5 presents the counter-argument to the four previous chapters. If the main argument of this book is that substantial elements of the social explosion never sought to extend hegemonic dominance across the national space of Chile, this chapter argues that there was a powerful thread that sought to organize an insurgent collective unity built around a shared national identity. This chapter principally accomplishes this goal by looking at how a shared collective memory of torture during the dictatorship informed various myths—not used in the slightest in a pejorative sense—during the social explosion that unified subaltern subjects. This helps explain, I argue, why the social explosion at times took a nationalist form.

Chapter 6 switches gears and addresses a shortcoming of the previous analysis. Namely, the body of this book is devoted to an analysis of how the social explosion represents a subaltern rebellion against neoliberal, patriarchal, settler colonial, and environmentally unjust hegemony; however, given that some days were marked by the attendance of literally millions of people, it would be inaccurate to argue that the social explosion was composed exclusively of subaltern elements. This chapter examines how members of the middle class put themselves into solidarity with the subaltern. Although there were some attempts to 'uplift' the subaltern through upward mobility into the middle class, a novel resolution to this issue arose with some non-subaltern participants seeking to create *relations between* collectivities in the post-hegemonic manner seen throughout this book (with the exception of Chapter 5).

A Note on Methodology

The very thesis of this book presents a certain methodological problem. If I were to follow the general protocol of a research text—the author collects evidence, analyzes it, generates a conclusion, molds that conclusion into a thesis, and then defines the object of analysis—then I would be undermining the very foundation of the book: that the social explosion represents an insurgent autonomous recoordination of social relations in which singular meaning developed by a cultural leader is exchanged for horizontal relationality in which meaning is co-generated by communal, collective, and individual subjects. This is an implied thesis of Magalí Rabasa's book on small presses. These presses, she argues, developed a novel political theory through cooperativism, dialogue, and the international networked exchange of texts. Her argument functionally demonstrates that autonomous politics calls for a novel methodology that goes beyond the purely thesis-driven monograph by the lone intellectual.

Rabasa is not alone. Both Holloway and Beasley-Murray have argued that traditional qualitative methods based on

> Opinion polls and other such instruments of technocratic observation are apparatuses of capture converting qualitative difference into quantity: they produce a statistical striation of social space that reduces experience to opinion and people to pop-sociological epithets ('soccer moms,' 'Essex man') so as to calibrate endlessly comparable differences.
> (Beasley-Murray 2010: 108)

The end goal of such studies are therefore to produce "a single set of policies" (Beasley-Murray 2010: 108) that reflect what has been learned by the objective academic in their fieldwork. These studies serve to assign an identity to a given movement that can then be contained within a policy position or law and implemented by the State. The form of the traditional understanding of the research monograph in which the meaning of a given phenomenon is precisely and methodically defined inevitably serves the State, regardless of the author's intention.

What, then, is the attendant methodology of autonomous politics? Of a politics based on horizontalist interdependence rather than the centralization of sovereign power in the State? I suggest that the literary-studies methodology of close reading offers us a possible methodological avenue. During the 2000s, the critique of this methodology formed the core of tense debates within the world of literary studies when Franco Moretti proposed a new methodology called "distant reading," "a patchwork of other people's research, *without a single direct textual reading*."[17] In this way, Maurizio Ascari (2014) summarizes, Moretti hoped to replace qualitative methods based on close reading with quantitative methods using computational analyses of larger data sets. Instead of the "very solemn treatment of very few texts taken very seriously," to cite Moretti's (2000) summary of close reading, we have the distant treatment of hundreds if not thousands of texts.[18] In initial evaluations of *On the Chilean Social Explosion*, this was the type of reading that was largely expected: I would gather dozens if not hundreds of cultural products in order to paint a broad picture of the revolt. When readers were confronted with various close readings of very specific elements, there was largely disappointment.

I follow Gayatri Spivak (2003), however, in noting that such a survey-based methodology is structured around creating "authoritative totalizing patterns depending on untested statements by small groups of people treated as native informants" (108). On the contrary, she continues, literary study is primarily based on accounting for the "texture" (108) of artistic works. As she describes the methodology of close reading through a discussion of Kant,

> [For Kant,] the investigating subject, the philosopher, takes the concept as a perspective, as on a hill, and sees a horizon, as a circle. The subject continues to develop the concept and finds more and more circles appear, newer horizons. When the case won't fit a circle, the seeker pushes the figure until it becomes an ellipse; and a parabola, and perhaps all the figures of geometry as a circle bent out of shape…, until he…comes upon the asymptote…You never get to empirical particularity when you are making logic palpable, says Kant, for the entire exercise is still only analogical.
>
> (Spivak 2006: 104–105)

Close reading, in other words, is dedicated to the interruption of "analogical classification" (Spivak 2006: 105) so as to allow the other to speak to us in their own language. As she summarizes elsewhere, although "we cannot—no self can—reach the quite-other…literature, as a play of figures, can give us imaginative access to the experience" (Spivak 2012: 352). Spivak (2012) argues that it is by careful attention to the texture of literary works and "the rhetoricity of language" that we can prepare ourselves for the "flexible epistemological performance" (353–354) of seeking to understand the other beyond the limits of analogical classification.

Spivak elsewhere links this to the field of politics. Through a reading of Derrida, Spivak (2003) asserts, "There can be no politics without collectivity" (28). Whereas the role of "capitalist imperialism" is to submit that collectivity to "calculation" (54)—i.e., analogical classification—she recommends the careful reading of literature in a manner that forces us to "detach" ourselves "from generalizations of collective identity" (70). To learn to read, in other words, is to illuminate those figures who disrupt a seamless collectivity (i.e., the subaltern), to illustrate that the "meaning of the figure is undecidable," and then "to learn to dis-figure the undecidable figure into responsible literality" (72). The central question of close reading, according to Spivak, is not only "Who are we?" but "How many are we?" (29). Spivak's methodology in this particular case is radically *anti-political* insofar as it interrupts and undoes any attempt to naturalize the collectivity on which politics rest. In Gramscian language, close reading interrupts a hegemonic conception of life.

In other words, close reading registers the conflict between the totalizing theory—which coheres an identifiable collectivity that can then be represented in the State—and the individual challenge to that totality—the subaltern who is without part within that totalizing theory. In Spivak's (2003) words, "Literature contains the element of surprising the historical" (55). As a result, to begin to understand the other on their own terms requires careful close reading of what they have to say. As she puts it simply and elegantly: "Literature is what escapes the system; you cannot speed read it" (52). It is through a close reading of individual texts—not the "speed reading" or survey of a wide variety of texts and cultural documents—that we can begin "to learn to learn from below" (50). To learn to learn from the social explosion, Spivak might tell us, requires that we dedicate ourselves to closely following what the literary, artistic, and narrative works of the agents of the social explosion have to tell us, not trying to collect a wide swath of the 'testimony' from various 'native informants.'

To put it polemically in order to drive the point home, in response to critiques that more cultural examples need to be included in order to support my argument—rather than deeper analysis of select intellectuals and artists—I say that such a methodology functionally perceives participants in the social explosion as 'native informants' to be mined for information in the formation of a new political collectivity. Initial critics of *On the Chilean Social Explosion*'s close-reading methodology implicitly saw Chilean protestors as informational content to be appropriated for grander political ends, not human beings with whom one needs to dialogue on an intimate level. What was implicitly sought was *the molding of a unified meaning* not *the registering of interdependence*. Moreover, such an attitude is at least in part what led to the political crisis at the heart of the social explosion. To perceive a person as having dignity, to perceive their socio-cultural paradigms as offering autonomous and legitimate modes of organizing social relations (see Chapter 1), is to accept that one must carefully, intentionally, and profoundly listen to what they are saying, not quickly appropriate what they say as one more expression or 'case study' in a long list of cultural examples. In the end, my methodology reflects just such an ethical relation.

In sum, the methodology of close reading is founded on the interdependency between author, text, and reader. Instead of engaging a wide variety and breadth of cultural materials that survey social explosion documents and testimony for purposes of sublating those diffuse materials into a general theory, I tend to focus on detailed readings of a few texts and events as well as proposing a cast of newly emerging artists and authors. This of course produces a serious problem: I cannot reasonably make a thesis about the social explosion in its entirety. Indeed, the reader should note that my discussions are situated primarily in Valparaíso—the region where I live—and Santiago. Yet this is also the point of my close-reading methodology: we need to abandon the hope for encompassing a phenomenon in its totality and reconfigure our ethical attachments with cultural actors in the realm of dialogue. I am not the scientist examining or representing the social explosion from the outside, I am in interdependent dialogue with various social actors.

Yet Spivak (2003), just like me, also insists that this does not mean that quantitative and information-retrieval methodologies should be dismissed. (In fact, much of my analysis depends precisely on such methods.) If she heavily critiques the tendency in much social-science research to reduce cultural products to "field research"—instead demanding that we treat the languages and art of the Global South as "active cultural media rather than as objects of cultural study" (9)—she also insists that such literary studies based in close reading needs to work with and supplement "area studies" based in social-science methodologies. Similarly, *On the Chilean Social Explosion* is not meant to replace social-science accounts of the social explosion; it is meant to supplement these studies, insisting that we take serious account of those in the streets in Chile in the later months of 2019 as theoretical agents and not just native informants.

As such, this study seeks to combine archival materials, so to speak, from three sources. First, as will be evident throughout the work, each chapter is based primarily on a set of primary texts. Second, there are what might be considered 'participant observation' sections. During the first two weeks of the social explosion I attended 10 marches, and subsequently I attended a combined minimum of three marches, meetings, assemblies, *cabildos*, and so on every week (for example, two marches and one assembly, or two meetings and one *cabildo*). These participant observation examples are drawn from these experiences. Methodologically, I *read* these events as if they were a literary text. The point here, as I've written elsewhere, is that we researchers need to abandon the concept of 'native informant' in order to recognize that those we are interacting with are constructing narratives and identities through complex rhetorical and discursive strategies in which they perform resistance through those narratives (Woods 2021b: 678). Not only are 'observed' participants and events complex constellations of social dynamics that require intimate attention to rhetoric instead of summary as quantifiable fact, but we also need to recognize our *interdependent linkages* with those who we are only ostensibly 'observing.'

Third, a notable amount of the activist networks that brought together participants occurred via social media. Various social media accounts became the sites to amplify calls for marches, advertisements for artistic performances, and announcements for *cabildos* and assemblies.[19] For instance, the Instagram account, @actividadesvalpo, published a daily list of every organized activity occurring in the Valparaíso area. On particularly busy days, dozens of activities would be listed, such as 7 December 2019 in which 42 different events were listed in Valparaíso alone. This pushes towards what was commonly known throughout the social explosion: there was no central organizing apparatus that held dominance, but rather there was a multiplicity of threads coming together. Gramsci's focus on the political party that unifies these threads was not operational; all threads were in some sense autonomous, and there was no central leadership. What remains to be seen in the body of *On the Chilean Social Explosion* is how these different threads were brought together.

This relationship between activism, virtual communication networks, and the politics of autonomy has been a field of intense interest since the Zapatistas launched their global communication strategy via internet communiqués in 1994 (Earl et al. 2012; Rabasa 2001; Rovira Sancho 2016). Since then, various autonomous social movements have sought to organize independent, horizontalist, and cooperativist media outlets, like Indymedia during the 2000s (Mosca 2008; Notes from Nowhere 2003). This has especially been the case in Latin America where movements like #NiUnaMenos (see Chapter 4) have depended upon the use of virtual communication networks (Accossatto 2018). Nonetheless, many have pointed out that these movements simply use the internet "as a broadcast channel for information distribution" and for "the online facilitation of offline activism" (Earl et al. 2012: 429–430). This was in large part the social-media activity I traced during the social explosion, not tracking potential 'hacktivism' like that of Wikileaks and Anonymous (Sorell 2015).

Following Rovira (2016), however, the case of the Zapatistas and later Latin American organizing points to how online activism is linked to a reconfiguration of social movements as *"connected multitudes"* rather than a traditional collective subjects. Although protests continue occurring offline, the connected multitudes formed through the Internet speak to a mode of collectivization beyond "the distinction [between] hegemonic publics/counterpublics," meaning that the central cultural struggle is no longer formed by "constructing 'public opinion,'" but rather by weaving together "the common dimension of singularities when they place their life as a shared problem" (Rovira 2016: 135–136). There are of course limitations to such an optimistic view—most notably that social-media activity is waged from within the confines of tech corporations like Facebook, not to mention the "digital divide" (Mosca 2008). Rovira's (2016) study, however, points to how the links between Internet activity and offline social movements speak to a new mode of decentralized collectivization without leaders, where each and every person is simultaneously producer and receiver of messages thereby permitting a "self-communication of the masses" (132). It is the argument of this book that such a reconsideration of the collective subject occupying streets during late 2019 and early 2020 was a substantial part of the Chilean social explosion.

Notes

1 For a fuller overview of the early part of the social explosion as well as a description of its dynamics, see Garcés (2020).
2 Not to be confused with the act of setting the actual subway on fire. As of August 2021, it is still unclear who committed this act.
3 This is of course drawing on Spivak's (2012) definition of agency as "institutionally validated action" (110) and of the subaltern as "the absence of institutionally validated agency" (326).
4 This history of anarchism in Chile is entirely from the wonderful research conducted by others (del Solar and Pérez 2008; Godoy Sepúlveda 2016; Grez Toso 2007; Muñoz Cortés 2013).
5 While outside the scope of this work, it is worth recommending that this concept of interdependency is similar to the Aymara concept of *ayni*, "an institution of help of non-remunerated work that demands strict reciprocity in its return [*devolución*]" (Fernández Osco 2000: 138). As such, *ayni* is founded on the values of "reciprocal correspondence" (Yampara Huarachi 2011: 7–8), equilibrium, and balance (Silverblatt 1987: 139) between systems. When Silvia Rivera Cusicanqui (2018) uses Aymara concepts to imagine a decolonized world in which the nation-State is replaced by equilibrium among the world's heterogeneous parts, she is, I would argue, in concert with Butler. The question to be asked of Rivera Cusicanqui, and which I ask in this book, is: How do we reconcile this desire for equilibrium with her historical account of armed militant decolonial action?
6 By discussing violence in terms of grievability and disposability, Butler tacitly defines all violence as lethal. That is, she makes no substantial distinction between the shove and the execution.
7 This is a tacit response to Slavoj Žižek's (2007) claim that the task of the revolutionary left is to embrace and critically redefine *revolutionary terror*. I follow Achille Mbembe's (2003) argument that terror has become an integral part of modern governance, and that such terror gives the sovereign the power "to define who matters and who does not, who is *disposable* and who is not" (27). The point here is that we need to imagine a politics that goes beyond such a logic of terror, a rebellion that is not based on the logic of terror, that does not define who is disposable and who is not.
8 Kautzer (2018) warns about transformative self-defense legitimizing the formation of a sovereign subject, yet he offers no theoretical guidance as to how to avoid that danger.
9 An exception to this is Negri and Hardt (2004).
10 After having written this introduction, I had the honor of reading Maria Laura Gutiérrez and Camila Arbuet Osuna's (2020) article that appeals to many of the same theorizations discussed in these sections—Schmitt, Butler, Benjamin—but arrives to a different conclusion. Potential debate between their and my readings of the social explosion is precisely what excites me about future research on the social explosion.

11 This useful distinction is thanks to Stuart Hall (1986).
12 This reading of Gramsci is highly indebted to Guido Liguori (2015b).
13 Trish Salah (2014) has more fully theorized the relationship between the subaltern and trans subjectivity.
14 The key phrase here is "and, with it, to the politics of autonomy." There is now a long bibliography tied to the question of a culture of networked relations dating back to Deleuze and Guattari's theorization of the concept of the 'rhizome.' Furthermore, Édouard Glissant's theorization of the *Poetics of Relation* is an implied theoretical base of much of this discussion. The question is not what a relational post-hegemonic culture looks like, but how such a culture is linked to a revolutionary politics of autonomy.
15 Though uncited in Mignolo's (2009) article, this idea of the multitude and singularities is fully theorized by Hardt and Negri (2000, 2004). As they say explicitly, the multitudes "are not peoples or nations or even communities" (Hardt and Negri 2004: 192). To polemically rework Mignolo's argument: enforcing a vision of the multitude onto the Aymara *ayllu* is a colonial act.
16 Mignolo is concerned with the same question. I have critiqued his response elsewhere and do not wish to revisit that critique here. In my estimation, we are concerned with the same problem, but have merely arrived at different responses. Just as in my critiques of his work elsewhere, it is impossible not to read my work without recognizing that this critique is inherently building off his work, not rejecting it.
17 Moretti would then expand upon this methodology in other articles and most notably a book in 2005.
18 To summarize this tension with one example. At a panel at the 2016 Modernist Studies Association, "Migration and the Modern(ist) City: Geographic and Computational Approaches," Elizabeth Evans and Matthew Wilkens presented a literary map of London, identifying various significant locations in the cultural imaginary of the population through a computational analysis of hundreds of books. Afterwards, Jason Finch presented a close reading of Sam Selvon's *The Lonely Londoners* in which he implicitly rejoined the previous presentation: many people may be discussing the same spaces and using the same language, but the articulation of those urban places takes on radically different forms based on the texture of the individual texts analyzed. For instance, Selvon's focus on Black Caribbean migrants' experience of central places in London drastically differs from white Londoners'. Finch's argument implied a rather paradoxical conclusion: to understand the general contours of a culture, one must first pay attention to the intimate details of individual texts. For a further development of this methodology see Finch (2016a, 2021).
19 In my personal case, I paid close attention to many accounts, including in the case of the Valparaíso area (i.e., not including major independent media outlets like @piensaprensa) but not limited to: @colectivo_bellavista_despiertx; @c.accionculturalvalpo; @colactiva; @actividadesvalpo; @difusionvina; @territorio.marimonjas; @movilizacionesvalpoyvina; @difusion.valpo; @contramedios; @rpivalparaiso; @acciongayvalpo; @cabildovina; @jovenesindigenasvalpo; @cordonesvalpo; @lascabras_movilizadas; @accionecosocialquintero; @cabildoquinteropuchuncavi; @mesa.social.valparaiso; @coordinadora8m.vina; @rival_medios; @concon_movilizado; @mums_valparaiso; @valposting; @resistencia.shishi. The reader will note that this list is *highly* heterogeneous including accounts that are representative of a well-organized and institutionalized social movement the likes of which I partly critique in Chapter 1 (e.g., @coordinadora8m.vina), others are simply run by individuals, others are sites that aggregate events organized by other people (e.g., @movilizacionesvalpoyvina),

and others are actually principally meme pages (e.g., @valposting). Such a list also misses a significant element of the early days of the social explosion: calls for marches were being circulated amongst friends, WhatsApp networks, neighborhood meetings, and so on. The point is not that the organizing was done exclusively by institutionalized social movements or by autonomous rhizomatic networks, but rather that none was dominant.

1 On the Barricade

In a video uploaded to the Internet on 19 October 2019, a group of about 50 people are gathered at an intersection in Santiago de Chile where they have collected together scraps of sheet metal, torn-up public-transport signs, bags of trash, and pieces of plywood in order to construct a barricade along a side street (Danza Ruiz 2019). Some have covered their faces and eyes with bandanas, neck warmers, goggles, and/or t-shirts for purposes that become clear later in the video: police enter along a central avenue with armored vehicles, tear gas, and pepper spray in order to break up the congregation. Upon the police's entrance, the protestors scramble behind the barricade in order to seek safety along the side street.[1] There is nothing particularly special about this video. It was an event I would witness personally dozens of times over the next months as part of what has come to be known as the Chilean social explosion [*estallido social*], a series of national-scale protests that placed Chile's postmillennial sociopolitical order founded on neoliberalism, patriarchy, colonialism, and environmental extractivism under structural crisis. Political congregations in urban centers confronting State forces with the erection of barricades became commonplace, and in the later months of 2019, seeing hooded individuals in streets next to flaming barricades had become routine, a basic element of protests that were being held multiple times a week by mobilized individuals.

The government's official response to barricades framed them as acts of criminality, with President Piñera's speeches tending to employ a discourse of the urgency for "armed forces" and "police" to protect "security," "order," "our government," and "the law" in the face of "violence," "delinquency," and "damage" (Navarro and Tromben 2019). This discourse was arguably made most evident in his speech on 20 October 2019,

> We are at war with a powerful and relentless enemy who does not respect anyone or anything and who is ready to use violence without any limit even when it means the loss of human life, with the only goal of producing the most damage possible.

DOI: 10.4324/9781003224594-2

This categorization of the social explosion in terms of criminality was later enshrined in law when the Chilean government passed an "Anti-Barricade" and "Anti-Looting" Law (Law 21.208, officially published on 30 January 2020) that declared in Article 268,

> Whoever, without being authorized, completely interrupts the free circulation of people or vehicles in a public thoroughfare [*vía pública*], through violence or intimidation of people or the installation of obstacles erected in that thoroughfare with various objects, will be sanctioned with the penalty of misdemeanor [*presidio menor*] in its highest grade.

Law 21.208 reveals the various cultural indices ("violence," "misdemeanor," "intimidation," "authorization,") that informed the government's legislative response to the social explosion. The State legitimized their criminalization of protest by appealing to a cultural perception of the barricade in terms of violence, delinquency, and the interruption of free circulation—implying that barricades (and with it the protests) represent nothing affirmative, that they were noise to be removed by the "authorizing" force of the State.

Representing the barricade as such, the government's brutal repression of protest during the social explosion should come as no surprise. Police violence was constant throughout the protests with Chile's National Institute of Human Rights registering as of 19 March 2020: 3,838 individuals injured by State armed forces and police (including 460 with serious ocular damage and 2,178 as a result of being shot by pellet, rubber bullets, or tear gas cartridges) as well as 1,465 judicial actions presented against the State (including 6 for homicide, 23 for attempted homicide, 206 for sexual assault, and 1,803 for torture). And though anecdotal, by November 2019 I began to assume that I would see police brutality at any protest I attended given the astounding number of cases I personally witnessed, many in complete disregard of Chilean law. For instance, on 18 November 2019, the Valparaíso court banned police use of pellet and rubber bullets against protestors (a decision that would later be overturned in February 2020), but on 26 November 2019, I found myself staring down the barrel of a police shotgun as an officer turned on us with pellet. All of this was legitimized under the official discourse that police were responding to "delinquency," "violence," and "intimidation" that was interrupting "the free circulation" of citizens.

But what of the protestors themselves? How did they perceive the barricade? Returning to the 19 October 2020 video of the barricade, we find that the protestors actively and affirmatively ascribed meaning to their congregation when they collectively joined together in singing "*El baile de los que sobran*" ["The Dance of Those Leftover"], a song that served as an anthem during the social mobilizations of 2019. "*El baile de los que sobran*" was released in 1986 by *Los Prisioneros*, a working-class post-punk Chilean band that "put lyrics, melody, and song" to the social process of protesting against and eventually ending the Chilean dictatorship (Duran 1999). By the time the song was written, the Chilean dictator, General Augusto Pinochet, had introduced a set of sweeping neoliberal reforms, and the inequalities generated by those reforms were beginning to be felt and seen with an economic crisis that began in 1982 and a wave of protest against the dictatorship that began in 1983. The lyrics respond not so much to the repressive politics of authoritarianism—though these politics are acknowledged in the music video—as to the affective register of the economic crisis of the 1980s, expressing frustration that while education had previously "ended for others with laurels and a future, they left my friends kicking stones." This affective register forms the foundation of the song's famous chorus, "Join the dance of those leftover…No one really wants to help us." In addition to recognizing material disparities under Chilean neoliberalism, the song expresses the specific experience of feeling leftover, an experience of watching a neoliberal culture forming and recognizing that you were being denied any "institutionally validated voice" (Spivak 2012). By singing "*El baile de los que sobran,*" participants were ascribing a particular significance to the barricade: Chile's leftovers were claiming their agency and presence in a socio-political landscape designed to deny that agency and presence. Whereas for the government the barricade was evidence of a "powerful enemy" wielding "violence" and "intimidation" against social order, for the protestors it was the dance of those leftover.

At the same time that the government was criminalizing protest, two powerful sympathetic narratives emerged in support of the protestors that I will explore in this chapter: (1) It was a condemnation of neoliberal governance that had reigned in Chile since the dictatorship, and (2) It was an extension of social movements that had been gaining momentum since the late 1990s. What I argue in this chapter is that these sympathetic modes of understanding the barricade, and along with it the social explosion, have been articulated in terms of "the reigning conventional wisdoms of political process theory, resource mobilization, and rational choice" (Calhoun 2001: 49). In other words, early analyses have attempted to understand the barricade in terms of politics of the State—What is the legislation and new political mapping that will result from barricades in the street?—and independent social movements leveraging for material gains—How is the barricade as a protest tactic used to win certain fights over political issues and access to resources? Within these readings, the barricade is a legitimate expression of discontent, but one that is waiting to be choreographed into proper political expression by social-movement and leftist leaders.

Following recent challenges to this material focus of many social movement analyses,[2] I argue that the barricades of the social explosion can be understood as Elisabeth Jean Wood (2001) theorized subaltern revolt in El Salvador, "The key to the logic of insurgent collective action…is the assertion of dignity and defiance through the act of rebelling" (268); the barricade was a subaltern assertion of agency and dignity.[3] To return to Walter

Benjamin's concept of divine and mythical violence from the introduction: the barricade was not a protest tactic of mythical violence to put pressure on the government to transform the law, it was *the ephemeral divine suspension of the law* that illuminated the prefigurative autonomous politics of the leftovers of Chile. More precisely, and departing slightly from Wood, I argue through an analysis of street art in Valparaíso during the social explosion that the barricade served not as a means for a unified collective to assert its univocal agency; instead, the barricade was a political locus that weaved together a variety of collective assertion*s* of agenc*ies* and dignit*ies*. The barricade was not only a protest tactic or a means of putting pressure on the State but also a means of various subaltern collectivities to assert their agency as the dance of those leftover.

Anti-Neoliberal Discontent and Beyond

Although the catalyst for the protests was the government raising subway fare, many have convincingly argued that the protests are more broadly condemning the neoliberal political-economic model initially installed in the 1970s under the dictator, General Augusto Pinochet (Panotto 2019; Rojas 2019; Valdivia Ortiz de Zárate 2003). Neoliberalism has frequently come to be the term used to describe processes tied to the recession or weakening of the State via the privatization of formerly public services and the deregulation of the market economy. Chile seemingly supports this understanding. When implemented in the 1970s and 1980s, neoliberalization served to undermine a previously strong centralized national State that "aimed at promoting industrialisation, regulating social conflicts and reshaping social structures" (Taylor 2006: 2). Trying to equitably distribute the benefits of national development and first emerging in the 1930s in response to pressure from the autonomously organized industrial working class, this State formation reached its zenith with the Socialist administration of Salvador Allende in the early 1970s. Between the 1930s and 1973, the Chilean State was a centralized institutional space in which certain elements of an empowered working class could collectively participate in the ordering of the national territory. Neoliberalism replaced this ordering of Chilean national space with a social landscape dominated by a deregulated, globalized, and decentralized marketplace.

To give just one example of the difference: during the 1960s and early 1970s, the Chilean State had nationalized the country's main natural resource and export, copper. Under neoliberalism, such national development built from working-class roots was dismantled, and copper rights were privatized and often sold to foreign corporations (Caputo and Galarce 2011). The broader list of phenomena privatized under neoliberalism is stark:

> almost all basic services (water, electricity, gas, telephone, medicine, banks); urban, rail and air transport; highway services inside and between cities; the pension system (except for the Armed Forces); the

> prison system; cubic meters of sea water given through concessions for the exploitation of marine resources; extensions of land, given through concessions for tourism; and also important areas of social welfare, such as the health and educational systems.
>
> (Cornejo et al. 2011: 153)

Within this understanding, neoliberalism signifies the substitution of a powerful centralized national State power, which the united working class could weaponize to realize significant material gains and articulate their collective demands, with a disaggregated marketplace constituted by atomized individuals and antagonistic to collective projects and working-class solidarity.

A closer look at Chile, however, betrays such an understanding. Beyond the basic fact to be explored later (see Chapter 5) that neoliberalism had to be installed with a dictatorship wielding brutal violence—i.e., If neoliberalism is merely the 'recession' of the State, then why is State violence so necessary for its implementation and functioning?—Taylor Marcus (2006) has effectively argued that neoliberalism is "a state-led project of social engineering that seeks to reformulate the institutional forms of state-society relations" (7). As Timothy Clark (2018) argues, Chilean neoliberalization began with the reorganization of the State in the mid-1970s in a manner that directed financial power towards business conglomerates who supported the mission of the new political-economic model. As a result, when the State subsequently privatized nearly 500 previously nationalized industries these capitalist elites were "well-positioned to snap up the most attractive and lucrative privatized assets" (28). These new capitalist elites, Clark continues, were built around multinational economic activities based on the importation of foreign commodities and the development of "new export sectors such as forestry, agro-business, and fisheries" (30). In the end, Chilean neoliberalization was and is marked by "the centralization of authority and the decentralization of production" (33), a social structure that enables a more diversified and globalized marketplace, weakens the power of organized labor, and strengthens the power of a select cadre of capitalist elites supported by the Chilean government.

Following Bob Jessop (2016), Chilean neoliberalism demonstrates that the State is not so much an identifiable subject as much as "a social relation" (53) defined by "the exercise and effects of *state power* as a contingent expression of a changing balance of forces that seek to advance their respective interests inside, through, and against the state system" (54). Neoliberalism, then, is constituted by "a changing balance of forces" in which capital transforms the State's "institutional architecture and strategic biases" (Jessop 2013: 67) in order to promote finance-dominated accumulation and to wrest power away from the (national, male, waged) working class (Jessop 2013, 2019). In contrast to the common image of neoliberalism as the recession of the State, the Chilean example demonstrates that the installation and maintenance of a neoliberal social landscape requires a highly active State that directs material resources into the hands of capitalist elites. Chilean neoliberalism is not the recession of the State; it is the evisceration of the *particular form* of the pre-coup centralized national State and the reconstitution of State power—the dictatorship rewrote the constitution behind closed doors in 1980 according to neoliberal principles—to enable its weaponization by a capitalist elite.

After the dictatorship ended in 1989, the new democratically elected government maintained this neoliberal model and its promises for economic development. The results of this policy decision have been lauded by many as a success, with Piñera less than a month before the social explosion describing Chile as an "oasis" of development in Latin America where, for instance, "the incidence of poverty fell from 45 percent in 1987, to 22 percent in 1998 and 21 percent in 2000" (Moreno Brid and Hernández 2004). Against this conclusion, however, others argue that this oasis is only a mirage: neoliberalization has in fact created massive inequality, exclusively benefitting capitalist elites at the cost of the working class (Klein 2007; Rojas 2019; Taylor 2006). For example, as of 2017, the top 1 percent of the richest individuals in Chile received 33 percent of the total earnings of the country, and half of all salaried workers in 2015 received pay "insufficient to cover the basic necessities of an average home" (PNUD 2017: 21–23). This structural critique of the inequality caused by neoliberalization helps explain one of the most popular slogans of the social explosion: *it's not 30 pesos, it's 30 years.* ("It's not 30 pesos"—referring to the subway fare hike—"it's 30 years"—referring to the post-dictatorship neoliberal governance structure.)

This anti-neoliberalism narrative was represented in liberal and leftist US media outlets like *The New York Times*, *The Nation*, and *Jacobin*.[4] Nearly every article in these publications followed the same basic format: The article was headed by a photo of a barricade, a burning building, police shooting tear gas, and/or hooded protestors, and the written narrative outlined the economic inequality of the country followed by a description of confrontations between State forces and civilians. For these media outlets, the protests were framed as a response to economic injustice in a nation that had successfully attained development during the 1990s and 2000s but had inequitably distributed the benefits of that development. As Pascale Bonnefoy wrote in the *New York Times* on 19 October 2019, "The [subway] fare increase, which went into effect on Oct. 6, came at a time when the cost of living for poor and middle-class families has been rising while wages have remained stagnant." Ben Ehrenreich, writing for *The Nation* on 25 November 2019, argued that Chile was part of a "global rebellion against neoliberalism," "All of the countries recently experiencing popular revolts...have for decades been ruled by a single economic model, in which the 'growth' celebrated by the pedigreed few means immiseration for the many." And René Rojas (2019) wrote in *Jacobin*, "while median monthly wages are $550, Chile's 1 percent earns at least ten times as much, controlling one-third of national income...Chile's obscene inequality, matched by the oligarchic concentration of political influence, is fueling the revolt."

Where these outlets varied, however, was in their representation of the affirmative politics being articulated within the revolt. For the *Times* and *The Nation*, discontent was framed as blind rage. Whereas Bonnefoy (2019) wrote about the protests "devolving into looting and arson" and Amanda Taub (2019), also of the *Times*, said there were "no effective channels for public anger," Ehrenreich (2019) described the Chilean population as, "so exhausted by austerity, so squeezed by low wages and long hours and debt, so fed up with the greed and blindness of the wealthy few who run the country that they were ready to burn almost everything down." To the contrary of the *New York Times* and *The Nation*, however, *Jacobin* identified emerging political alternatives to Chilean neoliberalism. Authors like Andrew Richner and Abigail Gutmann-Gonzalez (2019) painted a portrait of how anti-neoliberal discontent, first emerging in massive form with the student movements of 2006 (the so-called Penguins Revolution) and 2011, had eventually led to the formation of a new leftist political party in 2017, the *Frente Amplio*,

> a broad left electoral coalition composed of distinct left parties and social movements whose principal aim is to challenge the neoliberal consensus…[The] demands of the mass popular uprising mirror the coalition's political platform, opening the possibility for Frente Amplio to harness some of the energy.

Jacobin would later expand this vision beyond the Frente Amplio by including an interview with Daniel Jadue, the Chilean Communist Party mayor of the Recoleta neighborhood in Santiago who was a powerful political voice during the social explosion (Jadue 2019). For *Jacobin*'s contributors, *Frente Amplio* and the Chilean Communist Party were offering an affirmative articulation of the protestors' vision.

Inevitably, these articles were published alongside a photo of a hooded protestor(s) in front of or nearby a burning barricade. Prior to any word from the Internet version of Amanda Taub's (2019) *Times* article, for instance, the reader is greeted by an image of an anonymous protestor lifting their arms in front of a barricade burning in the middle of a Santiago street at sunset. The meaning assigned to the barricade within the narrative contexts of the *Times* and *The Nation* can be illuminated in the space between word and image: the barricade is an expression of legitimate discontent, but one that lacks any affirmative alternative. The barricade is part and parcel of "looting," "arson," and a willingness "to burn almost everything down" due to an underlying "public anger" "with no effective channels" for its resolution. For *Jacobin*, however, the barricade becomes not only a rejection of the dominance of neoliberal policy within the Chilean political economy, but an opening for the installation of a new political-economic model articulated by a leftist opposition; the barricade is "energy" to be "harnessed" by political parties like the *Frente Amplio* and the Chilean Communist Party.

If the protestors' act of singing *Los Prisioneros* at the barricade supports these narratives, insofar as they were effectively invoking the decades-long collective memory of the economic impact of neoliberalism, their song also points beyond that limited economic interpretation. Quite simply, to be leftover is not to be poor. The moment one shifts towards an examination of the leftovers in Chile, instead of the limited lens of anti-neoliberal discontent, a more diversified social field emerges. One might begin with the decolonial demands of Indigenous communities that ran throughout the social explosion. This decolonial element can be seen in a December 2019 stencil from Plaza Aníbal Pinto in Valparaíso, "It's not 30 pesos, it's not 30 years, this war started 470 years ago." After making initial reference to the common slogan already mentioned—it's not 30 pesos, it's 30 years—the stencil turns that slogan on its head in order to reframe discontent as a response to the continuing structure of settler colonialism ("this war started 470 years ago" with the colonial conquest). That this is a present critique of the structure of settler colonialism is clarified through the stencil's portrait of Camilo Catrillanca, a 24-year-old Mapuche farmer (the Mapuche form the largest Indigenous nation in the geopolitical space dominated by the Chilean nation-State) who was murdered by police on 14 November 2018. During the social explosion, one of the largest days of activity was in memoriam of the one-year anniversary of his death, with protests occurring in over 40 cities across the country.

There are also those who have arguably been the most active organizers during the social explosion: feminists and those looking to empower "sexual diversity" (see Chapter 4). One might look, for instance, at the "march of non-heterosexual discontent" that took place in Valparaíso on 6 November 2019. Furthermore, Diamela Eltit (2019) reminds us that the most recent precursor to the social explosion was feminist organizing in 2018 and 2019, organizing that additionally led to the formation of the Valparaíso art collective, LASTESIS, whose work from November 2019, "*Un violador en tu camino*" ("A Rapist in Your Path"), was subsequently performed across the globe (see Chapter 4). I could keep listing the various groups voicing that they feel leftover in the postmillennial social landscape of neoliberalism, coloniality, and patriarchy as well as their attempts to initiate a broad reconstitution of the country: those who live in the "sacrifice zones" of Chile that are demanding environmental justice (Woods 2020b), the Black communities of Chile's north who demand recognition (Henríquez Salgado 2015), those who are demanding water justice (see Chapter 3), and so on. Indeed, for those arguing that the social explosion is centrally about economic inequality, why were the most intense political debates during December 2019 about gender parity and reserved seats for Indigenous nations in the potential constitutional convention as well as about the need for a plurinational constitution that recognizes the multiple Indigenous nations occupying lands currently dominated by the Chilean State?

Social Movements and the Leftovers

What I am pointing to is that the social explosion cannot be understood exclusively as anti-neoliberal revolt and must also include the affects of being leftover that are tied to discussions of coloniality, patriarchy, and environmental justice. This diversity of discontents housed within the social explosion did not emerge out of a vacuum. Such decolonial and feminist elements built off activist organizing developed in the post-dictatorship era.

According to many accounts, official Chilean social movements after the dictatorship have passed through three phases. First, following the dictatorship, in which a multiplicity of social movements had united against the common enemy of Pinochet, collective social actors initially participated in the formation of the new democratic government. In this moment, utopian optimism reigned and many hoped that the transition would allow for a bottom-up mode of governance that recognized and resolved the various problems highlighted by social movements. Second, after this initial optimism many perceived that the new transition government was disempowering social movements by neutralizing and institutionalizing their organizations within liberal State apparatuses, in effect *depoliticizing* Chilean society (Forstenzer 2017; Pairicán 2012: 14). The result has been an explosion of NGOs and government ministries that serve to represent Indigenous and feminist concerns within the State (and thereby subordinate their autonomous demands to the institutional mechanisms of the State). Third, starting in the late 1990s and 2000s many began organizing independently[5] in order to confrontationally challenge the legitimacy of the State as a representative body for resolving social tensions and problems, leading to the eruption of new confrontational movements[6]—Mapuche organizers in Lumaco burning logging trucks in 1997, the student movements of 2006 and 2011, and the feminist protests of 2018 are often common examples. Within this frame, the social explosion can be understood as a response to the failure of post-dictatorship democratic governance to resolve the diverse issues brought forth by non-State, yet still institutionalized[7] in the sense of having a well-established organizational and hierarchical structure, social movements since the 1980s.[8]

Within this understanding, the barricade signifies a confrontational declaration by distinct non-State collective actors who engage in more confrontational "tactics" (e.g., the burning of forestry trucks in Lumaco in 1997 and student protests using barricades in 2006 and 2011).[9] This understanding of the barricade was expressed, for instance, by Gabriel Boric—a leader during the 2011 student protests, a member of the Chilean parliament as part of *Frente Amplio*, and president elect as of 2021—who in a series of tweets from 4 December 2019 defended voting for a law that "makes looting a crime" while simultaneously arguing that "barricades in the context of social struggle seem to us to be a legitimate expression of resistance" (@gabrielboric 2019), a rather common position that distinguishes between "peaceful and violent protests and criminal activity" (Somma, Bargsted, Disi Pavlic, and Medel 2021: 495).[10] Boric's statement generates its meaning by employing a cultural frame that defines the barricade as a legitimate tactic of non-State resistance distinct from both peaceful protests and criminal activity. That is, the representation of the barricade as a legitimate but confrontational protest tactic is by no means neutral; it reproduces and is founded on a cultural discourse generated during the 1990s and 2000s tied to institutionalized social movements' separation from State apparatuses. In this reading, the barricade is a tactic by non-State social movements to put pressure on the State to win certain material gains.

Such a cultural categorization of the barricade as a "tactic" of "violent protests," and its implicit links to a social-movement framework, is hampered by a serious limitation: these long-standing institutionalized non-State social movements were not the leaders of the social explosion. Indeed, one particular study of protestors at Dignity Plaza (one center of protests in Santiago) in November 2019 found that 64.2 percent of participants were not involved in any institutionalized social movement (Núcleo de Sociología Contingente 2020: 19). This is in large part unsurprising given that participants in postmillennial autonomous uprisings—Occupy, 2001 Argentinian protests, anti-austerity movements in Europe, and so on—tend to never have been politically active prior to the mass movement (Graeber 2009; Notes from Nowhere 2003; Sitrin and Azzellini 2014). Moreover, after publishing this tweet and voting to make looting a specific punishable crime, Boric was denounced by many participating in the social explosion.[11] Quite simply, this social-movement-based mode of understanding the social explosion in terms of peaceful protest, confrontational but legitimate resistance (barricades), and criminal activity (looting) seems to have been rejected by many.

Although some protests were organized in classic social-movement style—the International Women's Day March on 8 March 2020 was organized by the 8M movement, the general strike on 12 November 2019 was organized by various labor organizations, the January 2020 boycott against Chile's standardized college entrance exam was led by a high-school student organization (Coordinating Assembly of High-School Students [ACES]), occasional marches in Valparaíso were organized by the "Social Table" [*Mesa Social*], and so on—social-explosion protests were organized predominantly without any strict organizational structure, "October 2019 in Chile was celebrated massively in its character as a self-convened [*autoconvocada*] protest: a protest without recognizable leadership and expressing a manifest distrust towards institutional politics" (Richard 2021: 132).[12] Indeed, accepting that "the contents of the citizens' demands…were not programmatically articulated in a well-defined agenda of changes" (113), it is difficult to see the barricade as a protest tactic for leveraging material gains. Furthermore, some of the groups that did organize marches may not be commonly recognized as 'political' agents. For instance, the soccer-fan club for the team, the Santiago Wanderers, organized two marches in Valparaíso in late 2019: one on

31 October in memoriam of those killed by the State during the social explosion and another on 1 December in protest of unfair practices in Chile's national soccer organization. Both of these marches form part of the social explosion but would largely be ignored within social-movement narratives that would see the organization in general and the latter march in particular as non-political.

This is not to say that institutionalized social movements did not have an effect on the social explosion. That it was so easy for common demands and concessions to emerge in late 2019 is a consequence of earlier organizing already having inserted those demands into popular discourse. For instance, though writing a new constitution has frequently been discussed since the transition to democracy, it became a serious issue as a result of the 2011 student protests' placing it as a central element in their program (Donoso 2017), and the demand for specifically a *plurinational* constitution is a consequence of this discourse having already been circulated and developed within Indigenous Mapuche, Aymara, Diaguita, and Rapa Nui thought (Moraga 2016). Furthermore, each of these institutionalized social movements has been supported and legitimized by the generation of popular post-dictatorship cultures structured around questions of feminism and decoloniality (Carrasco 2000; Echeverría 2014, 2019; García 2012; Pisano 1996; Tricot 2013). Yet those working from within social movements are now faced with a difficult fact: the historical subject of the social explosion is not involved in institutionalized politics, whether that be from the 'inside' as State actors, from non-State institutionalized social movements, or from any space in between (Donoso 2017). This has led some researchers of Chile's social movements to comment that it is "surprising" that such social movements have played only a "marginal role [in the social explosion]...given their centrality in the protest campaigns of the past fifteen years" (Somma, Bargsted, Disi Pavlic, and Medel 2021: 496).

More polemically, what is "surprising" seems to be that the people might mobilize on their own initiative outside institutionalized social movements and State politics. Following Ranajit Guha's (1998) argument about both decolonial nationalist and neocolonial historical representations of decolonization in South Asia, many analyses of the social explosion by social movement leaders, leftist intellectuals and academics, and Chilean politicians account for the people of Chile only as "an inert mass deployed by the dominant elements to serve their ends" (x). Rozas Bugueño and Maillet's (2019: 4) discussion of the pension reform social movement (as well as the use of barricades as a "tactic" in that movement), for instance, analyzes: articles from the newspaper, *La Tercera*; speeches by politicians (Sebastián Piñera, Alejandro Guillier, and Beatriz Sánchez); information from the websites of organizations coordinating protests against the Chilean pension system; academic articles; and 16 interviews with "relevant actors in the Chilean pension sector." They do not, however, substantially ask how the pension-reform protests are actually understood by the people participating in and contributing to the movement. The people are passive evidence not active agents.[13] I contend that these leftovers—those who are denied any institutionally validated voice in Chilean society (i.e., not social-movement, political, or intellectual leaders)—have played a significant role in the social explosion and cannot be accounted for by social-movement and pure anti-neoliberal narratives.[14]

Reading the Barricade from the Bottom Up

So the question becomes: What does the social explosion mean to those who have joined the dance of those leftover? As I have recommended, this question can be answered by asking a more limited one: What does the barricade mean in this dance of those leftover? To respond, one might look to the cultural practices in which meaning is generated by and for the leftovers, one of which, I suggest, is street art. As one tag in Viña del Mar in March 2020 put it, "The streets will tell our story." During the social explosion, graffiti played a significant role in autonomous grassroots discussions. For example, during November 2019 an abandoned building at the corner of Avenida Libertad and 15 Norte in Viña del Mar was tagged nightly by forces alternatively thanking police for their attempts to re-impose social order and those thanking "the people" [*el pueblo*] for igniting the social revolt. Street art became a significant medium for popular conflictual discussion outside the elite discourses of political leaders.[15]

Tracing the genealogy of Chilean muralism and graffiti, this role of street art in the social explosion is rather unsurprising. Although popular historical narratives often trace the origins of Chilean street art to the visit by the modernist Mexican muralist, David Alfaro Siqueiros, in the 1940s (Bellange 1995; Bragassi 2010; Zamorano Pérez and Cortés López 2007), Chilean street artists have identified the beginnings of Chilean muralism with the Chilean Communist Party aesthetically "occupy[ing] public space" in the "open air" in the early twentieth century (Palmer 2015, 2016: 258). In either case, most agree that Chilean muralism flourished in the 1960s with the invention of *muralist brigades*: teams of laborers and students who independently learned how to collectively paint large-scale propaganda murals in support of Salvador Allende's presidential campaign (Bellange 1995; Mamani 2018; Rolston 2011; Villablanca Canales and Oyola Espinoza 2011). The official goal of these muralist brigades was to create a bottom-up mode of political information dissemination outside official media using a grassroots visual culture and language of doves, raised fists, hard hats, industrial equipment, and so on (Bellange 1995; Mamani 2018). Although these brigades would be broken up in the early years of the dictatorship, muralists returned to using street walls in the 1980s to encourage bottom-up community organization based on "the values of solidarity, community belonging, sacrifice, and struggle" (Bragassi 2010: 11). The murals during the late years of the dictatorship and into the post-dictatorship era maintained their dedication to a bottom-up visual culture of alternative information dissemination, but were now severed from the institutional structures of political parties (Páez-Sandoval 2015). Even today, Chilean muralists and graffiti writers complain about how both left- and right-wing political parties' and social movements' mural-based propaganda show little respect for street art insofar as they paint over artists' works (Palmer 2015).

In the post-dictatorship era, the dominance of muralism in street art was challenged by the entrance of graffiti to the Chilean social landscape (Palmer 2011, 2016). Whereas the muralism of the 1960s was founded on the desire to organize a new social totality (Mamani 2018), graffiti was founded on the desire by individuals of a disenfranchised subculture "to claim a symbolic presence" (Lennon 2016: 32). Graffiti is an insurrectionary aesthetic practice through which individual leftovers of a given social order can intervene in that world in which they have been denied any substantial participatory voice, making the conflict between graffiti practices and anti-graffiti campaigns one of control over public space and the revolt of the leftover individual (Austin 2001; Barnett 1994: 27; Dickinson 2008).

By the late 2000s, however, graffiti and muralism started entering into cross-pollinating dialogue, and by the 2010s a new synthesizing art form, the graffiti mural, was standard in Chilean urban space (Latorre 2019; Palmer 2011, 2016). What has often been noted is that the new aesthetic generated by the graffiti mural is one characterized by an eclecticism and a marked presence of "an artist's individual style" (Latorre 2019: 109), in contrast to the formalized collective language of 1960s and 1970s muralist brigades (Latorre 2019; Palmer 2015, 2016). Nonetheless, the graffiti mural still holds the function of an alternative means of cultural production and intra-community communication. For this reason, one sees the issues of Chile's leftovers ubiquitously represented within graffiti murals—patriarchy, neoliberalism, State violence, environmental injustice, settler colonialism, and so on—but done so using a bottom-up visual language that, since the 1980s, has been divorced from official politics and institutionalized social movements.[16] As such, the graffiti mural presents a unique insight into the autonomous culture and discourse of Chile's leftovers: no longer an expression of a unified and singular cultural voice or political party, a graffiti mural is an individual's articulation of a message to and of the people using a popular visual language, culture, and medium of communication of Chile's leftovers (Rolston 2011).

During the social explosion, various graffiti murals appeared in urban spaces across Chile representing and reflecting on the events at the end of 2019. I want to turn to one such graffiti mural, *Chile's Over* [*Chile se acabó*] by Danny Reveco, at a corner plaza underneath a bridge near the Barón Subway Station in Valparaíso.[17] If Reveco's graffiti mural appears chaotic with the quantity of images assaulting the viewer, for those familiar with the events of the social explosion each and every figure of the mural was immediately and easily identifiable and comprehensible. Using a black-and-white palette with a few splashes of color, *Chile's Over* is a functional encyclopedia of various events and symbols of the history of the social explosion including but not limited to: a protestor ripping off a water cannon from the top of a police tank, an image of *negro matapacos* (see Chapter 5), an image of *pareman* (see Chapter 6), Sebastian Piñera eating pizza (the president ate at a pizzeria during the first weekend of the social explosion in defiance of the social crisis), women preparing an *olla común* (a communal meal prepared in a "shared pot"), grassroots medic teams, and, most importantly for our discussion, a barricade (Figure 1.1).[18]

That is, the barricade within the work is a minor element—it occupies a negligible amount of space—yet its placement within the encyclopedic representation of the social explosion permits a close reading of its significance and meaning within the protests of 2019–2020. If we wish to understand the barricade as an integral and integrated element of the social explosion, it requires that we perform deep analysis of individuals' understanding of the barricade within their broader perceptions of the social explosion—i.e., atomized responses to survey questions are not sufficient—in dialogue with the movement as a whole. Reveco's carefully constructed graffiti mural permits just such an analysis.

By working within the Chilean tradition of street art and the recent phenomenon of the graffiti mural, Reveco articulated a meaning of the barricade from within a visual language and medium of communication by and for the leftovers of Chile. The very form of his work represents an autonomous understanding of the social explosion that, to rework David Graeber's (2009: 203) phrasing, communicates with the people as if the State, what in

Figure 1.1 Chile's Over [*Chile se acabó*] by Danny Reveco. Cerro Barón Subway Station, Valparaíso, Chile.
Source: Photo by Danny Reveco.

classic political theory is frequently perceived as the central apparatus for public dialogue and conflict resolution, did not exist. The street, not the parliament, is where autonomous political dialogue and organization takes place, and street art is one of the languages of that dialogue.

The barricade in *Chile's Over* makes visible both the social violence of the State—a point to which we will return to shortly—as well as the people's own autonomous collectivizations. Being the site of the only use of yellow in the entire work, the barricade serves as the mural's focal point. Functionally separating the left third of the mural occupied mostly by repressive State forces and the right two-thirds of the mural occupied by protestors and non-institutionalized community organizations, the barricade is a focal point in a double sense—it is the thematic center insofar as it divides right from left and is the visual center through its employment of yellow—and an illuminating point in a double sense—in addition to being the light source, it is the *knowledge source* insofar as the barricade's position in the mural makes it structurally possible to distinguish, and thereby see and know, the autonomous collectivizations on the right from the repressive violence of State forces on the left. In *Chile's Over,* the barricade makes possible knowledge of the social explosion in the sense that it allows us to discern certain elements to be known: the abuses of the State and the autonomous collectivizations of the leftovers.

What is just as significant in the mural is that the counter-cultural force of the people on the right side is marked by a diversity of collectivities coming together and not a singular, unified voice that challenges the State with a counter-hegemonic proposal. In *Chile's Over*, the viewer sees representations of pension reform protestors, feminist activists (one protestor in *Chile's Over* is carrying a sign with the lyrics from LASTESIS's "A Rapist in Your Path"), Mapuche youth, older activists making a shared meal, first aid teams, the front line of protestors with shields and non-lethal DIY weapons, and so on.

This diversification of the collectivities of resistance is embodied in a poster made by Reveco in collaboration with the FáBRiKa printshop at the start of the social explosion that reads, "BE MARGINAL / BE A HEROINE / BE A HERO,"[19] and is accompanied by a photo of police in riot gear in the bottom left-hand corner surrounded and being attacked by drawn figures—an elderly woman calling for the end of the privatized pension system, a Mapuche religious figure, a soccer hooligan, a mother with her face hooded accompanying her child, a protestor calling for the end of environmental violence ("no more sacrifice zones"), and other demonstrators (Figure 1.2).

While the stylistic difference—the realism of the photo versus cartoonish drawn activists—emphasizes a dichotomous distinction, the individual drawn figures emphasize a diversity of marginalized positions that have come together; what they share in common is being marginal. In Reveco's social explosion works, he is calling not for a unifying and coherent counter-hegemonic program—i.e., he is not offering a new *law*—but instead a congregated diversity of the marginalized.[20] What his graffiti mural, *Chile's*

Figure 1.2 BE MARGINAL / BE A HEROINE / BE A HERO. // THEY DECREE A STATE OF EMERGENCY. State of exception, resource that the government of a country can announce in exceptional circumstances, where the right is reserved to restrict or suspend fundamental rights relative to liberty and personal security, the inviolability of one's home and the freedom to assemble and move. During this state, armed forced can assume control of the internal order of the country.

Source: *Poster by Danny Reveco and FáBRiKa workshop.* "SEA MARGINAL / SEA HEROÍNA / SEA HÉROE," *by Danny Reveco and FáBRiKA workshop, Valparaíso, Chile*

Over, declares, however, is that while each marginal knowledge is distinct, they all share a common signification of the barricade as the light source that makes knowable these different marginal communities.[21] Returning to Butler's language from the introduction, the barricade is the site at which autonomous interdependency among Chile's individual, collective, and communal leftovers becomes manifest.

Reveco's representation of insurrection in terms of a multiplicity of marginal (collective and individual) subjects should not be surprising. Since the Zapatista uprising in Chiapas starting in 1994—the almost always cited beginning of this new mode of radical political organizing—autonomous and anarchist movements from the 2001 Argentina protests to Occupy in 2011, from the 2011 anti-austerity uprisings in Spain (the 15-M movement) and Greece to the anti-globalization protests in Seattle, Quebec City, and Prague have been structured around the Zapatista phrase, "a world in which many worlds fit," in order to prefiguratively imagine new horizontalist and cooperativist social relations in which multiplicity, diversity, and "the convergence of ideas and practices" are the goals (Graeber 2009; Notes from Nowhere 2003; Sitrin and Azzellini 2014). Multiplicity is the common element underlying these wide-ranging events. Reflecting on Notes from Nowhere's (2003) description of these movements as, "Not a homogenized band of revolutionary proletariat, but a diverse band of marginal people—vagabonds, sweatshop workers, indigenous peoples, illegal immigrants, squatters, intellectuals, factory workers, tree-sitters, and peasants" (24), we come to see that Reveco's work demonstrates that the social explosion was participating in a growing international tendency among radical activists to reorganize their guiding framework around autonomous multiplicity.

As was insisted in the introduction, however, the limitation of these autonomous movements has been their weak theorization of their relationship with the State. As others have noted, for instance, it is unclear what distinguishes Occupy from a political party (an issue to which I will return in the conclusion) (Dean 2012; Green 2015). Reveco's work directly confronts this limitation and identifies the barricade as the contact zone between the State and autonomous organizing. Although the easy interpretation is that the barricade in this mural is a weapon of self-defense—the State is violently attacking autonomous organizing, and the barricade is a non-lethal, but nonetheless violent, means to resist that aggression—it must be noted that the barricade is not directed against anyone in this image, nor is it impermeable. The barricade seemingly *slows* the advance of the State forces—it should be mentioned that we witness a snapshot of an event in motion—but it does not serve to mark off a stable territory to be defended. Violent self-defense is not a viable lens of interpretation.

If the barricade does not serve to defend the interdependent and multiplicitous autonomous organizing of Chile's leftovers, then what is it? To understand the barricade, we can turn towards Reveco's representation of the police: those who forcefully disrupt autonomous organizing by the leftovers. In the mural, the *law*—represented by Piñera on the telephone and, in the lower left-hand corner, Jaime Guzmán, one of the chief architects of Chile's neoliberal 1980 constitution—is not only an affirmative social ordering, but that which mobilizes police forces to eliminate other modes of coordinating social relations. Whereas the barricade is the light source making knowable the autonomous collective existences of the leftovers, the law is the darkness seeking to extinguish that illuminated autonomy. The barricade in *Chile's Over* serves not to mark off two distinct territories—one ruled by neoliberalism and one ruled by the autonomous leftover communities of the social explosion—but rather to suspend the negating function of the State and thereby ephemerally[22] make knowable the autonomous existence of leftover communities underlying the social explosion. The barricade is not a weapon of self-defense to install a new law[23], it is the light source that temporarily suspends the law so that we might briefly glimpse the sociopolitical possibilities offered by the leftovers. To use Benjamin's language from the introduction, the flaming barricade is the divine light annihilating all law and illuminating autonomous interdependency among the leftovers. For this reason, it is perceived as violent by the State, for it disrupts the violent, aggressive, and disruptive function of the law that serves to discipline those leftovers who do not abide by its prescribed social order.

Until Dignity Becomes the Norm!

To explain this further, one can look at a tag scrawled across the top of Reveco's *Chile's Over*: "Until dignity becomes the norm" ["*Hasta que la dignidad se haga costumbre*"]. The concept of dignity (and especially this particular phrase) was omnipresent during the social explosion, reflecting other postmillennial insurgencies like Arab Spring organized around a discourse of dignity (Marquand 2011; Schroeder and Bani-Sadr 2017). For many, the history of the concept of "dignity" is fairly straightforward. First invented in ancient Rome, "dignity" initially referred to the "elevated status of a few persons in a particular society" (Rosen 2012: 15) (i.e., the ruling class) and thereby served to legitimize their dominant position. This would eventually be challenged by Pico della Mirandola's implication that dignity refers to the "capacity for self-determination" (Rosen 2012: 15) that is present in all human beings "solely because they are human" (Rosen 2012: 12). This democratic thread would be more fully fleshed out in Immanuel Kant's now famous definition of dignity as the inner value of each and every human, a dignity founded on personal autonomy. Much later, this notion of dignity as the intrinsic value of each autonomous human being became the conceptual foundation for the United Nations' 1948 Universal Declaration of Human Rights in its opening line, "Whereas recognition of the inherent dignity and of the equal and inalienable rights of all members of the human family is the foundation of freedom, justice and peace in the world."[24]

This genealogy thereby ties the modern conceptualization of dignity to the historical emergence of bourgeois European democracy that grants autonomy and rights to all humans, but does so by taking a particular "ethnoclass (i.e., Western bourgeois) conception of human, Man," and "over-representing" it as if it were constitutive of universal humanity (Wynter 2003: 260). Against this, recent re-evaluations have emphasized how dignity has been differentially understood from within distinct cultural paradigms (Duwell, Braarvig, Brownsword, and Mieth 2014; Schroeder and Bani-Sadir 2017). This pluralizing reconfiguration of dignity was theorized especially by the Zapatistas in their insurgent moment in the 1990s in Mexico (Callahan 2016; Mignolo 2002). As John Holloway (1998) has argued, the Zapatista revolutionary idea of dignity is "essentially anti-definitional," and at its foundation is a "cry of 'here we are!'...Dignity is the cry of those who are not heard, the voice of those without a voice." In this way, "dignity's revolt" with the Zapatistas never principally aimed at winning power within the State and hegemonic institution, but sought to unite a variety of dignities of those whose presence is denied by the Mexican nation-State (the Zapatista revolt, for instance, focused intensely on Indigenous nations). Zapatista dignity is therefore more precisely the digniti*es* of those subjects and communities who are the leftovers of the dominant Mexican nation-State (Holloway 1998). In this way, and against the common narrative that sees the 1948 Declaration of Human Rights as the pinnacle of dignity discourse, Walter Mignolo (2011) can divorce claims for dignity from the discourse of human rights,

> Human dignity is something parallel to yet distinct from human rights. Discourse on human rights focuses mostly on the legal question of right while the issue of human dignity shifts to the human individual, and raises the question, 'Who speaks for the human in human rights?'
>
> (218)

Dignity is formed by the conceptual nexus of *human autonomy* within a particular definition of humanity and the *legitimacy* of respective cultural paradigms' definitions of humanity.

This concept of dignity was at work in Chile in the last months of 2019. For instance, authors have long noted that the Zapatista redefinition of dignity as the conceptual node where legitimacy and autonomy meet has had an influence on decolonial Mapuche organizing (Namuncura 2016; Tricot 2013). Additionally, critiques of so-called 'material' concerns such as public health, the minimum wage, and pensions were often reframed as a desire for a dignified life, with signs detailing: how the absence of proper medical care led to patients dying while on a waiting list for an operation, how retired members of Chilean society were forced to live off pennies due to inadequate pensions, and how workers were unable to support families due to the low level of their pay. As one poster by a nurse from Chillán put it in regard to health care, "How will you talk to your patients about a *healthy life* if you didn't fight for a *dignified life*?" The cry for dignity during the social explosion moved beyond questions of bare material existence and demanded that each autonomous individual's articulation of their desires from within their respective cultural paradigm(s) be accepted as legitimate.

This theorization of dignity can be exemplified through a particular example. On 30 October 2019, an intervention, "For a Dignified Dwelling," took place in Santiago's Dignity Plaza (formerly Plaza Italia, a central protest site in Santiago during the social explosion) in which a group of architects made the relationship between neoliberalism and dignified housing explicit. In this public square, the architects demonstrated the lack of dignity in Chilean housing by painting on the sidewalk at-scale blueprints of the incredibly small one-bedroom apartments in which many from Santiago are forced to live. As Tomás Bravo Urizar explained this intervention, architects reproduced plans for "two types of housing constructed for real-estate companies, 17 m^2 at about $81,000...and one type of social housing, 40 m^2 at about $20,000." He then called on the viewer to ask themselves, "Could I live there with my family? Could I buy housing?...Is it dignified to live like this?" (@tmbravo.scl 2019).

As this example shows, the discourse of dignity forces one to reconsider elements of neoliberalism beyond the terms of material inequality. More precisely, as the intervention makes clear, it forces the individual to consider their own autonomous definition of desirable housing ("Ask yourself") put into relation with the actual housing of others ("two types of housing...and one type of social housing") and placed within an economic context that limits the viability and possibility of actualizing that housing ("Could I buy housing?"). For instance, this intervention could apply to housing costs of an apartment-block unit in downtown Santiago just as easily as it could apply to Indigenous demands for the right to determine their own housing in accordance with their cultures of habitation (Calfio 2016; Sepúlveda and Zúñiga 2015). The question is no longer of a universal housing standard that the poor are unable to meet, but a diversity of housings desired by the people that are limited within a political, economic, and social context.

In other words, I am following Elisabeth Jean Wood (2001), who has argued with respect to peasant revolts in Guatemala that the conventional explanations for collective action, "with their varied emphases on material interests, benefits directly resulting from participation, and widening political opportunities" (267), do not adequately explain much subaltern Latin American political mobilization. Wood insists that peasants rebelled in order to assert their agency and dignity. That is, the leftovers' claim for dignity in Latin America is structured not only around leveraging material demands, but to autonomously assert their agency in their own terms and not the official terms of the State or institutionalized social movements. This, then, is the significance of the barricade that we see especially in Reveco's *Chile's Over*: various assertions of agency (the *olla común*, claiming Mapuche cultural practices, feminist modes of resistance, and so on) according to their own cultural paradigms, but all housed under a common cultural framework of dignity and illuminated by the barricade separating autonomous subaltern collectivities from anti-social State violence.

Dignity is therefore not a new law. It does not seek to impose a social order onto a territory and given population, but is rather the conceptual knot in which interdependent communities convene and affirm their autonomous existence. The particular phrasing, "Until dignity becomes the norm," is important in this regard. Rather than seeking to replace a dominant cultural paradigm—i.e., 'Make dignity the norm'—dignity is simply insisted upon "until" it becomes a norm. Autonomous existence, the declaration of 'here we are' or 'here I am,' is asserted and claimed, not enforced. The barricade—that divine light of "fleeting insurrectionary moments when the unfeasible becomes visible for a moment, like lightning illuminating the night sky" (Zibechi 2012: 44)[25]—is the activist form of this slogan, the revelation of a world changing without anyone taking power.

It is only in this way, for instance, that we can understand the organization of "breakfast barricades" in the Cerro Monjas and Cerro Mariposa neighborhoods of Valparaíso during the social explosion.[26] In November 2019, neighborhood organizations blocked the streets with a particular form of the barricade: tables, chairs, plates, pots, and cooking materials to provide free breakfast to the neighborhood. Furthermore, as one resident testifies, the "breakfast barricade" ended with "sharing the fanzine that we neighbors generated on the social problems and the issues of the neighborhood" (Jacobs 2019). The barricade was used to illuminate neighborhood organizing and self-determination, to affirm their autonomous existence. If the barricade were to be understood as self-defense, such neighborhood organizing would be unintelligible.

This cultural value of dignity provides us with a conceptual framework with which to understand the barricade from the bottom up: an intervention in the Chilean social landscape that gives discursive space to leftovers to represent their social, cultural, political, and economic demands on their own terms and from within their diverse cultural paradigms. What is therefore significant is not so much what dignity means in a positivist sense (one can remember Holloway's comment on the 'anti-definitional' quality of dignity), but that protestors' conceptually innovative use of the notion of dignity functionally allowed them to yoke together a variety of questions—health care, pensions, settler colonialism, housing, violence against women, and so on—and a variety of cultural paradigms—various Indigenous epistemologies (Diaguita, Mapuche, Rapa Nui, Aymara, Quechua, and so on), feminist knowledges, neighborhood-based communication and organizational networks, working-class traditions of resistance, and on and on—under a shared conceptual roof. Just as the barricade in Reveco's *Chile's Over* makes knowable a multiplicity of Chile's leftovers, the concept of dignity provides a common language differentially articulated by distinct cultures but around which varying leftover communities can convene. Whereas the barricade suspends the law and illuminates the leftovers' diversity of interpenetrating collectivities, the message scribbled across the top of the graffiti mural conceptually reconverges them: Until dignity becomes the norm!

Conclusion

The central argument of this chapter has been that we need to look beyond the material and political foundations, leading up to the social explosion in order to critically examine the cultural paradigms and narratives in which the social explosion is comprehended by the leftovers of Chile. I did this principally through an examination of how the barricade has been understood by various social forces. That is, the barricade (and along with it the social explosion) is not about delinquency (official government narrative) and it is not strictly about anti-neoliberal, decolonial, feminist, and environmental justice discontent waiting to be "harnessed" by leftist and social-movement leaders. Instead, the barricade should be seen as revealing a diversity of affirmations of dignity by the leftovers of Chile, where dignity is understood as the conceptual nexus of autonomy and legitimacy. More precisely, the barricade ephemerally suspends the law in order to illuminate the autonomous reality emerging from the social explosion. To set the barricade ablaze is not to attack the State, it is to make sensible the multiplicitous existence among interdependent subaltern communities.

In this way, I am implicitly arguing that the barricade during the social explosion resolved a central problematic of autonomous politics: How does one change the world without seizing power? How does one annihilate the State, defined at least in part by its monopolization of violence, without oneself becoming the State by insisting on one's own exceptional reasons for using violence? The implication is that the barricade is an affirmation of dignity that is perceived as violent by the State insofar as it disrupts the negative function of the law—to interrupt autonomous modes of coordinating social relations that do not abide by the rules it dictates.

I am not denying the significance of the Marxist and social-movement approaches, for there is no question that anti-neoliberal sentiment and social-movement-articulated discourse are at the heart of the social explosion. Indeed, despite my polemic tone against Somma, Bargsted, Disi Pavlic, and Medel's (2021) preliminary discussion of the social explosion—with my possibly too sensitive reading of their (perhaps accidental and unfortunate) use of the word, 'surprising'—their and other social-movement researchers' work has been fundamental to my understanding of the Chilean activist landscape. What I am saying, however, is that the elite representations of these concerns need to be eschewed in favor of how the people themselves are articulating those concerns in their own language, an articulation that appears, for instance, in the particular employment of the discourse of dignity and in street art. This is the underlying methodological insight of the

South Asian Subaltern Studies group that guides this book: researchers need to understand the cultural codes and paradigms with which the people themselves are understanding their activism rather than applying external methods to them. As I have argued elsewhere (Woods 2021b), we need a methodological framework that is waiting to be contorted via our dialogues with subaltern theoretical agents.

Notes

1 As I try to emphasize through illustration here—and through direct argumentation throughout this chapter—the traditional understanding of the barricade as a tactic that allows a social movement to seal off an area from State forces and thereby exercise territorial self-determination (Routledge 2017; Tombs 1999; Trotsky 2008; White n/d) was not at work during the social explosion. As we can see here (and as I saw demonstrated dozens of times during 2019 and 2020), the only tactical benefit of the barricade (in addition to the meaning assigned to the barricade discussed in the final section) was to slow the advance of police or hold them off for an extended period of time, but never to permanently detain them. At other times barricades were ignited in order to demand recognition—the claim of 'here we are!' discussed in the final section—rather than ward off the State; igniting barricades in working-class neighborhoods during moments of 'calm' precisely served this goal.

2 This challenge has largely emerged from research examining the affective elements of social movements (Calhoun 2001; Goodwin, Jasper, and Polletta 2001; Jasper 1999).

3 The Chilean social explosion is not alone here. Kristin Ross (2015) has also examined this side of the barricade during the Paris Commune.

4 The *New York Times* is especially notable insofar as they included articles by Chilean journalists and intellectuals (Dorfman 2020b; Peña 2019).

5 These movements are usually referred to as 'autonomous.' In this book, I am reserving 'autonomy' and 'autonomist' to refer explicitly to the post-hegemonic, horizontalist, cooperativist movements as described in the introduction. In much scholarly discussion of social movements in Chile, autonomy refers to any extra-State movement. For these movements, I use the term 'independent.'

6 See especially Bidegain (2017) for this movement from "cooperation to confrontation" and the importance of the "autonomist strand" in post-dictatorship social movements.

7 Institutionalized frequently signifies 'brought within official State apparatuses.' I am using the term here in a broader sense to signify the process through which a movement is established as an organization, whether that organization is an independent social movement or a State office. That is, a counter-hegemonic resistance group is just as institutionalized as the State.

8 This history is pulled together from a variety of sources. A comprehensive history of social movements can be found in Donoso and von Bülow (2017). For specific analyses of post-dictatorship social-movement organizing by feminists see Rios Tobar, Godoy Catalán, and Guerrero Caviedes (2003), Gaviola, Bedregal, and Rojas (2009), Valdés (2000), Pisano (1996), and Forstenzer (2019) and by Indigenous communities see Pairicán (2012, 2014), Tricot (2013), Hernández (2003), Pereira (2010), and Aravena Reyes (2008).

9 For a brief list of social-movement research that talks about the barricade as a "tactic": Medel and Somma (2016), Somma and Medel (2017), Donoso (2017), Rossi (2015), and Rozas Bugueño and Maillet (2019).

10 This discourse usually points towards the long history of the use of barricades in leftist protests in Chile (Bravo Vargas 2017).
11 In response to Boric supporting the anti-looting law, he received what is referred to as a *funa* (what in English might be termed "being called out") on 20 December 2019 in which dozens of people started yelling at him in a public park for 'selling out the people' and then dumped drinks on his head and threw the empty bottles, cans, and cups at him.
12 For a primary source demonstrating this, see Vamos hacia la vida (2021: 67–73).
13 In addition to Guha (1988, 1998), this critique of social science research of subaltern subjects is based on the work of Sarah Gelbard (2018), Gayatri Spivak (1999, 2003), and Maxwell Woods (2021b).
14 Even in sympathetic leftist accounts, there is a tension between oppositional leaders and academics on the one hand and the people on the other (i.e., the "leftovers"). According to Fernando Pairicán (2016), for instance, despite the fact that the Mapuche movement is a preoccupation for more non-Indigenous than Mapuche subjects, this is beside the point since the demands of that Movement for "collective rights...is a minority that has become consistent" (107). Nonetheless, this does speak to a disjuncture between elite articulations of the autonomous Mapuche movement fighting for hegemony against a settler-colonial nation-State and the grassroots articulations of that movement. Indeed, in this text Pairicán does not address those within the Mapuche movement who have sympathetically critiqued its tendency to invisibilize women, Mapuche counter-sexualities, and diasporic Mapuche subjects (Añiñir Guilitraro 2009; Antileo 2006, 2011; Aravena Reyes 2008; Catrileo 2016, 2019). Pairicán (2019) has addressed this issue in later writing. The point is not to critique Pairicán's articulation of the Mapuche movement, but to note the complexities, problematics, and relations of power within the movement.
15 The interested reader is *heavily* encouraged to see the project of Carol Ureta (2020): she photographed all of the graffiti between Plaza Dignity and the Governmental Palace (La Moneda) on 23 November 2019 and subsequently created a "virtual walk" online between the two sites. It is an incredible work and a lasting archive of the presence of street art in Santiago during the first weeks of the social explosion.
16 The relationship between (de)coloniality, Indigeneity, and Chilean graffiti murals has received much attention in recent discussions (Latorre 2017, 2019; Palmer 2015).
17 Rodney Palmer (2011: 9, 144) has talked about the particular significance of this space for Chilean street art.
18 Indeed, Reveco explained to me in conversation that each figure in the mural represents an individual story, person, or collective of the social explosion. They are not generic figures, but represent a specific element of the mobilizations. Again, as I repeat throughout this book, the social explosion was composed of multiple interdependent stories, not a singular unifying narrative.
19 As the FáBRiKa printshop informed me, this is a reference to Hélio Oticica's work, "Seja marginal, seja herói" (1968), a memorial to the *favela* resident, Manuel Moreira (alias "Cara de Cavalo"), who had been murdered by Brazilian police.
20 One can think here of a radicalized version of Edward Soja's (1996: 93) Thirdspace, "the reconstitution of difference as the basis for a new cultural politics of multiplicity and strategic alliance among all who are peripheralized, marginalized, and subordinated by the social construction of difference (especially in its strictly dichotomized forms)."

21 This representation of the barricade is also found in the work of one of Reveco's collaborators (for whom he designed illustrations for her literary work, *Guerra Florida*): Daniela Catrileo, a diasporic Mapuche intellectual and poet living in Santiago (see Chapter 4). As she writes,

> And where does poetry come from? Between the blocs, between the bodies of cement raised on Indigenous land, among the libraries of a city saturated with ghosts. Between muteness and noise...Between the police and the Church...*Between the train tracks and the barricades*...Poetry as a tool of evasion...Poetry as the first chosen language...Poetry as an improper [*impropio*] language
>
> [emphasis mine] (Catrileo 2019: 5).

The experience of the barricade makes possible the emergence of an "improper" poetry that grounds a decolonial urban culture of exile.

22 This is, of course, a reference to Camilo Trumper's (2016) thesis that there is a long tradition in Chile of "ephemeral urban acts, ranging from public protest to public art," used to transform "the city into a contested public arena where political discourse [is] made material, written in text and image directly on streets and walls" (2).

23 Of course, some did understand the barricade in terms of self-defense (see Vamos hacia la vida 2021); I am arguing against this understanding.

24 This history is found in Rosen (2012) and Hughes (2011). This simplified narrative has been nuanced in Debes's (2017) edited collection on the concept of dignity, where, for instance, the connection of Pico della Mirandola to dignity is heavily challenged (Pico and Manetti 2017) and the foundations of the concept of dignity are traced back to ancient Greece (Rankine 2017). This conceptualization absolutely holds weight in Chile as well: the concept of 'dignity' reappears in both official State Truth and Reconciliation Reports as well as grassroots reports about dictatorship-era abuses of human rights (see Chapter 5); Patricio Manns's musical homage to those tortured under the dictatorship is titled "Dignity Must Become the Norm" ["*La dignidad se convierte en costumbre*"]; and Ebe Bellange (1995: 54) noted the presence of the word, "dignity," in various murals during the dictatorship. The issue is not whether this discourse of dignity was present during the social explosion (it obviously was); instead, I am arguing that there was another conceptualization of dignity also being articulated.

25 This is an implicit rejoinder to Robespierre's famous saying that the people "do not hand down judgments, they throw lightning bolts." The lightning bolt is no longer a weapon of Terror, it is an illuminating mechanism.

26 This is not the only example of a creative barricade. The FáBRiKa workshop, for instance, produced a street-wide banner stating, "Murderous government, we're watching you," and that could be worn by a group of people like a t-shirt in order to block a thoroughfare. Images of flames then rose from the bottom of the banner. In conversation, they referred to this work as a barricade.

2 On Public Transport as Public Space

In Chapter 1, we saw how the Chilean social explosion can be understood as a bottom-up rearticulation of the discourse of dignity in a manner that allows social mobilizations to yoke together into a novel conceptual constellation critiques against a multiplicity of issues: neoliberalism, settler colonialism, environmental injustice, patriarchy, and so on. The corollary conclusion to this thesis is that, although a powerful narrative has emerged in the immediate wake of the social explosion explaining discontent in terms of economic inequality created under a neoliberal governance structure (i.e., the social explosion is a question of policy and economics), the event additionally consists of a cultural struggle by the subaltern to re-organize Chile's social relations in such a manner that they now hold substantial agency. The social explosion was the attempt to dissolve the elite/citizen/subaltern triad explored in the introduction. That is, though I will complicate this thesis in Chapter 5, the subaltern was fighting to become a legitimate and autonomous voice within social relations; not trying to subordinate the ruling class to their worldview, but rather demanding the capacity to substantially participate in the horizontalist and multiplicitous co-generation of a shared geopolitical space.

Chapter 1 served another purpose as well: to outline the foundations of the social explosion—the rise of anti-neoliberal discontent as well as the emergence of feminist, decolonial, and environmentalist social movements—and how dominant narratives of these foundations tend to serve a State- and/or material-centered interpretive framework that ignores important cultural-political elements of autonomous movements. Against this, I offered the history of street art and a close reading of Danny Reveco's mural, *Chile's Over*, as an alternative: the social explosion is a post-hegemonic autonomous insurrection by the leftovers of Chile. In this way, Chapter 1 largely served to examine the pre-history of the social explosion.

Such an explicit thesis was based on another tacit argument: the so-called neoliberal hegemony that reigned in Chile after the dictatorship never existed. Put differently, post-dictatorship Chile represents one more version of what Ranajit Guha (1998) in his against-the-grain reading of Gramsci calls "dominance without hegemony." Despite the post-dictatorship Chilean

DOI: 10.4324/9781003224594-3

State's attempt to consolidate power by unifying the country's population around a program of neoliberal modernization, autonomous subaltern worlds resisted and persisted. One novelty of the social explosion is the weaving together of a plurality of cultures subalternized by the dominant colonial, patriarchal, and neoliberal paradigm. Neoliberalism has never been hegemonic in Chile; significant elements of the social body have always been organizing autonomously, and the difficulty of the Chilean social explosion was how to link together these marginalities.

But how to show this? How to demonstrate that there were alternative subaltern worlds that were silenced and suppressed, but never eliminated, by post-dictatorship neoliberalism? Although this has been repeatedly shown with regard to Mapuche and other Indigenous struggles for cultural re-existence in the face of the post-dictatorship Chilean State's "armed neoliberalism" that hegemonically insists on its mode of social relations over and above all others (Mansilla Quiñones and Melin Pehuen 2019; Mondaca 2013; Nahuelpan Moreno and Antimil Caniupán 2019), these decolonial struggles are not the social explosion's only instances of enduring autonomy. For example, and this is the central argument of this chapter, the initiating act of the social explosion—the fare-evasion movement of October 2019—can be understood as the occupation of public space based on already existing autonomous cultures of public transport. In other words, this chapter continues the discussion of the pre-history of the social explosion, arguing that a public culture of public transport fed the evasion movement.

Taking a more overarching perspective of the situation, although the Chilean social explosion was ignited on 18 October 2019 with massive national-scale protests against Chilean neoliberalism, patriarchy, settler colonialism, and environmental injustice, this (not incorrect) chronology misses that the movement had taken its first steps during the week of 6 October. During this week, high-school students in Santiago started organizing protests of the government's imposition of a subway fare raise by collectively evading metro turnstiles and occupying subway stations, effectively transforming the Santiago subway into a public space of insurrection.

This public-transport-oriented beginning has frequently been used to connect the social explosion to the 2013 Brazilian protests, which similarly started with insurgent occupations of public transport in order to protest against a fare raise. Such a connection, however, ignores that the insurgent use of public transport as a public space[1] is by no means novel. Laura Kemmer (Kemmer 2020, forthcoming; Kemmer and Simone 2021) has shown that there is a long history in Brazil of protests in the public space of public transport, and Tonio Weicker (2020) has traced such a history of the use of public transport as an insurgent public space in Ukraine. Similarly, it is little remarked that one of the most significant elements of the US civil rights movement of the 1950s and 1960s was based on using public transport as a public space of insurrection: the Montgomery Bus Boycott and Rosa Parks's insurgent occupation of a public bus. That the social explosion started with the use of public transport as an insurgent public space is rather banal in itself.

Theoretically, this chapter makes a triple intervention of interest to social movements. First, the insurgent occupation of public transport as a public space is a common and serious mode of resistance and not, as it is frequently represented in academic discussion, a preliminary element of social movements. The evasions were not part of the 'lead up' to the social explosion, they were an integral element of the social explosion. Second, following the work of Kemmer and Weicker, we require a more robust theorization of insurrectionary uses of the public space of public transport, a theorization which this chapter makes in the particular case of the Chilean social explosion. Third, this theorization revolves around the following conclusion: public transport serves as a public space for forming a public culture which can subsequently feed insurrectionary occupations of public transport. What researchers and activists can therefore be asking, and what is the guiding question of this chapter, is the following: What type of culture is formed in the public space of public transport, and how does that culture generate a radical politics?

More precisely, this chapter traces the history of urban segregation and modern public transportation in Santiago through a reading of the chronicles of the queer and poor Chilean author, Pedro Lemebel, in order to demonstrate how Santiago's interlocking histories of urban segregation and modern transport have long been setting the stage for contemporary social mobilizations; it is no accident that the Chilean social explosion emerged from students' use of public transport as a public space. Lemebel's writing shows that Santiago's public transport has regularly been used as a public space for the autonomous collectivization of the capital's subaltern communities, but the State's neoliberal modernization of public transport during the 1990s suppressed that oppositional spatial practice. By occupying subway stations, then, Santiago's subaltern communities were reclaiming that space as one in which they could reactivate a public culture that had already previously been cultivated in the cultural crucible of public transport as a public space. In the end, the initial steps of the Chilean social explosion represent the return of the repressed of Chilean neoliberal modernization and urban segregation, the return of those bodies expelled from Santiago's modern neoliberal center and public transport system who occupied public transport as a public space with their alternative visions of living in common.

The History of Santiago's Public Transport

To move in broad generalizations, Santiago's history of public transportation follows the basic periodization of twentieth-century Chilean history. First, following the horse-drawn busses, early electric trams, and unsanctioned "gondolas" (the precursor to the motorized bus) of the late nineteenth and early twentieth centuries, the Chilean State started formally intervening in Santiago's mass transit system in the 1940s by forming the National Transport Enterprise in 1945 and subsequently replacing this enterprise in 1953 with the State Enterprise of Collective Transport. In 1965 the national State then founded the Santiago subway, whose construction was officially approved in 1968 (but which wouldn't start running until 1975).[2] From Chile's initial dispersed and informal forays into public transport, the State eventually assumed a central role in public transport's development. Following the discussion in Chapter 1, this history mirrors the general tendency starting in the 1930s and continuing until 1973 of the development of a strong, centralized, interventionist State in which social tensions and relations were resolved through "the establishment and subsequent expansion of new state institutions" (Taylor 2006: 16) like the State Enterprise of Collective Transport.

In 1973, however, this vision of State-driven modern mass transport development would be upended when Chile suffered one of the most traumatic elements in its national history: the coup led by General Augusto Pinochet. Discussions of Pinochet's dictatorship are often divided between those who highlight the dictatorship's authoritarianism and those who highlight its neoliberal modernization of the country, in which Pinochet introduced a series of policies that effectively terminated State-driven developmentalism and instituted a new privatized socio-political landscape: "public spending was reduced by more than a quarter," money supply was reduced, nationalized State-controlled corporations were privatized, and foreign direct investment was encouraged (Collier and Sater 2004: 366–369; Klein 2007; Tironi 1990). This project of rapid neoliberal modernization also affected public transport. Under the new neoliberal model, the bus system of Santiago allowed private companies to open up new routes, to increase the number of buses in circulation (thereby increasing the frequency at which buses arrived to stations), and starting in 1983 to freely determine the cost of bus fare. As a result, by the end of the dictatorship in 1989 bus fares had skyrocketed, bus companies refused to update their now dangerously old buses due to the cost of replacement, there was major traffic congestion due to multiple private companies fighting for space within the marketplace, and there was massive inefficiency even according to neoliberal analyses (Díaz, Gómez-Lobo, and Velasco 2004: 9–11).

The post-dictatorship era was marked not by the elimination of this policy framework, but by the attempt to refine and regulate the neoliberal modernization model started by Pinochet but without the authoritarian politics; the post-dictatorship Chilean State maintained the same neoliberal political-economic model as the dictatorship, but tried to do so by winning consent through hegemony rather than enforcing it through authoritarianism (Taylor 2006). Within this logic, the buses of Santiago had come to be an embarrassment, with the Chilean Transportation Subsecretary, Guillermo

Díaz, co-writing in an article from 2004, "Many citizens of Santiago have come to think that the buses—with their chaos, congestion, and pollution—are like the Andes: immutable" (Díaz, Gómez-Lobo, and Velasco 2004: 6). To be fair, the subsecretary and his co-authors have a point: in addition to continued problems of high fares and traffic congestion, one survey found that on a scale from 1 to 100 the buses received an average score of 11.9 by Santiago residents (7). In addition, there were serious security issues given that in the year 2000 there were nearly 5,000 accidents in Santiago that included buses with "4,668 persons injured and 116 killed" (16). The government responded by, in addition to regulating bus routes and the transportation industry, replacing old buses with new ones (11).

This reorganization and continued neoliberal modernization of public transportation eventually culminated in the creation of the Transantiago public transport system in 2007, which still regulates public transport in Santiago today (though as of 2019 with a new name, The Metropolitan Mobility Network [*Red Metropolitana de Movilidad*]). As this reform was justified in a proposed 2000–2010 Urban Transport Plan of Santiago in the lead up to Transantiago's creation,

> The problems of public transport in Santiago are widely known, and their negative consequences for the quality of life of its inhabitants as well. The informality of services and of the entrepreneurial organization of operators, the inefficiency and lack of rationality in the exploitation of the total means of transport derived from the lack of integration, the lack of correspondence between the supply and demand of services, the intense externalities produced in terms of atmospheric and acoustic contamination, and the aggression of the system with respect to users are all elements that, among others, characterize this activity.
>
> (Abedrapo Bustos, Correa Díaz, González Tagle, and Solís Mateluna 2000: 10)[3]

In response to this crisis, the Urban Transport Plan repeats a constant refrain of needing to "moderniz[e] the public transport system of Santiago" with "efficient businesses administered professionally and with modern systems" (44). With the city represented in terms of chaos, pollution, aggression, and a lack of systematization, the logical response is therefore the construction of an urban transport plan founded on a discourse of modernity, efficiency, rationality, and professionalism. The State tried to generate hegemonic consent for their public transport policy by culturally legitimizing their project of the neoliberal modernization of transport infrastructure through a conceptual "investment in crisis" in which the city is painted as in chaos so that the State "can come into [its] own as [an] authoritative agen[t] that can restore order" (Li 1992: 262–263; Ureta 2015).

So far, I have recounted the official history of public transport in Santiago, one which is framed in terms of a process of successful modernization through neoliberal policy and that won broad-based support in Santiago.

This narrative is betrayed, however, by a basic fact: discontent with the Transantiago system has been registered since literally the first day of its operations, 10 February 2007. With major confusion over new routes, riders angry about being forced to walk extended distances to official bus stops (previously, buses would frequently pick up passengers at any point along their route), and intense overcrowding, the implementation of Transantiago was almost universally decried as a political catastrophe (Morandé y Esteban Doña 2007; Muñoz and Gschwender 2008; Olvarría-Gambi 2020). Anger among citizens ran so high that many government officials were even expecting a "massive social revolution" in response (Ureta 2015: 114–115).

Elite discourse—both by those heavily critiquing the system and by those trying to downplay its problems—responded by framing the event as a "matter of failed *politics*" and the "incompetence" of politicians with regard to "technical expertise." By doing so, however, they also reproduced the dominance of neoliberal modernity; despite the catastrophe of Transantiago's implementation, the narrative that public transport needed to be modernized was never questioned, and the possibility that the 'non-expert' subaltern might offer different viable cultural foundations on which to construct a public transport system was never entertained (Ureta 2015: 138–139). The elite maintained the foundational narrative that they had used to try to win consent for the project of neoliberal modernization, but argued that ineptitude in the realization of this (legitimate) cultural paradigm was to blame. To frame the failure of Transantiago as a problem of failed policy or political incompetence, however, is largely to miss the point. The failure was more precisely a consequence of elites' implicit hegemonic insistence that these discontented riders' alternative urbanist visions represented a "depleted form of urban life" (Simone 2016: 11) that needed to be erased or modified.

As such, we should not be surprised that the 2019 social explosion began as a fight over public transport. Indeed, one might argue that the social explosion's first steps represent both an extension of this long-held discontent and an attempt by subaltern voices to legitimize their distinct cultures as viable foundations for thinking through questions of urban public transport. Yet one might reasonably ask: is there actually such a coherent subaltern culture of public transport? Are they really offering an alternative, or are they simply expressing anger over what currently exists? I want to argue during the rest of this chapter that the chronicles of Pedro Lemebel outline one such autonomous subaltern culture of public transport. More precisely, a reading of his chronicles reiterates the refrain of this book: the discontent underlying the Chilean social explosion—discontent whose roots are found at moments like the commencement of the Transantiago system in 2007—is not only a question of policy but also a question of *whose* socio-cultural systems hold legitimacy when determining how to coordinate social relations. Lemebel's chronicles demonstrate precisely that (1) The post-dictatorship Santiago subaltern does indeed have an alternative public transport culture, (2) Elites justified their monopolization of the authority over public transport policy by delegitimizing such subaltern public transport cultures, and

(3) Conflicts over and within public transport can be seen not only as resistance *to* the installation of specific policies, but also as the attempt to legitimize subaltern public transport cultures in the discussions in which spatial practices in and of public transport are determined.

Pedro Lemebel and Peripheral Public Transport Culture

Writing during the late-dictatorship and post-dictatorship eras, Pedro Lemebel is principally remembered for being a poor and queer literary voice that critiqued "the excesses of the dictatorship" and the failures of post-dictatorship democratic governance (Uribe Ugalde 2018). Additionally, he has been championed by many activists during the social explosion, with streets being renamed after him, public statues of Chilean national heroes being redesigned in his likeness, and the third annual Pedro Lemebel Festival being hosted in January 2020 in the midst of the social explosion. His position as both *poor and queer* is central in many ways to his cultural work. As he writes in, "Manifesto (I Speak for My Difference),"

> I speak for my difference / I defend what I am / And I'm not so weird / Injustice stinks / And I suspect this democratic dance [*cueca*] / But don't talk to me of the proletariat / Because to be poor and queer [*maricón*] is worse / One must be acid in order to bear it.
>
> (Lemebel 1997: 83)

In this manifesto, Lemebel carefully carves out: how his class status disqualifies him from participating in the formation of elite neoliberal culture, how his sexuality disqualifies him from participating in the major leftist opposition to neoliberalization and authoritarianism, and, nonetheless, how he *embraces and speaks for* his difference, defending what he is. Lemebel develops a cultural voice on the margins of—but not separate from—official Chilean culture in the post-dictatorship era ("I'm not *so* weird"—he admits that he's weird, but just not *so* weird). As Vek Lewis (2010) summarizes, Lemebel's allegiance is "toward all those linked by their nonideal status" (187) and toward all those who are the leftovers of the hegemonic culture of post-dictatorship Chile.

It should therefore come as no surprise that Lemebel's chronicles explore urban marginality in Santiago (Cabrera 2017; Pastén 2009; Uribe Ugalde 2018). More precisely, they represent the worlds of what Lucía Guerra (2000), borrowing from Lemebel's own phrasing, calls the *anal city*, that urban space extending beneath and on the borders and gaps of Santiago's neoliberal center that consists of

> residential blocks where workers and *lumpen* are stacked, [as well as] suburbs and slums [*barriadas*] in which the cultural images of neoliberal society acquire other meanings...The anal city configures in this way

> another historical becoming marked by delinquency, poverty, and exclusion, by the clandestine force of transgression against the order and authority of the neoliberal State.
>
> (Guerra 2000: 87)

The anal city is the urban space of those deposited outside the culture of post-dictatorship neoliberal modernity.

Moreover, this urban space segregated from Santiago's neoliberal center was enabled by the neoliberal modernization of Chile's public transport (De Mattos 1999). Following a common story of Latin American urbanization, as the population of Santiago began to rapidly increase in the 1990s, the poor were forced into the city's periphery.[4] This peripheralization of urban poverty was aided by the rapid expansion of public transport since the poor could still work within the neoliberal center, but would now be forced to travel long distances on buses and subways in order to get there (Hidalgo, Alvarado, and Santana 2016). Due to this spatial peripheralization, however, there emerged in the anal city a form of public space that is only now slowly starting to receive dedicated attention in research: *public transport as a public space*. It is in this public space of public transport that we can find the formation of a subaltern culture of public transport in Lemebel's chronicles.

For instance, in the chronicle, "Beetles on the Windshield," from his collection of chronicles, *The Corner Is My Heart*, Lemebel (2001) explores the popular culture found on the old city buses of Santiago. In this work, Lemebel does not focus on public transport as a mobility machine, but rather talks about the public culture of the buses on the fringes of the neoliberal city, describing them as "putting wheels on a shack and trafficking its shrill aesthetic through the urban viaducts...Almost a roving museum of domestic kitsch that wobbles on the tiny shoes hanging from the mirror" (139). Lemebel does not stop there, talking about how the rider is forced to listen to music, "imposed by the driver, who has been trained as a disc jockey, a formula one driver, or a relentless collector of those who try and enter through the back door without paying" (140). He concludes by describing this public space of outmoded Chilean buses as "the shine of the *bus party*...As if the bus were a rolling Wurlitzer that liberated its resentful pulse in the fever of the song, that all...accompany by moving their feet below the seats" (143–144). In other words, he describes the formation of a public culture within the public space of public transport on the fringes and with the residues of the official modern neoliberal culture of post-dictatorship Chile. In response to the question, 'Is there an active culture of public transport in Santiago other than that offered by hegemonic neoliberal modernity?,' Lemebel's chronicle gives a definitive answer: yes.

This public culture within public transport is formed, Lemebel insists, by specifically *peripheral* subjects of Santiago. As he writes, "The bus is a cup of soup that rolls around in the intestines. A pastiche of belches, faults, and farts that color the hard transit falling over a precipice *into the periphery*" [emphasis mine] (Lemebel 2001: 141–142). The public culture of the public bus is not high neoliberal culture, but is precisely the culture of the periphery, of those who have been excised from the modern neoliberal center but still nonetheless metabolize products circulating in the global marketplace that have arrived to Chile through neoliberal avenues. Even further, the Spanish Lemebel uses ("*eructos*," "*flatos,*" "*peos*," and so on) would likely be considered a 'low-class' Spanish by elites. As Francine Masiello (2001) writes,

> What captures the imagination is deviance from the linguistic norm; and in Lemebel's case, the marginal figure of the barrios, whose language has not yet been incorporated by high fashion or official discourse, initiates a contestatory voice, a defiance of institutional order.
>
> (195)

The very language that he employs expresses his peripheralization from the official culture of post-dictatorship Chile.[5]

The Hegemony of Neoliberal Modernity

To clarify through contraposition, we can distinguish Lembel's chronicles with the work of another post-dictatorship author from Santiago, Alberto Fuguet (Pastén 2009). In a 1996 manifesto co-written with Sergio Gómez, Fuguet distinguishes his experience of the neoliberal Latin American social landscape (what he calls 'McOndo') from the previous magical realist representations of Latin America of the 1960s and 1970s embodied in the fictional setting of Gabriel García Márquez's *100 Years of Solitude*, 'Macondo,'

> Our McOndo is as Latin American and magical (exotic) as the real Macondo...Our country McOndo is larger, overpopulated, and full of pollution, with expressways, metro, cable TV, and slums. In McOndo there are MacDonald's, Mac computers, and condominiums…five star hotels built with laundered money and giant malls.
>
> (Fuguet and Gómez 1996: 15)

In this manifesto, Fuguet and Gómez are concerned with locating Chile's particular place within planetary-scale networks of commodity exchange, carving out an independent self-created identity for Chile within a potentially homogenizing globalization whose cultural articulation in a discourse of postmodernism is largely dominated by the North Atlantic. In this way, their discourse critiques a global distribution of cultural power disproportionately controlled by the North Atlantic.

Yet as his representation of 1990s Santiago also demonstrates, Fuguet's mappings of Santiago are "isolated from the radically different realities" represented in Lemebel's chronicles that "dispute and dispense with [Fuguet's] privileged cartographies, which not only erase Latin American differences but represent Santiago as part of a prosperous, postmodern global village" (Palaversich and Allatson 2002: 101). Fuguet's vision for post-dictatorship neoliberal culture makes no adequate place for the worlds represented by Lemebel. This is not to argue for a "militant particularism" (Harvey 2000) of the spaces and concerns represented by Lemebel in diametrical opposition to those of Fuguet. For as Guerra (2000) notes, Lemebel uses the "cultural images of neoliberal society" (86)—for example, Lemebel admits that the public culture of public transport uses kitsch objects from a market of cultural commodities enabled by neoliberalization—however, the question is about who holds the cultural power in the processes of valorizing and narratively controlling that cultural content, who is authorized to assign cultural meaning to the postmodern Chilean social landscape. Lemebel and Fuguet are differentiated precisely here, in their contrasting modes of envisioning a post-dictatorship culture through the narrativization and valorization of the global flows of commodities in which Chile is embedded. Such a basic differentiation is rather innocuous. Strictly speaking, there is nothing worthy of critique in the simple fact that Fuguet represents other spaces than Lemebel. The issue is that the culture of post-dictatorship "neoliberal narrators" for whom Fuguet "represents the leader," to use the words that Lemebel (García-Corrales 2005: 26–27) himself employs in an interview to describe Fuguet's work, "only privileges his country of McOndo while it looks down on [*desprecia*]" the "underdeveloped" [*subdesarrollado*], poor, Indigenous, and/or marginalized areas that continue being the reality for "the majority of Chile and the rest of the continent" (Palaversich 2005: 36). More bluntly, the privileging of such neoliberal spaces serves to delegitimize cultures of the anal city.

To see one particular example of this hegemonic process through which anal city culture is silenced, one can look at post-dictatorship developments of Santiago's public transport system. In another representation of the ongoing process of the neoliberal modernization of Santiago's public transport in the chronicle, "The Santiago Subway," Lemebel implies that Chilean elites were successful in repressing anal city modes of socio-cultural relations that had been developed in the public spaces of Santiago's old public buses. As he writes,

> the Santiago subway is the disciplined evidence that the dictatorship left us. A subway as clean and shiny as the kitchens of the rich. As neat and tidy as if it's never used…A subway that…[still] appears as new in its celestial blue and its radiant speed.
>
> (Lemebel 2010: 245).

In other words, modern neoliberal public transport in Chile is a space of discipline, a way of enforcing the modernity of neoliberal urbanism onto its users. The Santiago subway insists on *its* particular brand of "transport behavior" (Schmucki 2012) over and against all others, such as those of the "bus party" described by Lemebel. The result, as Lemebel highlights, is a highly impersonal and cold space in which passengers "avoid looking forward, trying to maintain a pride of keeping a fixed look on the window covered with the darkness of the tunnel" (Lemebel 2010: 246). The difference could not be clearer between the frigidity of the hegemonic modern neoliberal culture of the subway on the one hand and, on the other, Lemebel's anal city culture built in the public space of public transport with its disc-jockey drivers, domestic kitsch, and passengers dancing in their seats. The neoliberal modernization of public transport becomes a means of disciplining Santiago citizens into conformity with the demands of modern neoliberal social relations.[6]

To further demonstrate this cultural struggle between the subaltern anal city and the hegemonic neoliberal center, one can look at another chronicle by Lemebel, "The Death of Madonna" in *Loco afán*, which tells the story of a trans[7] woman from the poor Santiago neighborhood of San Camilo[8] who admired and imitated the famous *gringa* pop star (Lemebel 1997: 33). She even knew all of the *gringa* Madonna's songs by heart; and although "she had no idea what the songs were saying" since she did not speak English, she gave them "the charm of her illiterate inventiveness [*cosecha analfabeta*]" (Lemebel 1997: 34). In this way, Madonna of San Camilo goes beyond merely copying the *gringa* Madonna by revalorizing and restructuring that North American cultural material.

In the chronicle, Lemebel recounts when Madonna of San Camilo participated in a performance art piece during the dictatorship where various artists held a mock red-carpet event. During the event, she posed nude, "as God sent her into the world, but hiding the embarrassment of the member between her buttocks" (Lemebel 1997: 36). According to the chronicle, Madonna of San Camilo would die of AIDS before the end of the dictatorship, but after the return to democracy the Chilean National Museum of Fine Arts hosted an "Open Museum" event in which any artist, performer, film director, and so on could exhibit their work. Meant to demonstrate the new freedoms of Chilean democracy, "the exhibit had no previous censorship" (Lemebel 1997: 37). As a result, a video of Madonna of San Camilo from the red-carpet performance was included. As Lemebel writes, "the naked body of Madonna...her Native profile, her Hellenic shoulders" (Lemebel 1997: 37), caused a scandal at the exhibition and the curator quickly removed this video in which Madonna "simulat[ed] a modest Venus for the museum of fine arts" (Lemebel 1997: 37). Lemebel then asks the obvious question, "Why the censorship now that we are in democracy?" (Lemebel 1997: 38).

Lemebel is therefore implying a double claim. First, post-dictatorship Chile quickly erected its own dominant culture in which certain expressions of beauty, sexuality, gender, race, class, and art were acceptable—a culture in which Madonna from San Camilo was branded as obscene. Second, Madonna of San Camilo, like the old buses of Santiago, was pointing towards another culture that autonomously restructures, processes, consumes, and valorizes the residues of that dominant neoliberal culture. For example, Lemebel describes Madonna's room in which she had plastered thousands of images of the *gringa* Madonna as, "reiterations of the same infinite image, in all its forms, in all its sizes, in all its ages; the star was revived in the beloved velvet of the homosexual [*coliza*] eye" (Lemebel 1997: 35).[9] This queering of aesthetics can be seen, for example, in Lemebel calling Madonna of San Camilo a "modest Venus for the museum of fine arts." This is not to petition for her inclusion in the new official postmodern culture of Chile, but rather to argue that the post-dictatorship culture of Chile would need to be restructured so that this valorization of Madonna's performance as beautiful could hold legitimacy and could be seen as autonomous from (rather than derivative of) the *gringa* and high-art Madonnas.

To state this argument polemically: the "Open Museum" event and the disciplinary technology of the subway demonstrate how post-dictatorship Santiago has been characterized by the ongoing attempt by elites to erase or silence autonomous subaltern cultural practices in the process of maintaining the dominance of neoliberal modernity. Lemebel, however, *dis*places (rather than *re*places) this cultural hegemony by reconceptualizing the references of this 'high' culture (the "Venus," the Madonna, the "Hellenic shoulders," the profile of the "nymph," and so on) in terms of Madonna of San Camilo (in contrast to conceptualizing Madonna of San Camilo in terms of these references). Whereas a hegemonic struggle would consist of the cultivation of a *distinct* anal-city culture that can then occupy the museum and advocate the *replacement* of neoliberalism with a new State founded on the novel cultural values found in the occupied museum, Lemebel is offering something different: the reconstitution of the museum—and with it the cultural foundations of Chile—around a decentered kaleidoscope of meanings, values, readings, interpretations, and codes. Not the replacement of Madonna, but the reconstitution of a *pluralized* Madonna as defined by classical 'high' art, the postmodern pop art of neoliberalism (to be discussed in Chapter 5), and the peripheral queer art of Madonna of San Camilo.

The point is not to argue that the anal city represents a utopia. Lemebel's description of the Santiago bus ending with a crash in which multiple children die and his chronicle of Madonna of San Camilo ending with her dying of AIDS both demonstrate this fact. What is at stake is an engagement with the culture of the anal city, of the leftovers of the post-dictatorship era with their own systems of conceptual and cultural valorization, as a legitimate and autonomous mode of conceiving of social relations. The point is not that Madonna of San Camilo and the people interacting in the anal city public space of public transport are perfect, the point is that they have dignity. As Lemebel would say explicitly in an interview,

> That is what moves me, my [queer] friends from the *Zanjón* neighbourhood [the lower-class Santiago neighbourhood where Lemebel was raised]...there, where you can find the prostitute transvestites [*sic*]. I am not interested in those who perform in shows in discos; I have nothing to do with that, nothing. What interests me is the prostitute, the one who gambles her life in the street, a life for at risk...Not as a metaphor. The street is cruel. I turn my writing into this: a sharpened way of seeing oneself in these spaces.
>
> (Pino-Ojeda 2006: 400–401)

His chronicles are not a romanticization of poverty, of being queer in Chile, of growing up in what the middle- and upper-class would likely consider a slum. Instead, they are engaging the cultures of these worlds as legitimate and autonomous ways of social interaction as well as critiquing the hegemony of high postmodernism that delegitimizes the participation of Chile's leftovers in the formation of a shared post-dictatorship culture.

Lemebel's works can therefore be understood as illuminating the relations of power articulated in the conflict between elite hegemonic culture and subaltern subcultures, a conflict that in his chronicles becomes particularly exposed in the act of cohering a public culture within Santiago's public transport as a public space. For if the process of forming an official post-dictatorship culture of rational neoliberal modernity in the Transantiago project is countered by Lemebel's kitsch culture of the "bus party," the hegemonic function of the expansion of elite notions of public transport through policy and through the installation of hard infrastructure is to threaten the life of this anal city public space of public transport. Lemebel's mode of engaging public transport as a public space is delegitimized under the hegemonic culture of post-dictatorship neoliberal modernity.

As he concludes the chronicle, "Beetles on the Windshield,"

> So, the buses were exiled in their scrapped-out old age. Aerodynamic buses erase the Cinderella carnaval, tracing new routes without risk and codified numbers for the routes that replace the poetry of the old lines. The city bursts into a megalopolis hurried by the daze of these pachyderms that leave the city coughing their deathly vapors, reflecting in their patched windows *the golden ribbons of modernity.*
>
> [emphasis mine] (Lemebel 2001: 145–146)

On the one hand, Lemebel recognizes in this chronicle the reasons behind the modernization of the public transit system—the old routes were confusing, inefficient, and unreliable, and the old buses were wildly unsafe. On the other hand, he laments all that is lost with this modernization of the peripheral public culture of the "bus party": the "poetry of the old lines" and "the Cinderella carnaval." The issue is not that the Chilean government transformed Santiago's public transport system (Lemebel himself raises critiques of public transport), but that the subaltern culture of public transport was suppressed and delegitimized under the post-dictatorship hegemony of neoliberal modernization ("the golden ribbons of modernity"). If the social explosion and the Transantiago implementation in 2007 are two particularly spectacular expressions of discontent over public transport, Lemebel's chronicles demonstrate that such discontent has always been present in the post-dictatorship era. The dictatorship and post-dictatorship modern public transport system represents a dominance of the subaltern without the elites' hegemony ever fully winning consent.

The Social Explosion and the Resurgence of the Public Culture of Public Transport

Lemebel identifies one moment when this hegemonic suppression of the anal city culture of public transport as a public space fails. In the chronicle, "The Santiago Subway," wherein he describes the frigidity of modern neoliberal public transport culture, Lemebel describes a moment during the campaign to remove Pinochet as dictator when the Santiago subway "was overcome by civilian passion." With "screams and flags for the return to democracy," Lemebel paints a picture of the energy inside the subway car,

> All the world singing, jumping with: 'whoever doesn't jump is Pinochet.' And the train also hopping like a rabbit on its wheels of rubber...The train was bursting with dudes in revolt tagging it with spraypaint...before the horrified eyes of the guards who couldn't control this human storm.
>
> (Lemebel 2010: 246–247)

It is in this instant, Lemebel concludes, when the subway "crossed the city like a blackboard of discontent" that it "escaped the untouchable showcase, because later, they washed it, they shined it up, returning it to its flaming vehicular hypocrisy" (Lemebel 2010: 247). Neoliberal modernity, in this view, is not a set of policies, a state of affairs, or a historical period, but rather the cultural structuration of social relations in a manner that requires constant renewal by repressing all challenges to its dominance, and public transport as a public space is one site at which this conflict between neoliberal modernity and its leftovers is waged. Lemebel identifies moments when the suppressed anal city public culture of public transport reappears as well as how neoliberal modernity reproduces its dominance by re-suppressing these insurrectionary moments.

If, as Lemebel implicitly argues, post-dictatorship neoliberal modernity has traditionally won this conflict in public transport as a public space, the

2019 social explosion shows both that Lemebel's diagnosis was correct—there was deep-seated discontent within Chile against neoliberal modernity and this discontent is at times manifested in the public space of public transport—and that he was too pessimistic. We can see the error in his pessimism, for instance, in the conflict over the Baquedano subway station in Santiago during the social explosion. This subway stop is in what today is referred to as Dignity Plaza, formerly known as Plaza Italia, which was a central space for protests in Santiago. In a video uploaded to the internet on 18 November 2019 ("El que no salta es paco"), a large group of protestors have gathered at the entrance of the subway station which has been covered with graffiti. In the video, the protestors start collectively jumping together while chanting, "*el que no salta es paco*" ["whoever doesn't jump is a cop"], an alternative version of the chant that Lemebel noted on the subway ("whoever doesn't jump is Pinochet").[10] That is, we see the return of the exact phenomenon Lemebel described as happening at the end of the dictatorship and that was repressed by neoliberal modernity. The occupation of public transport as a public space of insurrection during the social explosion is part of a long history of subaltern cultures of resistance and collectivization.[11]

Once again in 2019, neoliberal modernity tried to repress this explosion of discontent and this persistence of subaltern cultures of public transport as a public space. Early one morning on 25 October 2019, a group gathered to paint over the graffiti that had collected in the Baquedano subway station during the social explosion and to clean up the barricades that had been erected at the station's entrance, reproducing the desire, as Lemebel notes, to maintain the "showcase" of the modern public transit system. The head of the Chilean government's communications team, Karla Rubilar Barahona (2019), would celebrate this act in a tweet, "Once again in #Baquedano station of @metrodesantiago and nearby, youth collaborating in cleaning up sectors in which public property that belongs to all of us has been destroyed." The political act of re-installing modern neoliberal public transport was being supported by the elite attempt to relegitimize themselves as the proper stewards to hold power over the "public property that belongs to all of us"; if the youth cleaning up the entrance to the station were materially reproducing neoliberal modernity, Rubilar's comments acted as State support. By that same afternoon, protestors had re-graffiti'd and re-barricaded the entire metro stop. That is, in contrast to the event discussed by Lemebel, during the social explosion neoliberal modernity was struggling to maintain its disciplined control of public transport as a public space, and the suppressed anal city culture formed in the public space of public transport was returning in full force.

Yet, developing a further reflection on the barricade and the politics of autonomy, what is significant is the form that public-transport protest took: the evasion. The opening salvo of the social explosion did not seek to replace or even topple the dominant cultural coordination of public transport in Santiago, it sought to *evade* it. What was desired was the right to use public transport according to distinct autonomous cultural configurations like those highlighted by Pedro Lemebel. The evasion was the public-transport version of the barricade: the divine violence that suspends law in order to allow for the illumination of the autonomous subaltern cultures of the anal city developed in the public space of public transport. The response by the Chilean government was expected: the attempt to reinstate the law with police repression. Just as described by Lemebel, the subway transformed into a "blackboard of discontent" was reordered with clean-up crews "shining it up, returning it to its flaming vehicular hypocrisy," though the State in 2019 had to support this task with police buckshot and tear gas. As such, it is unsurprising that the mathematics professor, Roberto Campos, faced a possible[12] eight-year prison sentence for smashing a subway turnstile while participating in an evasion and was potentially prosecuted under the "Law of State Security," which is used against acts that threaten "national sovereignty" (Diario Uchile 2021). The evasion was not the attempt to usurp the position of the sovereign to define the order of the public transport, it was the attempt to suspend sovereignty in order to give space for the autonomous public culture of the anal city, as is described by Lemebel, to participate in and co-generate the life of public transport.

Conclusion

I have been arguing that we need to reorient current understandings of the Chilean social explosion which have tended to coalesce behind discussions of policy and economic inequality. While this is undoubtedly part of the discontent fueling protests, it is not all. Instead, behind much of the discontent are questions of cultural hegemony, of who is perceived as having the legitimacy to participate in establishing the rules that determine social relations. This cultural conflict is particularly manifested in the initial event of the social explosion: public transport policy. My argument is that the discontent embodied in the fare-evasion movement was not only about the material problem of a fare hike—though it was about this too!—but also about the delegitimation of subaltern cultures of public transport. Against the hegemonic culture of neoliberal modernity that has dictated post-dictatorship public transport policy, the subaltern's use of public transport as a public space of insurrection reinscribed the city with their own particular urban cultures like those found in the chronicles of Pedro Lemebel. The social explosion's fight for dignity in regard to public transport policy includes the fight to reframe subaltern cultures of public transport as autonomous and legitimate foundations for the development of transport infrastructure.

Beyond ethnographic interest for the Chilean social explosion, the chief theoretical consequence of this chapter is its insistence that public transport serves as a public space that can enable the formation of an insurgent autonomous public culture. Social-movement researchers have not adequately taken this into account. For instance, studies of the politics of autonomy tend to focus on one particular public space as the epitome of organizing:

the assembly in the plaza or square. In its most celebratory accounts like that of Andy Merrifield (2013), this "liberated, autonomous realm" (105) serves as a place of encounter "without an absolute center" (41) in which "mass occupation expresses political ambitions before the political means necessary to realize them is created" (97), making the plaza the site at which "new communes bloom and the realm of the possible—another possible world—might be glimpsed" (105). Rather than seeing the assembly as the exemplary public space, however, we must look at *all* autonomous uses of public space. This chapter has principally focused on proving that the evasions were not merely a protest tactic, but were an expression of an autonomous public culture of Chile's leftovers formed in the public space of public transport.

The implied corollary is that studies of the politics of autonomy need to rework their definition of public space beyond that implied by the assembly. Elsewhere, I have more properly focused on Lemebel's conception of the publicness of public transport—hence the absence of a full theoretical discussion of public space in this chapter—arguing that he sees public space as a space of *exposure* rather than encounter.[13] In public space, not only are we exposed to new perspectives and expose others to our perspectives (i.e., the common theory of encounter), but our vulnerabilities are exposed to hostile others. Being in public space thereby becomes a process of managing one's vulnerability and complicity when exposed to the public. In public space, we do not only expose ourselves to those with similar interests (e.g., forming an autonomous decision-making body), we are exposed to hostile forces who want to silence those autonomous social relations. To give just one example, reflecting the "paradoxical logic of the closet" in heteronormative society (Creech 1993: 136), queer subjects in public space often simultaneously expose themselves complicitly to other queer subjects while shielding themselves from the attacks of a hostile heteropatriarchal society. Public space is marked by a kaleidoscope of complicities, vulnerabilities, and contestations articulated within the intersecting matrices of heteropatriarchy, racism, and capitalism. This helps explain why, as David Graeber's (2009) ethnography demonstrates, autonomous assemblies are not spaces of pure encounter but are always sites of conflict and tension articulated by gender, race, and class. By looking beyond classic public spaces to those like public transport, it may be easier to understand how assemblies work.[14]

Following this already existing exploration of Lemebel's understanding of public transport as a public space, the public space experience is one of ephemeral and thrown together alliances that are constantly emerging, disintegrating, shifting, reconfiguring, de-constituting, and re-constituting. Take the example of the massive evasion. All those entering into the subway station at the moment that the evasion is happening are *exposed* to the action of the students, and various choices are made available to each rider. Participate in the evasion by quickly sneaking through the exit door the students are holding open. Critique the students because the evasion is holding up the subway and potentially making one late to a meeting or work. Perform solidarity by joining in the students' chants and responding to critics. Support the State imposing order by taking photos, calling police, or otherwise interrupting the evasion. And yet, this momentary alliance, conflict, and/or inconvenience is dissolved only moments later when one exits the station or the train departs. There is no *we* of the massive evasion, there are riders exposed to the evasion and their varying vulnerabilities and complicities at that moment. Collectivization is ephemeral, unstable, and never clear.

The point of this conclusion is not to dismiss the importance of the assembly. Indeed, the next chapter is based on the assumed importance of this political formation. Rather, I am arguing that autonomous explanations of public space need to expand beyond the highly limited experience of the assembly to account for other spaces. In this sense, the massive evasion was not a protest tactic; it was the insurgent occupation of one type of public space as a space of exposure. Through the evasion, those in Chile were exposed to an underlying collective discontent with neoliberalism, to shared autonomous cultures that had been dismissed by elites, to their capacity to insurgently affirm that distinct coordination of social relations, and to the repressive measures taken by the Chilean government to silence threats to its dominance. Through massive evasions, the leftovers were exposing themselves both to others who participate in that leftover culture and to the hostile forces of the State.

Notes

1 In addition to already existing studies examining public transport as a public space (Grossman 2012; Ocejo and Tonnelat 2014; Schmucki 2002, 2012), the HERA-funded research project, PUTSPACE (2019), has been actively developing a theorization of how public transport is "at the frontline of contesting what is, can be, or should be public in the city."

2 This history of Santiago public transport is found on the *Micropolis* website.

3 I thank Ureta (2015) for his initial analysis of this document. I want to insist: my analysis of the Transantiago in this and the following paragraphs is highly indebted to Ureta's work.

4 See Link, Valenzuela, and Fuentes (2015) and Dattwyler, Rivas, and Link (2019). Their analysis is particularly valuable insofar as it nuances the strict center-periphery model that has been revised in Latin America since at least the publication of Teresa Caldeira's *City of Walls* (2001).

5 The concepts of marginalization and peripheralization with respect to Latin American urbanization have come under heavy criticism due to how they fail to account for how many urban spaces are formed by *many* centers. What might be the margins or periphery for one citizen could be the center for another. I am following recent reconsiderations of this topic by Niall Geraghty and Adriana Massidda (2019: 2) who argue for its use in Latin America and redefine it as

> a condition whereby an individual or a group is placed outside decision-making structures; where their relative income hinders their access to elementary goods, spaces and opportunities (which is to say, access to their

basic rights); and where it implies that some cultural, physical or bodily trait is deemed to be lesser value than the 'norm.'

6 This is still seen today (early 2020) on the Metro insofar as there is currently a campaign by the subway system to ban informal salespeople who sell the various goods of "domestic kitsch" that formed the foundations of the public culture of Santiago's old public buses; there is a constant attempt to discipline the subway according to the script of neoliberal modernity.

7 I am using "trans" here insofar as Madonna of San Camilo is always addressed by Lemebel using feminine pronouns, and no other name other than Madonna is assigned to her. As Vek Lewis (2010) argues, however, this is not entirely appropriate,

> What has become historically differentiated out as 'transgender' in other (notably U.S.) spaces is often visualized as part of the 'homosexual' in Latin American cultures. Even subjects who live as another social gender and adopt feminine expressions, modes of dress, and address (*travestis*) are frequently seen to exist on a homosexual continuum.
>
> (6)

8 The neighborhood was also known for being a red-light district for queer sex workers of Santiago.

9 Lemebel uses the concept of the "homosexual eye" in a variety of contexts. For those familiar with the piece, for instance, he uses the phrase to describe how Juan Dávila's *El Libertador* "reconstructs with a homosexual eye [*ojo coliza*] the mythological ghosts of independence" (Lemebel 2006).

10 I cite this video so that the reader has hard evidence of such an event; however, it was remarkably common during the social explosion. I must have heard the "*el que no salta es paco*" chant hundreds of times, often at the entrances to metro stations and bus stops.

11 In addition to the 2007 protests against Transantiago, I also mention the 2006 student movement fighting for free student fares on public transport (Gómez-Barris 2018) as well as the 1949 *Huelga de las Chauchas* and the 1957 "Battle of Santiago,"

> We could mark a milestone on August 13, 1949, when schoolchildren and university students went out on the streets to protest the increase in the price of public transport fares by 20 cents. This event was called the *Huelga de las Chauchas* (Strike of the Cents). Eight years later, in the first days of April 1957, the so called 'Battle of Santiago' took place, in which the increase in public transport fares caused general unrest, manifested through massive secondary and university student protests.
>
> (Cornejo et al. 2011: 157)

12 His case is still under consideration as I write this in August 2021 with the possibility that his case will be deemed unconstitutional.

13 See Kemmer, Sgibnev, Weicker, and Woods (forthcoming). Though I say 'I' for ease of reading, this was a co-written article in which Kemmer was the team leader.

14 This paragraph is entirely based on a co-written article with Laura Kemmer, Wladimir Sgibnev, Tonio Weicker, and myself.

3 On Water

"*No es sequía, es saqueo*" ["It's not drought, it's looting"]. So runs a protest slogan commonly repeated during the Chilean social explosion. Since 2010, Chile has been subjected to major drought, and water demand is quickly starting to exceed supply in various places throughout the country (Muñoz et al. 2020). For example, in the Copiapó River Basin, the river dries up halfway to the ocean (Bauer 2015: 157), and in the particularly affected rural area of Petorca, most rivers and water basins are now empty leading to dramatic shortages of water for some residents (INDH 2014; Muñoz et al. 2020; Panez-Pinto, Faúndez-Vergara, and Mansilla-Quiñones 2017). Yet as has been repeatedly pointed out, this water crisis is a human-made crisis insofar as water has been more and more diverted to external ends including but not limited to the heavy water-use economic sectors of mining and industrial agriculture (INDH 2014; Muñoz et al. 2020). By crying out, "*No es sequía, es saqueo,*" protestors were not only redirecting critiques of the so-called destructive elements of the social explosion—illuminating that the elite were the actual looters (in this case, looting water) and not the protestors—but were also highlighting that the current Chilean water crisis is a highly artificial consequence of particular political-economic decisions. With the chant, protestors were arguing that the political-economic model of Chile, not natural water cycles, had produced the water crisis and that the transformation of Chile's socio-political relations also required the transformation of socio-environmental relations.

A central element of the social explosion was its frequent condemnation of environmental injustice. In Valparaíso alone, various events were held in the final months of 2019 in relation to environmental injustice: an environmentalist march through Valparaíso, "Let's defend our Earth," was organized for November 30; the "No More Sacrifice Zones" Coordinator hosted an open-air "environmentalist forum" on November 29 on a central street in Valparaíso in order to have a panel of environmental activists, scientists, and economists discuss questions such as the environmental impact of globalization, "Sacrifice Zones," climate change, glacier protection, and the water crisis; protest signs in Valparaíso marches frequently addressed the question of "Sacrifice Zones"—the name given to Chile's contaminated

DOI: 10.4324/9781003224594-4

industrial areas that are becoming more and more inhospitable to humans, "places that, to their extractors, somehow don't count and therefore can be poisoned, drained, or otherwise destroyed, for the supposed greater good of economic progress" (Klein 2014: 169)—a particularly relevant issue in Valparaíso since the Quintero-Puchuncaví region to the north of the city plays host to an Industrial Park founded in the 1960s that has contaminated the area, transforming it "from a summer tourist destination into a reservoir of waste" (Balcazar 2016; Resumen TV 2019; Valenzuela Pérez 2016; Woods 2020b); and various socio-environmental *cabildos* were held in both Valparaíso and the nearby town of Villa Alemana, where *cabildos* are open, self-convened town-hall meetings dedicated to autonomously generating communal consensus with regard to a particular issue. (The *cabildos* will be described in more detail later in this chapter.) Water was a particularly present and significant element in these dialogues about environmental justice. For instance, on 15 December 2019, a Civic Enquiry [*consulta ciudadana*] was held throughout Chile to determine public opinion on various issues. One of the questions on the enquiry was "What three social demands are the most important?" Two of the possible responses were "expand access to water" and "care for the environment and natural resources."[1]

The social explosion therefore resonates with much recent interest across the globe in regard to questions of *water justice*, which can be defined operationally as the struggle for the equitable distribution of "rights to access water and [the struggle to] participate in decision making on water management and governance" (Zwarteveen and Boelens 2014: 143).[2] As this definition implies, and as others have explicitly argued, to question the hegemonic cultural significance of water is also to question dominant "water-society relations" (Budds 2020) and, with them, the very foundations of dominant sociality that determine those relations; fights for water justice are not only about access to a material substance, but "*recast* social relations through water" (Budds 2020: 166; Gandy 2002; Swyngedouw 1999, 2015). To imagine new "water-society relations," to use a phrase of Jessica Budds (2020) that will appear throughout this chapter, is to imagine new forms of living-in-common in general (Rubenstein 2010; Swyngedouw 1999, 2015; Woods 2017).

Central to this task of 'recasting social relations through water' has been the formation of a hegemonic conception of water through the production, circulation, and popularization of literary and artistic representations of water. Erik Swyngedouw (1999), for instance, argues that late nineteenth-century literary representations of Spanish "drylands" served as "a symbol of the decline of Spain and its failure to modernize" (455). This re-conception of (the lack of) water enabled the generation of a powerful centralized Spanish State that could implement a national water system. The cultural task of representing "the scale of the river basin as the geographical basis for exercising control and power over the organization, planning, and reconstruction of the hydraulic landscape" was in effect "one of the central arenas through which" elites legitimized the formation of the modern Spanish nation-State (459). Similarly, Michael Rubenstein (2010) has argued that the envisioned socio-political form of decolonized Ireland was dependent on Irish literary representations of public water infrastructure. The political struggle over the form decolonized Ireland would take was a cultural struggle over which representation of water would become popular: John Mitchel's representation of public works as a colonial imposition undermining the decolonial "ideal of an agricultural idyll," or James Joyce's representation of Ireland's lack of public works as a consequence of British colonization meaning that a modern water system was in fact a decolonial expression of independent Irish development (28).

These arguments are implicitly based on a classic relationship between culture and politics: hegemony. Literature in these examples serves to generate a consistent conception of the world—or, in this particular case, of water—which then can be materialized in, for instance, public works like Spain's and Ireland's water infrastructure. As such, although these examples demonstrate how art, politics, and water are intimately intertwined, they offer little help for understanding the relationship between art, autonomous politics, and the communal self-administration of water. In contrast to Rubenstein and Swyngedouw's implicit dependence on a theory of hegemony, the Chilean social explosion calls on us to ask: What does an *autonomous* and *horizontalist* administration of water look like, and what is the non-hegemonic role of art in that political project? What is the task of the cultural worker committed to water justice in the midst of an insurrection founded on an autonomous politics eschewing the logic of hegemony?

Other autonomous social movements provide possible responses. The communal self-administration of water as a foundation for autonomous politics has been a consistent element since the *Coordinadora de Agua* [Water Coordinator] in Cochabamba, Bolivia sparked massive grassroots mobilizations by seizing control of the management of Bolivian water systems (Graeber 2009; Gutiérrez Aguilar 2008; Notes from Nowhere 2003). As they wrote in their declaration,

> Water is best protected by local communities and citizens, who must be respected as equal partners with governments in the protection and regulation of water. Peoples of the earth are the only vehicle to promote earth democracy and save water.
>
> (qtd. and translated Graeber 2009: 103)

Raquel Gutiérrez Aguilar (2008) has most closely traced the activity of this group and its importance for the politics of autonomy, arguing that their activity is based on

> a local ancestral knowledge of the use, management, and care of water, embodied in a complex and differentiated mosaic of 'uses and customs'

> whose principal axis is the autonomy to regulate the use of water based on complicated supra-community agreements that are decided in assemblies and become obligatory for all who depend on and use [*usufructúan*] the same water source.
>
> (64)

The Cochabamba Water Coordinator is evidence of how autonomous politics seeks to self-govern and self-regulate communities' use of water in an egalitarian, horizontalist, and cooperativst manner.

Nonetheless, these discussions do not comment on the role of art and literature in such an autonomous politics of water justice. What is clear, however, is that such administration of water does not depend on a common conception of water, as was the case with the struggle for hegemony in Spain and Ireland, but rather requires making broadly conscious the idea that a water system is metabolized by a given community and that they have the power to self-regulate that metabolization. The *Coordinadora de Agua* shifts the role of art and literature from one of popularizing a political project's cultural foundation to making a community conscious of the fact that they can collectively determine how to self-administer their water. In the former, art *coheres* a given population around a shared conception of water; in the latter, art *convenes* a given population to autonomously make their own decisions with regard to how to administer water-society relations. How artists during the Chilean social explosion accomplished such a task is the theme of this chapter. In other words, this chapter shifts from the focus in Chapters 1 and 2 on the pre-historical cultural and political foundations of the social explosion to how artists actively responded to and intervened during the social explosion.

The goal of this chapter is double. First, I demonstrate that the generation of neoliberal dominance during the dictatorship and post-dictatorship eras required a corollary water culture that reflected, reinforced, and reproduced that neoliberalism. To challenge the dominant perception of water was to challenge the very foundations of Chilean neoliberalism and vice versa. Second, I explore how Valparaíso artists during the social explosion responded to concerns of water justice, examining the alternative water cultures they were proposing as well as their corollary water-society relations.

Neoliberalism and Water Justice in Chile

> *¡Uf! ¡Uf! ¡Qué calor! ¡Un guanaco, por favor!*
> *[Oof! Oof! It's so hot! Send a water cannon, please!]*

I have forgotten how many times during the social explosion I heard this chant that playfully mocked the Chilean State's brutal use of water cannons against protestors. It seemed that every time that Chilean police turned a corner in their armored busses mounted with water cannons that protestors who had been walking in the drought-stricken summer heat would start yelling this chant. I remember specifically hearing this chant on 26 November 2019 right before the police turned on protestors in Plaza Victoria in Valparaíso with a water cannon. As protestors fled, I waited and observed on a nearby street corner. Not hearing the warnings being screamed at me by others and not seeing the other police bus arriving at the plaza, I was hit point blank with a water cannon. I had heard rumors of the cannons' water being filled with chemicals—one study (*widely* critiqued by other independent chemists, it should be mentioned) found that the water was filled with lye (Equipo El Siglo 2019)—and as I shook on the ground for 30 minutes as it felt like someone had set fire to my skin, those rumors flooded my head. With just a half an hour of pain I consider myself lucky: photos of bodies covered with blisters, hives, and rashes as a result of being hit with the police's water cannons were not uncommon sights on social media and in the press during the social explosion.

This macabre humor—the mocking of and joking in the face of State brutality—was not the only use of this chant. I also remember the march of 22 December 2019 between Valparaíso and Viña del Mar. A smaller demonstration attended by only a few hundred people, we realized that we were marching straight into a congregation of police and, in order to avoid confrontation, diverted the march's route through the middle-class neighborhood of Recreo (a neighborhood that was largely avoided by marches due to the extremely narrow streets and lack of high-visibility public spaces). I remember seeing people coming to their doorways who could not march—people with oxygen masks, the elderly, the disabled—so that they might briefly participate by banging on a pot as we marched by. The day was particularly hot, drinking water reserves were quickly depleted, and many participants started overheating. Yet protestors were soon invited by local residents to fill water bottles with the water from their houses. Moreover, in one particularly memorable event, a resident watering their garden turned their hose on the protestors in order to cool them off. In this moment, the protestors burst into the chant at the heading of this section, joking about how they were being hit by a 'water cannon.' This fluid and creative use of the protest chant is representative of the underlying water conflict and the environmental justice vision of the social explosion: the State weaponizing water to maintain a social structure that benefits elites (water cannons filled with chemicals), and protestors not only resisting that water injustice (the first use of the chant) but autonomously appropriating and resignifying the cultural significance of water from the bottom up in order to propose democratized water-society relations (the second use of the chant and the communal sharing of water).

The overarching context in which this cultural struggle over the significance of water occurred is what Alex Loftus and Jessica Budds (2016) have referred to as Chile's *neoliberalization of water* (Bauer 1997, 1998, 2004, 2005,

2015). This neoliberal socio-ecological vision dates back to the implementation of the 1981 Water Code—written behind closed doors during the dictatorship with no democratic input[3]—the basis of which is, as stated in Article 5, "Waters are national goods of public use and the rights of use of them are granted to particulars in conformity with the dispositions of the present code." What this meant in practice was that "water rights were privatised and separated from landownership" and "government regulation of water use was weak and restricted" (Bauer 2015: 147–148). Under the 1981 Water Code, "the Chilean state grants a petitioner's rights for the use of surface water and groundwater. Once all water rights have been allocated..., the management of water rights at the watershed scale is overseen by water users' organizations" (Herrera et al. 2019: 303). Furthermore, water rights were sub-divided into consumptive and non-consumptive use. For instance, irrigators diverting and consuming water is an example of consumptive use whereas power companies sending water through hydroelectric turbines is a non-consumptive use (Bauer 2015: 155–156). In this way, the Chilean State's neoliberalization of water generated a private property market of water rights and curtailed the government's role to an administrative, rather than regulatory, capacity among water-rights owners (Loftus and Budds 2016).

As Sara Larraín (2012: 82) notes, there is an underlying contradiction in Article 5 of the 1981 Water Code, "despite the definition of water as 'a national public good,' at the same time it authorized the [*sic*] privatization, granting unlimited water rights for free and in perpetuity." As Budds (2013) argues, this ostensible contradiction in the description of water as both a national *and* private good can be resolved when one notes that "it was not Pinochet and [his] military advisors" (308) but rather the so-called "Chicago Boys"—a group of Chilean economists trained under Milton Friedman at the University of Chicago who adopted the free market neoliberal philosophies of the Austrian School and who were subsequently appointed to the National Planning Office by Pinochet (305)—who, in collaboration with non-State business elites, "directed the neoliberal economic reforms" (308). The dictatorship's particular privatization of water rights was instrumental for the broader privatization of natural resource industries—mining, chemicals, water supply, electricity companies, and so on—since the latter depended on cheap access to water and "counted private water rights among their capital assets" (Budds 2013: 309–310). It should therefore be unsurprising that the largest owner of water rights in 2012 was the private company, ENDESA (today ENEL), "with 80.4 percent of the total national water ownership for non-consumption use," water rights that were formerly State-owned but were sent to the private sector during the dictatorship (Larraín 2012: 84). Combined with ENEL's reputation for unjustly raising electricity rates, it is consequently of little surprise that on the first night of the social explosion protestors set fire to one of their large office buildings in Santiago.

Budds also notes a second rationale underpinning this neoliberalization of water. The act of privatizing water rights and the particular industries that obtained and used those water rights, she argues, guaranteed both that neoliberalism would continue after the transition to democracy and that the Chicago Boys would be granted "top executive positions" within those very industries after the dictatorship (Budds 2013: 310). In this way, mirroring the discussion of neoliberalism in Chapter 1, the neoliberalization of water is not so much the withdrawal of the State from the public sphere as the reformulation of "the institutional forms of state-society relations" (Taylor 2006: 7) in such a way that guarantees the maintenance of power by a certain elite. Against common views of neoliberalism as the "privatization of public services" in a way that witnesses the recession of the State (Arena 2012: xxvii), neoliberalism can more precisely be called capital's weaponization of the State in its drive to accumulation that concentrates political-economic power. In this way, it is by no means a contradiction to say that water is at the same time a "national good" and defined in terms of private water rights; these two poles, as Budds's work elegantly shows, have always been intertwined. Liberally using chemical-infused water cannons against people protesting neoliberalism during the social explosion is therefore just one more example of this phenomenon of the neoliberalization of water: Water is a "national good" insofar as it is weaponized by the State in order to protect the stability of elites' position within the privatized neoliberal landscape that has constituted Chile's dominant national project since at least 1975.

That water has been weaponized against the people can be seen in the material consequences of the neoliberalization of water. To give just a few examples of the consequence of this overlap of environmental injustice and neoliberalism: "By 2015...river flows and reservoir levels...were between 50 and 80 percent below normal" as a result of both 'non-consumptive' and 'consumptive' use (Budds 2020: 170); by the 2000s the Chilean government had granted rights "to several times more groundwater than was annually recharged" (Bauer 2015: 157); as of March 2020, 136 communities in Chile were under a state of agricultural emergency (Fernández 2020); and in the Antofagasta Region, "mining uses over 1,000 litres per second of surface water and owns almost 100 percent of the groundwater rights" (Larraín 2012: 83) in addition to mining accounting for "about 64 percent of total water demand" (Herrera et al. 2019: 304).[4] In certain particularly affected communities, due to the overuse of water by specific industries—a consequence of their disproportionate ownership of water rights—it is now the norm for households' water use to be functionally rationed since their water has to be trucked in (Bauer 2015: 158). To repeat the protestors' own formulation: The Chilean drought of the 2010s was more accurately the looting of communities' water.

This reference to the national project of neoliberalism opens up a corollary postulation: the neoliberalization of water was not just a political-economic project, but a cultural one that redefined dominant national understandings and perceptions of water. Indeed, a fairly basic problem emerged of justifying a socio-ecological model that was designed by an elite to concentrate and subsequently maintain power in their hands; culture would have to play the hegemonic function of convincing people to consent to the environmental injustice of neoliberal governance (Babidge and Bolados 2018). Loftus and Budds (2016) precisely argue this: the Chilean neoliberalization of water—the shift from the State-driven developmentalist model of the 1950s, 1960s, and early 1970s to the neoliberal project starting with the dictatorship—required the hegemonization of a redefinition of individuals as consumers and owners of water rights rather than as citizens of a community who collectively co-generate the nation's socio-environmental water systems.

That the neoliberalization of water is additionally a cultural project can be seen by taking even a glancing look at Indigenous defenses of waterscapes across the geopolitical space dominated by the Chilean government. Communities from multiple Indigenous nations have opposed the neoliberalization of water and land not only because it signifies economic dispossession but because it represents "losing the unique material base, the land, associated with individual and collective [Indigenous] development," given that the land was and is "the gluing element" of Indigenous communalities (Caniuqueo 2006: 179). As José Millalén Paillal (2006: 28) argues with regard to the Indigenous Mapuche nation, "The *Mapuche* culture in its entirety—language, customs, beliefs, notions of time and space, socio-political and territorial organization—only has coherence and sense in its origin in the occupation and relation with the historical territorial space." To impose neoliberal water relations within Mapuche geopolitical space is functionally to attempt to erase the Mapuche nation from the map.

Reflecting this conflict, Indigenous nations have heavily resisted the neoliberalization of water in order to empower the re-existence of their own socio-environmental visions.[5] For instance, the partly State-directed practice of cleaning irrigation ditches in mining areas in Chile's north has become a means for Aymara communities to covertly conduct water rituals that reproduce their Indigenous relations to water and the earth (Babidge and Bolados 2018). Perhaps more famously, however, has been Mapuche resistance to hydroelectric dams in the south, insofar as the dams' so-called non-consumptive use of water in fact threatens the integrity of ecosystems at the center of Mapuche cultural practices, politics, and sociality.[6] If this is most famously embodied in the Mapuche leader, Alberto Curamil, whose organizing efforts stopped "the construction of two hydroelectric projects on the sacred Cautín River in central Chile" during the 2010s and garnered him the Goldman Environmental Prize in 2019 (Goldman Environmental Foundation 2019), it should also be noted that this struggle has especially been fought by women such as Macarena Valdés and Millaray Huichalaf.[7] The response by the Chilean State and capital to this activism has been clear: the imprisonment of both Millaray Huichalaf and Alberto Curamil under questionable charges and the suspicious death of Macarena Valdés after she organized against the construction of a hydroelectric plant on Río Tranguil. The Mapuche fight not for equal representation within Chilean neoliberalism but for the recuperation of Mapuche land—a struggle sustained and legitimized by the empowerment of a coherent socio-environmental vision unassimilable by Chilean governance—has been met with intense State and business-conglomerate repression (Correa, Molina, and Yáñez 2005).

I emphasize this decolonial environmental resistance and re-existence in the leadup to the social explosion for two reasons. First, I want to re-emphasize that decoloniality was a key element of the popular insurgent culture in the years preceding 2019. To understand the social explosion, it is not enough to look exclusively at economic discontent. Second, as Jessica Budds (2013) writes, the neoliberal relationship between water and society was an essential element of the stability of popular consent with regard to the neoliberal program. As such, to oppose or critique the neoliberalization of water was to critique the very basis of post-dictatorship Chilean governance, and to affirmatively imagine alternative water-society relations was to imagine a new sociality. In the next two sections I want to demonstrate that both elements—the critique of the neoliberalization of water and the affirmative generation of alternative water-society relations—were substantial elements of the social explosion.

Critiquing the Neoliberalization of Water

On Monday, 2 December 2019, I attended the "Water Assembly" hosted in *Espacio Warhola*, a former (now abandoned) luxury hotel transformed into a gallery and art space in the center of Valparaíso, and part of the festival, "2019 Encounter: Sound Practices in Contexts of Crisis," set up by the Valparaíso Sound Art collective, Tsonami. Like any festival, it had been in the works for more than two months, meaning that Tsonami was in the position of carrying out a sound art festival imagined for times of calm in a moment of major social upheaval. Hearing the organizers introduce the artists and the event, it seemed that they were genuinely struggling with a difficult question: *How do we, as sound artists, confront and approach the major social, economic, political, and cultural crisis unfolding outside the doors of the festival?* Their insistence that we were attending an *assembly*—in reference to the popular self-convened assemblies that had been occurring across Chile for the previous month and a half—was part of their attempt to redesign a sound-art festival for the social explosion.

More precisely, the Water Assembly was concerned with how to produce sound art in relation to water in a moment when water-society relations were undergoing significant change. This should be not entirely surprising given that sound art has often addressed socio-environmental relations (Woods 2019). The very mission of the Water Assembly reflected these overlapping fields of shifting socio-environmental relations, water crisis, the social explosion, and sound art. As they describe the event, "On this occasion we desire to hear what water has to say." In order to achieve this objective, the group had erected a "hanging canal" that moved "a tiny volume of water in the form of a trickle." More precisely, a canal suspended in and running through the space of *Espacio Warhola* contained the average amount of water consumed by an individual on a daily basis. Though this water represented "an insignificant shadow of that which farm workers [*campesinos*] [work with] in the valleys," the Water Assembly imagined this installation as a catalyst to generate "a meeting…to provide the conditions for water to speak to us" and thereby permit "a group of friends—poets, residents, artists, activists" to "hear the water" (Tsonami 2019). In sum, the goal of the Water Assembly was to generate a poetic space in which to hear water and in which our shared sense perception of water might be altered in order to reflect what water is demanding of us and what we might demand of water.

The night opened with an explanation of the hanging canal referenced in the citation above as well as an opportunity for the public to see the other sound-art installations—such as Ozzo Ukumari's "Trawunko" ["meeting of waters or rivers" in Mapudungun] which "tries to amplify [the] experience [of feeling another presence through closeness] by using water as a medium placed in a copper pot that functions as an antenna and permits one to feel how water gets close to your skin" (Galaz Ulloa and Ukumari 2019).

The first full performance of the Assembly, however, was by the Brazilian sound artist, Luisa Lemgruber, whose work, "Novel Ecosystems," "consists of the creation of an ecosystem directly connected to the current habits of exploration."[8] Lemgruber's work started with a nearly empty and clean terrarium with a few rocks inside and situated next to the hanging canal. She then started filling the terrarium with more rocks, then dirt, then trash, then more rocks, then more garbage, and so on until it was full. At the same time, she diverted water from the hanging canal into the terrarium in a reference to the use of water by various industries (mining, waste removal, and industrial agriculture) in a way that disrupted the careful equilibrium of water that represented daily water use for an average person. As she describes the act, "In this intentional diversion, there is a risk of unbalancing or even destroying this system, since it is necessary that it has a specific volume of water in order to keep working" (Lemgruber 2019). All of this was then amplified using a contact microphone.

Lemgruber was elegantly and effectively making the effects of extractivism and contamination on carefully equilibrated water systems available to the senses. In contrast to the abstract and theoretical scientific documents and activist and government papers written on the Chilean water crisis, Lemgruber made the crisis visible and audible to the audience at the Water Assembly. The relationship between sound art, the water crisis, and the social explosion in "Novel Ecosystems" was precisely that imagined by Jacques Rancière. Rancière (2010) argues that the politics of art has nothing to do with individual artists' position with regard to certain political issues, but rather has to do with what he calls a "partition of the sensible, of the visible and the sayable, which allows (or does not allow) some specific data to appear; which allows or does not allow some specific subjects to designate them and speak about them" (152). The work of art is political insofar as it challenges "what can be said, thought and practised" (Routledge 2017). A work of art is a *dis-sensus* that ruptures a shared sense perception that otherwise serves to support a hegemonic *con-sensus*. In the case of Lemgruber, she shattered neoliberal sense perception by *making sensible* the effects of extractivism and contamination.

This act of making water injustice sensible was a common thread running through the Water Assembly. "Infiltration of Water in the Radiosphere" by Barbara González is another example. González used a contact microphone to amplify the sound of water running through the hanging canal. She then fed this sound into handheld radios throughout the space which she subsequently handed out to individual members of the audience. These individuals then circulated their sonic cyborg bodies—formed by the hybridization of sonified water, radiosphere, handheld radio, and kinetic organic body—through the space. Perhaps more provocatively, González was making audible the neoliberalization of water. The use value of water in the hanging canal was transformed into an electrified sound package which could be exchanged over the radiosphere. Water became a sound-package contained in handheld radios, guarded by individual 'owners,' and circulated with those owners' sonic cyborg bodies within the bounded space of the gallery. In some sense, however, this circulation was controlled and organized by the overarching 'governing' body of González. The playful, free circulation of sonified water was, in fact, the top-down directed privatization of water. González made sensible how the neoliberalization of water worked by transforming an equilibrated water system into an exchangeable private package, a transformation that could be justified in terms of the 'free circulation' of private property, but which also decoupled that free-circulation system from the water-ecosystemic roots on which the circulation was founded.

The Water Assembly was in this sense a profound critical intervention in the neoliberal partition of water's sensibility. This should in part be unsurprising given that the artists often maintained a similar stance in general. As Ozzo Ukumari ("Statement") states,

> I am interested in the relations, the ability to generate nexus not only between art and society or object and subject; I am interested in the relations between the forces and wills of the matter and the being; in the environment. *I believe in a Social Sculpture able to transform and produce consciousness.*
>
> [emphasis mine]

In this way, the role of the sound artist was fairly clear: they were an expert intervening in and thus transforming shared sense perception. The very *framing* of the Water Assembly—held in a gallery with performances by artists before a listening public—supported this social relationship.

Under the circumstances in which the Tsonami festival was imagined prior to the social explosion, when it appeared that there was relative consensus around the hegemonic project of the neoliberalization of water, this role of the artist was easily justifiable: they were a lone *dis-sensus* rupturing and critiquing the shared sense perception on which that hegemony rested. Yet in a moment of major social upheaval, when that hegemony had been thrown into crisis, this same intervention held a surprisingly conservative tone: they were no longer rupturing *con-sensus*, they were protecting the role of the professional artist as an expert in altering sense perception. This is not a critique of the Tsonami festival in itself (the reader hopefully notes that this section is largely a celebration of the innovative and revelatory work of the sound artists) but rather the significance of the Tsonami festival generated as a result of its framing during the social explosion. For however illuminating the sound artists' interventions may have been, the social explosion was demanding something else: a reformulation of the role of the artist in society.

Taking Water Action

For those familiar with Walter Benjamin it may be clear that this analysis is highly influenced by his lecture, "Author as Producer" (1996b [1934]). Benjamin makes the following claim, "the bourgeois apparatus of production and publication can assimilate astonishing quantities of revolutionary themes—indeed, can propagate them without calling its own existence, and the existence of the class that owns it, seriously into question" (774). More precisely, insofar as "left-wing literature" serves only "to wring from the political situation a continuous stream of novel effects for the entertainment of the public" (774), such directly political works of art serve only "to supply a productive apparatus without changing it" (775). Benjamin (1996b: 770) concludes that what is important is not the "attitude of a work" *towards* social relations or a social context, but rather how it reconfigures its position *within* them. The issue I raise with the Water Assembly is that it did not adequately reflect on this different problematic. They analyzed the sound artist's position *towards* the social explosion and the water crisis, but not sufficiently the sound artist's position *within* the social explosion. More precisely, they did not consider what the artist's position would be within the social explosion's politics of autonomy.

We can use the example of the Cochabamba Water Coordinator from the introduction of this chapter to explain Benjamin's idea. During the revolts provoked by the Coordinator, there was no need for artists to critique the privatization of water rights because the Coordinator had already effectively destabilized the dominant neoliberal representation of water as a 'natural resource' to be administered by the State. The role of the artist, instead, was to *convene* Bolivia in order to participate in the autonomous re-administration of water. What was needed was not another work of art that transforms how water systems are perceived (e.g., the sound artists at the Water Assembly) because the water coordinator had already accomplished such a feat. What was needed was to make conscious that those in Bolivia could autonomously self-administer their communities' water. No longer rupturing common sense, the artist was called upon to autonomously convene the population.

During the social explosion, this problematic would be addressed by the Valparaíso Coordinator for Cultural Action [*Coordinador Acción Cultural Valparaíso*] (CAC). A grassroots, horizontally structured, and self-convened organization, the CAC emerged in the first days of the social explosion. Their mission was founded on

> the necessity to meet as workers in the arts, culture, and Chilean heritage in response to the social crisis...a space of action based in reflection, that brings together demands from [this] sector...This is a living space that today is found in resistance.[9]

The goal of the CAC was to meet as *workers* within a system of production who, in the midst of revolt, believed that "from our capacity to organize ourselves as a community we can self-determine ourselves [*podemos autodeterminarnos*], exercising in this way our legitimate right to decide how we want to live." Recognizing that "the elite promotes a hegemonic culture" that is served by a corresponding "artistic elite," they sought "to connect ourselves with our communities." As a result, they perceived their struggle in terms of "the necessity to position culture within social demands as a category alongside health, education, work, and so on, since we understand that its relation is symbiotic." What was being rethought was not what art has to say with respect to the social explosion, but rather the position of artists within the society being constructed in the streets during the social explosion.[10]

In Valparaíso, the CAC is perhaps best known for having organized on 10 November 2019 the *cabildo* for arts, culture, and heritage [*patrimonio*] in a local school (Liceo Pedro Montt, Avenida Alemana 5196). As already mentioned, the *cabildos* are a form of assembly or open town hall that were popular during the social explosion as a means for people to self-convene in order to autonomously generate their political, cultural, and social collective imaginaries.[11] The methodology of the *cabildos* often used was one developed by *Unidad Social* [Social Unity], a collection of "the principle social organizations" formed in 2019 prior to the social explosion and which aimed "to represent the needs of the Chilean people before the offensive of the business sector...[and] to construct a juridical framework that sustains this model for decades" (Gajardo 2019; NODAL 2019; Reyes 2019).[12] Their *cabildo* methodology was notable precisely because it could be dynamically appropriated and reconfigured: Valparaíso developed its own *cabildo* methodology in dialogue with local municipal governance (El Desconcierto 2019); a leftist political party, *Revolución Democrática* (2019), offered its own methodology; and in every *cabildo* I attended a separate subgroup had previously worked out the methodology, which was then presented to the *cabildo* at the beginning of the meeting.[13] By November 2019 the *cabildo* had become a particularly popular form of autonomous political organization, with over 15,000 people from over 142 communities in Chile having participated in a *cabildo* by 7 November 2019.[14] Topics of *cabildos* ranged widely, including: neighborhood and municipal organization, environmental justice, cultural labor, migratory justice, writing a new constitution, and so on. In short, the *cabildos* were grassroots and autonomous means of constructing a mode of coordinating a life in common outside the bounds of the State.[15] The assemblies and consensus-building processes that have received so much well-deserved attention in discussions of the politics of autonomy were at the foundation of the social explosion as well.[16] The dialogues and materials specifically generated by the cultural *cabildo* in Valparaíso were systematized by the CAC over the course of three months and released in February 2020 (CAC 2020a). In the document, one can find not only the methodology and context of the *cabildo*, but the common issues faced by cultural workers in the region such as the extreme precarity of the cultural labor market.

Beyond the *cabildo*, the CAC also organized their own artistic and cultural actions that were effectively generating new forms of art to reflect Chile's shifting socio-political and cultural landscape. One of these, the "Water Action," was dedicated precisely to the shifting relationships between the social explosion, the water crisis, and aesthetics. Unfortunately, the "Water Action" was cursed. Initially planned to take place on the final weekend of December 2019, it was delayed due to forest fires raging throughout Valparaíso that required a redirection of organizing energy to help those affected. The CAC then planned to realize the action on 22 March 2020, the International Day of Water, when various marches and actions were to be realized throughout Valparaíso as part of the social explosion and in recognition of the water crisis. This was also postponed because of the installation of quarantining measures for the COVID-19 pandemic. The "Water Action," fully written, planned, organized, and even partially rehearsed—and therefore eminently available for analysis[17]—was never carried out. What follows is therefore a discussion only of the planned event.

The "Water Action" was a five-part theatrical narrative to be realized in the streets, plazas, and buildings of two Valparaíso neighborhoods, Cerro Yungay and Cerro Bellavista. The first part of the narrative would have started in Cerro Yungay with a "river of bottles": two lines of performers were to march down a neighborhood street while blowing on empty bottles (a representation of the drought and the water crisis), a singular dancer would march with a river of empty bottles trailing them as a cape and train, and "exploiters of water" would observe them all.[18] After arriving to the small public space of Plaza Yungay, the action then would have developed the second part of the narrative: in a representation of the ongoing drought, the performers were to spread out and start performing various everyday water-related acts—bathing, brushing their teeth, cleaning dishes, sharing water, and so on—but would be forced to perform them with the dirt from the plaza's ground since they lacked water.[19] In the third part, they would then have marched from Plaza Yungay to Cerro Bellavista and along the route asked for water from those in the neighborhood, "with the goal of collecting water for their community." Though under duress, the performers and the community were claiming their right to equitably distribute water. After arriving at their final destination, a public amphitheater within the "Open Air Museum" in Cerro Bellavista, the fourth part of the act would have consisted of performers drinking a little bit of the communally collected water to refresh themselves, caring for the water, and then deciding to rest and sleep. As they slept, the exploiters were to arrive, steal half of the water, and "contaminate" the rest. After waking up, the people were then to confront the exploiters, and the "river of bottles" was to unfold into a banner that contained information about the water crisis that was then to be raised and delivered to the community. Finally, in what can be termed the 'coda' of the work, a brief seminar was to be held in which information about the water crisis could be shared and those present could ask questions to a few participating individuals who had extensively studied the Chilean water crisis.

As can be gleaned from this summary, autonomous water justice—the self-determining community's right to equitably distribute water—was at the center of the "Water Action." From the communal collection of water in the third part to the demonstration in the fourth part of how the contemporary drought was a consequence of political-economic decisions by the elite (i.e., "*no es sequía es saqueo*"), the question at the center of the narrative was that of who controlled water-society relations. More precisely, the CAC was showing both that water justice could be achieved by the community collectively claiming their right to self-determine water-society relations *and* that the Chilean elite's actual determination of water-society relations (i.e., contamination and extractivism) was both unjust and undemocratic.

Returning to Benjamin, what is just as significant as the "Water Action's" message about the water crisis is its position *within* social relations. Effectively, the street narrative deconstructed the distinctions between stage and audience, performer and public, the removed world of art and the everyday world of the community. Through the act of community members giving water to the performers, the distinctions between these dyads were collapsed; community members were also performers within the narrative fulfilling a specific function—they were actors who delivered water to a caravan of thirsty people—and the performers were community members asking for generosity from their neighbors. By including community members as performers in the narrative, the structure of the "Water Action" forced those community members to analyze their actual communal relationship to water as if they were analyzing a theatrical work of art.

In other words, this was not a narrative performance before a community, *this was the narrative emplotment of that community's actual water-society relations.* For instance, the water contaminated and stolen was not symbolic or representative water within the world of performers on stage, but was the very water of the communities of Cerro Yungay and Cerro Bellavista. The "Water Action" threw a narrative frame around the entire community itself, forcing those present to analyze their relationship to water as one would a theatrical narrative and to perceive themselves as audience, actors, and writers of that narrative.[20] The CAC was raising to consciousness the fact that the community at any moment could claim the power to determine how water was distributed, accessed, and managed and that the "exploiters" had stolen that power from them. In this way, the CAC was proposing a new place for the artist in society: no longer the expert intervening in shared sense perception, the artist now served to open a discursive space in which the community (not the artist) could examine and claim the right to determine social relations as well as the cultural paradigms that supported them. The CAC had *convened* the community around water-society relations.

In the case of the "Water Action," cultural action did not only serve the Brechtian drive to raise to consciousness the relations of power that determined water distribution, access, and management—i.e., the employment of artistic techniques that allow the performer and audience "to underline the historical aspect of a specific social condition" (Brecht 1964: 98) such as water injustice—but in addition it served to raise to consciousness that the community itself had the power to self-determine its collective metabolization of water. Whereas Brecht (1964) was concerned with the fact that "the necessity and the possibility of remodelling society loom ahead" and that theater should lay the groundwork for that remodelling through "its social criticism and its historical reporting" (98), the CAC during the social explosion was actually in the midst of remodelling society and therefore the demands on the work of art were different: they had to catalyze not social criticism, but the act of taking control of social relations. The framing of the "Water Action"—i.e., the 'breaking of the fourth wall,' or, more precisely, re-positioning the narrative frame around the community itself—served not to rupture a shared sense perception, as it functionally did for Brecht, but instead to redefine the people of the community as the agents of the narrative in which they claim the right to determine equitable distribution and access to water. The "Water Action" illuminated not only "the historical aspect" of the water crisis but also that the mobilized community of the social explosion was positioned to claim the right to determine water-society relations.

In this way, it is significant that the 'coda' of the "Water Action" occurred *after* the theatrical narrative that raised to collective consciousness that the community held the power to claim the right to autonomously self-determine their relationship with water. Those individuals sharing information with the community about the water crisis were not acting in the form of experts instructing unenlightened masses, but instead were delivering the democratized knowledge tools necessary for the community to actualize novel socio-environmental visions of water. This was not necessarily a new socio-epistemological form for the region. For instance, various social movements in the "Sacrifice Zone" of Quintero/Puchuncaví organized "days of socio-environmental education" within the community in order to share knowledge and to allow community members to directly interrogate scientific experts. One such day on 22 June 2019 allowed residents to speak with oceanographers, engineers who could explain how to read air contamination graphs, and lawyers who were presenting environmentalist cases before the Supreme Court. The CAC was generating a new cultural paradigm to reflect, enable, and legitimize this popular and autonomous seizing of socio-environmental relations, raising to consciousness that the information delivered to the community was to be actively used in their democratic reconfiguration of water-society relations and not to be consumed as a justification of and instruction manual for navigating already existing water-society relations.

The work of the CAC had a double effect. First, they were generating a cultural paradigm that reflected, legitimized, and enabled popular, democratic, and autonomous socio-political relations. The cultural *cabildo* is one such example: they were no longer considering how the artist should respond to the social explosion, they were interrogating how the social explosion challenged the very position of the artist in society. Second, given that this irruption of autonomous modes of living-in-common also correlated to recasting water-society relations, the CAC's "Water Action" represents one manner of reconstituting artistic production that aids such a vision of direct democracy. The artist is no longer the expert intervening in shared sense perception, they are constructing a narrative frame that facilitates a community in autonomously examining and subsequently taking control of water-society relations.

Conclusion

This chapter makes a triple argument with respect to the social explosion. First, a repeated refrain throughout this work: neoliberalism was a central, but not the only, element of Chilean unrest. The presence of environmentalist mobilization, especially around questions of water justice, demonstrates the breadth of the protestors' vision. Second, as Fernando Gaspar and Guillermo Jarpa (2019: 18) write, one of the main responses by protestors was not to appeal to the State to resolve social issues, but rather to autonomously organize "under the form of assembly, *cabildo*, or other methodology of meeting with the perspective of discussing social demands, channeling discontent, and advancing towards concrete proposals emanating from the citizenry [*la ciudadanía*]." Part of this autonomization of the process of configuring a novel mode of living-in-common was the reconsideration of water-society relations. Three, such a recasting of social relations required the recasting of the relationship between art and society. What was needed was not a response by artists to the water crisis in the midst of the social explosion, but a reconsideration of the artist's role in society in the midst of a social and water crisis. In this way, the elegant critical pieces of Tsonami's Water Assembly were ironically conservative: they reinforced the role of the professional artist in society rather than questioning what art would be in a society democratized by the empowerment of subaltern communalities. The CAC, on the other hand, through the cultural *cabildo* and the "Water Action," sought to redefine art as that which enabled power being autonomously claimed.

The point here is not to say that this particular event by Tsonami is 'bad'—and I would like to emphasize that I am critiquing a particular *event* and not Tsonami itself given that some people collaborating with Tsonami also were involved in the CAC's "Water Action" and were in the streets participating in the social explosion—and the CAC's water action is 'good.' Instead, I am making a specific argument: art must be conscious not only of its content and form, but how the framing of the work of art either reproduces already existent art-society relations or pushes towards new visions of the position of art and artist in society.[21] In this way, the CAC illuminates how an artistic work's framing (re)produces social relations through its implied art-society relations. In other words, the *framing* of a work of art generates a relation between the speaker and receiver—two subject positions that, I argue, were broken down by the CAC insofar as the framing of the "Water Action" transformed performers into community members and vice versa—that further implies generalizable social relations. The frame is a microcosmic embodiment of the social relations proposed by a work of art. To rework Rancière's thinking, the politics of the work of art is not in what it says about a given social issue; the politics of the work of art is how within its very framing are embedded social relations that prefiguratively posit broader modes of living-in-common.

Nonetheless, the CAC left undiscussed a significant question: *Who* was convened through their "Water Action" and at their *cabildo*? This particular inquiry generates a broader one: What is the identity of the collective brought together during the social explosion? What yoked these widely ranging individuals, collectives, and communities into a coherent 'we'? The CAC was functionally agnostic towards this question, only convening but never questioning who specifically was being convened. In the next chapter, we will explore why this agnosticism needed to be concretely resolved as well as the proposed resolutions to this problematic by various artists and activists during the social explosion.

Notes

1 It should be stated: of the 13 possible options on the Civic Enquiry, access to water scored lowest and care for the environment in the bottom half. Nonetheless, this does not signify that water was not an important issue, only that it was not as important as, for instance, increasing pensions.
2 For more on the idea of water justice see: Robinson et al. (2018); Sultana (2018); Sultana and Loftus (2011, 2019); Wong (2018).
3 There have been various reforms to the Water Code in the post-dictatorship era, but they have done little to actually transform the framework of water-society relations (Bauer 2005, 2015).
4 For more evidence beyond these examples see Larraín, Poo, and Programa Chile Sustentable (2010).
5 This resistance/re-existence conceptual dyad is thanks to Walsh and Mignolo (2018).
6 For instance, for the significance of swamplands (*Menoko* in Mapudungun, the Mapuche language) in Mapuche sociality, see Adkimvn (2011).
7 For more on the relationship between Mapuche socio-environmental vision and Millaray Huichalaf, see Zurlatente Producciones (2014).
8 This text is taken from Lemgruber's *Vimeo* page where one can also see a video of the performance (Lemgruber 2019). I have chosen to translate "Nuevos Ecosistemas" as "Novel Ecosystems" in reference to the term introduced by Chapin III and Starfield (1997). A "novel ecosystem" is a species combination emanating from "changing species distributions and environmental alteration through climate and land use change" (Hobbs et al. 2009: 599) that results in the ecosystem departing "entirely and irreversibly from its historical analogs" (Hobbs et al. 2014: 645; Murcia et al. 2014: 548). Though likely, I am uncertain as to whether Lemgruber was intentionally referencing this concept.
9 I participated in CAC actions and assemblies. Although it is my duty to inform the reader of my position, I mention this in a footnote as I want to emphasize as heavily as I possibly can: *I am a reader of the CAC's actions, not their representative.* I repeat, in writing this book I am a reader of the CAC's actions and should *never* be perceived as their representative. Indeed, the CAC *explicitly* decided against having a representative voice. I request that the reader perceive this reading as if it were coming from any other audience member.
10 All citations in this paragraph from CAC ("Declaración de Principios").
11 A different cultural *cabildo* was also held in Santiago (Facuse and Cavalcanti 2019). The *cabildo* was not invented during the social explosion. For instance, the Quintero-Puchuncaví *cabildo*, initiated to address the environmental injustice of those living in the "Sacrifice Zone" of Quintero-Puchuncaví, existed before the social explosion, and former president Michelle Bachelet had convened *cabildos* throughout the country to generate in-put with regard to a potential new constitution. The *cabildos* were originally a colonial-era institution in which municipal residents could consult among themselves to discuss certain issues and present recommendations to the colonial government; more recently, since 1991 they have been an established part of the Colombian constitution (Cogollos Amaya and Ramírez León 2004).
12 *Unidad Social* was in many ways the culmination of the independent institutionalized social movements discussed in Chapter 1, with all their associated problems. For instance, the feminist organization, *Coordinadora Feminista 8M* [the Feminist Coordinator for the 8th of March (International Women's Day)], left the organization in January 2019 since, according to their critique, the "Labor Bloc" of *Unidad Social* sought to subordinate all other concerns to their mission (Coordinadora Feminista 8M 2020).

13 For a description of one such methodology, see CAC ("Cabildo"). The details of such assembly processes are outlined by Graeber (2009).

14 Information from Iglesias and Valdés (2019). This article is particularly recommended as it includes testimony from *cabildo* participants. See also Albert and Köhler (2020).

15 Though as the Valparaíso case makes clear (El Desconcierto 2019; Iglesias and Valdés 2019), there was often a dialogue with the State. For this reason, some far-left participants in the social explosion critiqued the *cabildos* as an attempt by "traditional political parties and the 'new left'" to "coopt and supplant the self-direction of the movement" in order to "impose their positions and transform themselves into validated interlocutors for negotiating with those in power" (Vamos hacia la vida 2021: 71).

16 These other discussions have said everything about autonomous assemblies in a much more elegant and compelling manner than I ever could. I urge readers to go to these other wonderful theorizations and ethnographies (Butler 2018; Dinerstein 2015; Graeber 2009; Gutiérrez Aguilar 2008; Hardt and Negri 2017; López y Rivas 2011; Sitrin and Azzellini 2014; Zibechi 2010).

17 The analysis of the "Water Action" is based on my reading of the script, initial partial rehearsals, and my having witnessed the successful performance of an earlier action by the CAC, an "Artistic Candlelight Vigil" held on 31 October 2019. In other words, though the official performance was never conducted, the planning of the work can be analyzed, and their previous actions demonstrate that the "Water Action" would similarly have been realized successfully.

18 Quotes are from the script used to coordinate the action.

19 CAC organized a revised version of this part of the "Water Action" in a video created during the pandemic (CAC, 2020b).

20 I have more fully discussed the CAC's insurgent use of the narrative frame elsewhere (Woods, forthcoming b).

21 As my reference to Benjamin—who was specifically thinking of DADA in the lecture cited—makes clear, the historical avant-gardes already accomplished this by challenging the *institution* of art (Bürger 1984). I argue that the CAC not only questioned the position of art and the artist in society but were pushing towards new art-society relations that legitimized and enabled subaltern democratization and autonomy.

4 On Collectivization

MUERTE AL CISTEMA
DEATH TO THE CISTEM
[Graffiti in Valparaíso during the social explosion]

As discussed in Chapter 1, explanatory narratives are already emerging of the social explosion, and perhaps the dominant one explains the movement as a critique of the neoliberal Chilean State. Social-movement experts are rejoining these narratives by pointing to evidence like this graffiti: yes, the neoliberal State was a key element of the protests, but not the only one. To the anti-neoliberalism of the social explosion, these researchers add feminist, queer, decolonial, and environmental-justice narratives. Indeed, LASTESIS (2021c) has suggested that we (at least partially) frame the social explosion as part of an "avalanche of continuous unstoppable changes and processes" started with feminist protests in 2018. In this way, despite my critiques of the social-movement narratives in Chapter 1, this book might be understood as critically building off the latter, arguing that the popularization of these narratives largely transformed independent social movements into an autonomous rebellion.

I am, it seems, implicitly following Foucault's (1978b) insight that

> there is no single locus of great Refusal, no soul of revolt, source of all rebellions, or pure law of the revolution. Instead there is a plurality of resistances, each of them a special case: resistances that are possible, necessary, improbable.
>
> (95–96)

There is no single source of the social explosion, but rather a multiplicity of factors that combined in late 2019 to generate mobilizations in the street. Foucault's phrasing has proved particularly enduring because it allows for a way out of the myopic focus of some Marxism on class and economics. As McNaughton (2008) notes, "While dynamics of gender, race, nature, nation, ethnicity, sexuality, ability et al. are framed by capitalist political economy they cannot be simply reduced to this dynamic" (15). As McNaughton

DOI: 10.4324/9781003224594-5

continues, however, this analysis frequently poses "the relationship between class analysis and difference in a dualistic either/or fashion" (16)—*either* the rebellion is about the class-based critique of capitalism *or* it is based on social movements structured around so-called 'cultural' questions of difference such as feminism, racism, and so on. As McNaughton then concludes, "the most pressing theoretical task" becomes the capacity to take "both class and difference seriously" in such a way that

> adequately address[es] the epistemological and ontological implications that difference and *the struggles for recognition* pose to a Marxist understanding of power. This is not to suggest that we should reject the category of class or class analysis—on the contrary. But reimagined class struggles within the conditions of postmodernity need to take the challenges of difference more seriously.
>
> (16)

In the case of the social explosion, then, we need to consider the structural relationships between, for instance, neoliberalism, feminism, and coloniality.

In five sections with a particular focus on feminist elements, this chapter argues that the social explosion is not a rebellion against neoliberalism *and* hetero-patriarchy *and* settler colonialism, but is instead a critique of the heteropatriarchal-colonial-neoliberal State. That is, we cannot separate anti-neoliberalism, feminism, and decolonial threads of the social explosion; instead, they are interlinked and mutually reinforcing. The critique of the patriarchal State is a critique of the neoliberal State is a critique of settler-colonial State. Starting with a theoretical overview of how these connections have been theorized in the past, with a particular focus on the relationship between feminism and capitalism, I will then analyze a collection of short stories by Daniela Catrileo, *Piñen*, to argue that prior to the social explosion there was a profound awareness of the deep links between settler colonialism, heteropatriarchy, and neoliberalism. An analysis of Catrileo's work demonstrates how racism and misogyny are not 'cultural' issues in contrast to the 'material' concerns of class; instead, settler colonialism, patriarchy, and neoliberalism are mutually reinforcing fields structuring social relations. I then close by analyzing three attempts during the social explosion to re-coordinate social relations beyond the limits of capitalism, patriarchy, and settler colonialism by imagining a novel collective subject formed by Chile's leftovers: LASTESIS's "Un violador en tu camino," Cheril Linett's *La Yeguada Latinoamericana*, and the Catrileo+Carrión community's *Poyewün Nütramkan* [*Caring Conversations*].

Gender, Race, and Neoliberalism

In a 1997 article, "Merely Cultural," Judith Butler critiqued "the tendency to relegate new social movements to the sphere of the cultural, indeed, to dismiss them as being preoccupied with what is called the 'merely' cultural, and then to construe this cultural politics as factionalizing, identitarian, and particularistic" (265). More precisely, they had in mind class-based and Marxist critiques that feminist and anti-racist movements were secondary concerns that in themselves, "fai[l] to address questions of economic equity and redistribution, and fai[l] as well to situate culture in terms of a *systematic* understanding of social and economic modes of production" (265). Against this, Butler argues that gender and sexuality are integral elements of the capitalist mode of production insofar as "the production of gender" serves to normalize the institution that reproduces the labor force: "the heterosexually normative family" (271–272). For Butler, to fight the heteropatriarchy is to fight the reproduction of the labor force is to fight capitalism.

This relationship between gender and capitalism would be more fully theorized in Silvia Federici's *Caliban and the Witch* (2004). Focusing on the transition from feudalism to capitalism, Federici argues that the implementation of capitalism resulted in: (1) the forced "exclusion of women from waged-work," (2) their subsequent relegation to labor dedicated to "the reproduction of the work force," and (3) the ideological reconfiguration of that labor as an act of love rather than labor, thereby legitimizing their continued unpaid exploitation (12). In sum, capitalism requires the reproduction of the work force, that reproductive labor has been relegated to women, and the patriarchal gender system ideologically enables that ruthless exploitation of women's work.

White men's waged-work and "the expansion of the unpaid part of the waged working-day" (104–105) thereby came to depend on the existence of unpaid labor forces: women and, Federici also argues, African slaves. These "divisions within the working class" structured around race and gender "became constitutive of class rule" (63–64) insofar as they permitted privileges for the waged white male laborer and disincentivized his aligning with working-class women and enslaved people. Under this theorization, gender and race serve to divide laborers in order to impede working-class solidarity and maximize capitalists' profits by increasing their capacity for exploitation (Chibber 2013). As Stuart Hall (1986) puts it, race and gender "provided the means for differentiated forms of exploitation of the different sectors of a fractured labour force" (24). Gender and race are not 'cultural' concerns, they are imminently material.

Like any hegemony, such a gender and racial system produces elite/citizen/subaltern distinctions. If the elite are those who define[1] this gendered, racialized, and classed system upholding a capitalist mode of production, its citizens are those who develop their identities as subjects within this system: the loving mother, the white male breadwinner, and so on. The subaltern, then, are those who are unidentifiable within this system: sex workers whose labor insists on the linking of waged labor and sexuality (that apparently 'private matter' that belongs to the 'loving' realm of reproduction), women who do not marry, queer men whose sexual orientation does not serve to reproduce the nuclear family, trans men and women whose sexual identity does not permit their recognizable identification within the gendered mode of capitalist production, and so on (Edelman 2004; Smith 2020).

So what happens to those who refuse this hegemonic gender system? Working-class women who refuse to become unpaid laborers of reproduction, homosexual men who refuse to participate in the reproduction of the labor force, trans men and women whose identities are "rendered unintelligible" (Edelman 2004; Federici 2004, Smith 2020: 75)? The State weaponizes violence to enforce compulsory acceptance of the system. For instance, witch hunts, Federici (2004) argues, disciplined women into accepting their new position within a capitalist mode of production and to attack working-class women's "resistance" (170). In short, witch hunts were class warfare against working-class women. Following Nicola Smith (2020), to this we can add the State's persecution of queer men—Smith notes in an examination of England's Buggery Act that in 1806, "more men were put to death for sodomy than for murder" (70)—as well as the court's inability to recognize non-cisgender subjects. The State instrumentalizes violence in order to guarantee compulsory acceptance of the gendered ordering of reality that supports capitalism's sexual division of labor.

For some, this linking of patriarchy and capitalism has been disproven by feminism apparently thriving under neoliberalism. This is the conundrum addressed by Nancy Fraser (2013). Why does neoliberal capitalism apparently permit the loosening of the patriarchal order of social relations to the contrary of previous forms of capitalism? Fraser's response is that this is made possible through the reconfiguration of feminism: no longer primarily concerned with transforming the mode of production in which the reproduction of the workforce was relegated to the unpaid (or, at the very best, underpaid) labor of women, feminism under neoliberalism shifts towards "claims for the recognition of identity and difference" (219). Hegemonic feminism under neoliberalism no longer challenges the capitalist mode of production, it fights for the recognition of (certain) women's rights *within* that mode of production. As Lee Edelman's (2004) analysis implies, the same might be said about the fight for gay marriage: dominant queer activism stopped its critique of social reproduction and fought for the right to participate *within* the existing capitalist mode of (re)production.

Within Chile, Fraser's thesis has been adopted, critiqued, and reworked (Godoy Ramos 2016; Ruiz Encina and Miranda Medina 2018; Schild 2016). As these authors note, neoliberalism has permitted a greater participation of Chilean women in the waged-labor force as well as in the higher education system; however, this has not meant the emancipation of women "from their subaltern condition" (Ruiz Encina and Miranda Medina 2018: 196). Instead, neoliberalism has signified the transformation of "the codes of such a subaltern condition: it brought them from their place in the family to their current anchoring in the market, bringing over…the ancient conservatism to contemporary narratives" (196). Women are pushed to pursue 'feminine' careers (ones that are less valued, as shown through their lower salaries and higher precarity) (Ruiz Encina and Miranda Medina 2018: 195–196), they are still expected to fulfill the labors of reproduction in the household (Ruiz Encina and Miranda Medina 2018), and the neoliberal evisceration of public infrastructure has been supplemented by an increase in "feminized work" (Gago 2019: 236). As Schild (2016) puts it, "The autonomy provided by the neoliberal model of the family with two salaries and 'flexible' work has its costs: emancipation serves to feed the motor of capitalist accumulation… while care work [*el trabajo de cuidados*] continues falling…on women" (42). To rework for our purposes Vivek Chibber's (2013) phrasing, neoliberalism regains legitimacy after the dictatorship "by opening a space for subaltern groups to articulate and pursue their interests—albeit within the limits of" (42) neoliberal social relations. As Godoy Ramos (2016) summarizes, Chilean women are now neoliberal citizens, but they are not treated as *political subjects* who can participate in the ordering of social relations.

This *gattopardist* understanding of the relationship between feminism and neoliberalism in Chile—for neoliberalism to remain the same, gender relations must completely change—is complicated by another factor: the settler colonial character of the Chilean State. For instance, during the late nineteenth and early twentieth centuries the Chilean State's colonization of Indigenous Mapuche lands took the form of forcefully 'reducing' Mapuche families to small shares of land. Such a mission, which sought to transform Mapuche into "petit bourgeois via becoming owners of [their] means of production" (Caniuqueo 2006: 172), disrupted the distinct mode of agricultural production and social reproduction underlying Mapuche communality (Marimán, Caniuqueo, Millalén, and Levil 2006). By the 1930s, such reductions no longer supported those growing families, thereby producing a massive wave of Mapuche migration to urban centers, especially Santiago (Aravena Reyes 2008).

Indigenous women in Chile, then, experience not only patriarchal control—the denial of their being as political subjects within neoliberalism—but additionally colonial *dispossession* both in terms of land as well as in terms of the power of communal self-definition. As Gayatri Spivak (1999: 30) insists, patriarchal exclusion of white women and the racist exclusion of Indigenous Others are based on distinct logics: "the Woman…is argued into that dismissal" whereas the Indigenous Other is dismissed in "a casual rhetorical gesture"—their presence is not even taken into account. Maria Lugones's (2010) concept of the *coloniality of gender* precisely expresses this fact: Indigenous women are judged and defined by "a normative" and alien "understanding of 'women'" (744), thereby denying them the right to define themselves according to gender frameworks within a distinct mode of (re)production. Indigenous women are therefore provided two options. First, work within the lines of dominant Chilean feminism—in which they will fight for their inclusion within neoliberalism or, perhaps, for the transformation of the gendered mode of capitalist production. In this case they will have to deny Indigenous modes of production and their attendant gendered social relations (i.e., they will have to accept settler colonialism). Second, work within the lines of Indigenous organizing—in which they will work within the government organizations mentioned in Chapter 1 that institutionalize Indigenous organizing or within decolonial autonomous organizing in which feminist and diasporic migrant organizing often takes a backseat. The migrant Indigenous woman embodies the subaltern condition: not those who are occupying an oppressed position, but those whose position is rendered unintelligible by the dominant ordering of social relations.

This ties into a little-discussed element of Federici's argument. She mentions on more than one occasion that in the transition from feudalism to capitalism, those who

> did not peacefully agree to work for a wage...[often] became beggars, vagabonds or criminals...In the 16th and 17th centuries, the hatred for wage-labor was so intense that many proletarians preferred to risk the gallows, rather than submit to the new conditions of work.
>
> (Federici 2004: 136)

Federici notes here that those subaltern subjects who are forcefully introduced to, but do not accept, capitalist social relations—witches, colonized subjects, and so on—become those who have no place within the dominant ordering of social relations ("beggars, vagabonds or criminals"). Moreover, they are then subjected to brutal disciplinary measures ("...preferred to risk the gallows"). Indeed, as I've argued elsewhere (Woods forthcoming a), there are always those who cannot cohere themselves as subjects within modern capitalism and therefore must be violently disciplined into accepting those social relations. These leftovers—not capitalism's oppressed, but those who are without place in capitalism—are the subaltern, and they are constantly subjected to the disciplinary forces attempting to shape them into recognizable subjectivities.

Chile's post-dictatorship neoliberalism is therefore a complex system that permits the re-coordination of gender and colonial relations of power as long as that system's existing self-definition goes unchallenged. Such a process, however, creates a wide set of leftovers constituted by those who refuse to abide by those gendered, racialized, and classed definitions afforded to them: working-class women generating autonomous social relations, Indigenous migrant women, counter-sexual subjects who reject the reproduction of labor power under the nuclear family, and so on. These subjects are not oppressed citizens of neoliberalism, they are subjects that neoliberalism refuses to acknowledge. To speak of the leftovers, then, is not to speak of a 'merely cultural' concern. It is to speak of those whose existence is unintelligible within the dominant forms coordinating social relations in Chile. What remains to be seen is therefore double: 1.) Was there consciousness of this subalternization in Chile on the eve of the social explosion? 2.) If such consciousness existed, what were the alternative collective social formations offered by the leftovers during the social explosion? How did the leftovers reimagine gendered, racialized, and classed collectivization? For to imagine the collectivization of the leftovers is to imagine a world beyond patriarchy, capitalism, and settler colonialism.

Daniela Catrileo and the Subaltern Experience

The reality of this subaltern experience was embodied in a collection of three short stories published in October 2019, the same month as the beginning of the social explosion: *Piñen* (a word with Mapuche origin referring to dirt stuck to the body) by Daniela Catrileo. Part of the Mapuche diaspora following the reductions, Catrileo grew up in Santiago. Her writing—especially her 2016 work of poetry, *Río Herido* [Wounded River]—reflects on growing up poor on the periphery of Santiago as well as the diasporic Mapuche experiences of maintaining a collective memory, "the loss of language, and the place-between that many of us who were born in *fütra waria* (Santiago) inhabit" (Blanche 2019).

In interviews, Catrileo has frequently reflected on how dominant feminism in Chile does not encompass the realities of Indigenous, Black, and migrant women, "Colonial or white feminism is not fighting for the demands of our peoples [migrant, Black, and Indigenous women], this is because they are centered on gender as a unique form of oppression. Sometimes they introduce the discourse of intersectionality, but they don't use it as a tool of action, but rather as a statement of moral correction" (Huenchumil 2021). It is at least partially for this reason, she explains elsewhere, that she did not participate in the women's strike on 8 March 2019, "In that space there are no migrants in precarious situations [*migrantes precarizadas*], Black, Indigenous, children, imprisoned women, etc. Those who do not have rights are not there, because their bodies do not matter" (Blanche 2019). Dominant feminism, Catrileo implies, does not take into account the historical conditions of existence[2] of Black, Indigenous, migrant, and incarcerated women.

Moreover, she argues that "being Mapuche…[on] the Santiago periphery" sees one's Indigeneity erased insofar as this Indigenous subjectivity is ignored within dominant Indigenous narratives tied to the ancestral Mapuche territory in the south and is re-categorized within Santiago according to class-based identities (Montesinos and Gálvez 2020). While an Indigenous cultural movement has existed in Santiago since reductions-provoked migrations (Aravena Reyes 2008), others have noted that there is still a policing of Mapuche identity that excludes discussions of diaspora, urbanism, counter-sexualities, and so on (Antonio Catrileo 2019: 61). In short, Catrileo articulates the double bind of the diasporic Mapuche woman: politicize oneself within feminist, Indigenous, and/or Marxist organizing and accept a social position (woman, Indigenous, working-class, etc.) that does not represent the material conditions of one's existence, or remain on the apolitical outside. Empowerment means a denial of one's subjectivity; an affirmation of one's particular subjectivity means subalternization.

This is a theme of the last short work in *Piñen*, "Warriache" (the Mapuche word for city-dwelling subjects), which tells the story of two Mapuche women, Carolina Calfuqueo and Yajaira Manque, growing up in housing blocks on the periphery of Santiago from the perspective of Carolina. Both growing up in poor and peripheral neighborhoods while coming of age under a racist social structure—for instance, Carolina tells the story of fellow students inviting her to participate in a lip-sync of a Spice Girls' song for a school talent show, but only if she plays the part of Mel B ("Scary Spice," who is Black[3])—the story distinguishes their adolescence and early adulthood. While Yajaira joins a Marxist political association (*Jóvenes Comunistas* [Communist Youth]), becomes the director of a school dedicated to Mapuche youth in southern Chile, and eventually returns to Santiago where she embraces upward mobility as exemplified by her living in a middle-class condo, Carolina embeds herself in punk and post-punk subcultures while experimenting with drugs and struggling to find an adequate place in the world, "I [Carolina] felt that my whole life dealt with verifying [*comprobar*], once and again, my existence on this piece of earth" (70). Whereas Yajaira eventually functions well within this social system, but in a way that denies her existence as a poor, urban, diasporic, Mapuche woman, Carolina is disciplined: medicated by psychiatrists (and self-medicated in order to enter into a "trance") (64), indebted to pay for her college education, chased by police, and eventually asked by Yajaira to not be a part of her life. As Carolina summarizes, she is "like a wound that learned to reside on the skin" (47). Whereas Yajaira reconstitutes her subjectivity according to the demands placed on her identity by others (working-class youth, the NGO-ization of Indigenous organizing in southern Chile, neoliberal upward class mobility, etc.), Carolina is that which is leftover, that which never has a place in dominant social relations and therefore must be disciplined.

In "Warriache" there is only one moment when Carolina apparently successfully forms herself as a subject. After refusing to play Scary Spice in the talent show, Carolina and other rejected youths decide to do their own lip-sync of Michael Jackson's "Thriller" by playing the zombies, "A dance to say that we were not all alone, that there were more weirdos [*raros*] than us [*nosotras*]. Those without a group" (56). Rather than forming a contestatory counter-identity, the dance gives collective identity to the leftovers' identitylessness as identitylessness. As zombies, their social body is the living dead, precisely those whose lives cannot be fully taken into account as lives. Rather than insisting on their inclusion as a distinct life to be taken into account, the dance uses the language of neoliberalism—pop music arriving from the North Atlantic enabled by the globalized marketplace—to collectivize those who exist under neoliberal Chilean domination but whose lives' existence are denied within those social relations: the living dead.

What is just as notable is how neoliberal hegemony is experienced by the leftovers in *Piñen*: as violence. The collection's other two stories, "¿Han visto cómo brota la maleza de la tierra seca?" ["Have you seen how weeds grow from dry soil?"] and "Pornomiseria" ["Pornomisery"], represent the experience of growing up as a poor woman on the periphery of Santiago as one of being embedded in an environment of violence. Whereas "Have you..." speaks of the firearms-fueled civil violence in peripheral housing blocks, "Pornomiseria," speaks of the domestic and street violence to which women are constantly subjected. Catrileo confronts what James Tyner (2012) calls the paradox of how "violence in our everyday lives...and here I mean *actual, physical violence* is pervasive...[but] we often don't associate violence as a mundane feature of our existence" (2). Catrileo's stories, I suggest, illuminate that an environment of "actual, physical violence" in which leftovers are embedded engenders their isolation, thereby impeding the potential for a contestatory united front formed, for instance, by working-class women of the urban periphery. Why do the leftovers not collectively contest neoliberal hegemony? Catrileo is clear in this regard: because they are constantly subjected to violence as a "mundane feature of [their] existence" that interrupts that collectivization.

This is especially the case in "Have you..." The story opens with the murdered body of a neighborhood resident, Jesús, laying in the street as neighbors gaze from their respective windows. Nonetheless, "at that hour no one dared to leave...their houses." Such a death, the narrator concludes, "was common" (Catrileo 2019: 13). Silence and isolation caused by an environment of omnipresent violence are the qualifying experiences of the housing block. As others have argued, this civil-violence-fueled isolation is a consequence of neoliberalization. Prior to the dictatorship, Santiago was marked by the growing autonomous territorial organization of various working-class neighborhoods, but this was interrupted during the dictatorship and post-dictatorship period through two avenues: torture (see Chapter five) and the relocation of residents to housing blocks on the periphery of the city (Zibechi 2012). As Juan Carlos Skewes (2005) implies, the housing blocks served to disrupt collective territorial organizing that could challenge the neoliberalization of the Chilean landscape, a form of "spatial disciplining" (102) to make the "most marginal component...accustomed to modernity" (121) that in the end generates "individualism and reciprocal distrust" (118). The rise of intra-neighborhood civil violence can be read as a consequence of the neoliberal dissolution of collective neighborhood organizing (Gago 2019; Skewes 2005: 121–122; Wieviorka 2009; Zibechi 2012). We see the symptoms of this State-based process in *Piñen*.

This enforced isolation via the disruption of neighborhood organizing and via the racialized othering of the diasporic Mapuche individual (as Carolina experiences in "Warriache") is furthered via one other avenue: gender. "Pornomisery" opens with the description of a pornographic scene in which a woman's body is violently penetrated by numerous men and in which the camera itself dissects the body into fragmented parts, all while "no one cares…Imagine that others say that it's nothing. In the end it's just a penis entering" (30). This image becomes the overarching metaphor of the short story: the violence to which women are subjected in the household and in the street. For instance, the narrator[4] tells of: the first time a man exposed himself to her and forced her to feel his penis; the men who take it upon themselves to protect women on the street, redefining citizenship in a masculine register ("the conception of the citizen as the defender of the polity and protector of those—women, children, the elderly—who allegedly cannot protect themselves") (Fraser 2013: 37) and thereby relegating women to carrying out strictly domestic work in which it becomes "normal to hide everything behind domestic actions" (Catrileo 2019: 39); and the inability to say or do anything about it, with the narrator confessing that, upon seeing her abused neighbor grown up, "I wanted to say something to her, but whatever word was absurd when my eyes were pointed towards her like a camera and her towards herself" (43).

These stories reveal three things. First, as Tyner (2012: 21–22) argues, violence is "a practice of both social and spatial control." Violence disciplines subjects into behaving in a certain way by determining where they can be and under what conditions. Second, as Allen Feldman (1991) argues in his discussion of (de)colonial violence in Northern Ireland during the Troubles, the body is "a spatial unit of power, and the distribution of these units in space constructs sites of domination" (8). Power is exercised on the body by determining where it is permitted to be at any given time and under what conditions. Third, "Pornomisery" insists that women are subjected to the violent power that determines where isolated bodies can be and when, and are never active participants as a collective subject in that spatialized corporal distribution. In short, following Raquel Gutiérrez Aguilar (2018), "patriarchy…is the daily and reiterated manner of reproducing and fomenting separations among women, installing once and again some type of masculine mediation between one woman and another, between each woman and the world" (38). The same can be said of Carolina as an Indigenous subject in "Warriache": she is dispossessed, making her Indigenous experience under Chilean settler colonialism the denial of the right to collectively determine how to corporally occupy one's territory according to Indigenous paradigms.[5] Indeed, the moment when Carolina realizes she is Mapuche is when her non-Mapuche teacher informs her of the meaning of her last name (51). The meaning of her very name is imposed upon her by a settler, stripping her of the right to self-definition. In this experience, to be Mapuche in Chile is not to participate in an autonomous communal life, it is to be defined as Mapuche by—and thereby atomized, othered, and individually isolated from—settler society.

Reading *Piñen* allows the reader to see the why the social explosion was experienced as a shock even among the subaltern and the oppressed who were well aware of the material foundations of discontent: the leftovers had collectivized despite the violence to which they were subjected that interrupts that collectivization. The additional question posed by Catrileo is therefore how the subaltern might come together to form a collective force without that collectivity itself subalternizing another population. *How can the left-overs of the heteropatriarchal, neoliberal, colonial social order collectively offer an alternative coordination of social relations without itself subalternizing a new community?* Catrileo's work shows that traditional feminist organizing subalternizes Mapuche women; traditional Indigenous organizing subalternizes diasporic Indigenous women; and traditional class-based organizing subalternizes both with its ideal of the male proletariat as the heroic "soldiering" citizen (Fraser 2013: 39). On the eve of the social explosion, Daniela Catrileo was implicitly positing the need for a new mode of collectivization by, for, and of the leftovers. The rest of this chapter is dedicated to analyzing three different prefigurative collectivizations of the leftovers of neoliberal, colonial, heteropatriarchal Chilean social relations that occurred during the social explosion.

LASTESIS: Towards a Feminist Collectivization

If the barricade was the ubiquitous metonymic image for the social explosion, the choreographed performance, "Un violador en tu camino" ["A Rapist in Your Path"], a play on the official slogan of the Chilean police, "A Friend in Your Path," by the feminist performance-art collective, LASTESIS [The Theses], is perhaps the social explosion's most widely-known cultural-activist product. First performed outside a police precinct in Valparaíso on 18 November 2020,[6] "A Rapist in Your Path" consists of a multitude of women simultaneously carrying out a series of choreographed movements and reciting lyrics regarding how the patriarchal State, by providing "impunity for my murderer," enables violence against women—the song names "femicide," "disappearance," and "rape." The performance implicates "the police, the judges, the State, the President, the oppressive State" as rapists themselves—"you are the rapist"—and absolving each performer of their culpability in the violence—"the guilt was not mine, nor where I was, nor how I was dressed."

Although "A Rapist in Your Path" became known across the world after being performed in dozens of other countries, it emerged from a wave of postmillennial Latin American feminist organizing.[7] Perhaps the most obvious—but by no means the only—recent precursor was the #NiUnaMenos movement. Initiated with marches in 2015 in Argentina but quickly spreading across Latin America, #NiUnaMenos started as a collective protest against femicide.[8] As protestors made clear, "violence against women does not refer to a personal problem between aggressor and victims but rather is defined as structural violence against the feminine collective" (Sciortino 2018: 38). Soon after, #NiUnaMenos started making a conscious effort to visibilize the relationship between capitalism, patriarchy, and violence against women. The activist form given to this effort was *the women's strike* in 2017, "We decided collectively to appropriate the tool of the strike…to link machista violence to the political, economic, and social violence that results from the complex but fundamental logic of current forms of exploitation" (Gago 2018: 158–159). The effect of the women's strike was to "multipl[y] the question of labor, [make] it multiple, without diluting its historical density" (Gago 2018: 162, 2019). Moreover, the strike served to compose "a common body: a politics that makes the body of one woman the body of all us women" (Gago 2019: 31), a reconstituted social body that was, as Marina Montanelli (2018) summarizes, "a multitude, differentiated, irreducible to One, whether that be of the State, of the Party, or of the People" (86).[9]

The feminist activist backdrop against which LASTESIS emerged was therefore one in which the links between anti-capitalism and feminism were well-established (Gago, Malo, and Cavallero 2020). Indeed, LASTESIS insists that they are not the vanguard of feminist theory, with their work being dedicated to the circulation and popularization of feminist theory beyond the academy, hence their name, 'The Theses,' a reference to the feminist theses they are sharing with the public. The thesis explored in "A Rapist in Your Path"—only one of their numerous works—is that which has been fully explored in this chapter: women are embedded in an environment of patriarchal violence that serves to discipline their bodies in support of a gendered division of capitalist labor legitimized by the State. Although violence against women is perpetrated within so-called civil society, LASTESIS's performance asserts that the State and its various representatives are equally rapists insofar as they enable gender-based civil violence by granting impunity to those exercising violence on women's bodies. Here, I specifically use the term, 'bodies,' because LASTESIS makes the control and place of women's bodies in space a central element of the work, "The guilt is not mine, *nor where I was, nor how I was dressed.*" As they elaborate in their manifesto, *Burn the Fear* (LASTESIS 2021b), through a reading of Federici, this control of the spatial distribution of women's bodies has a specific purpose: to guarantee the sexual division of labor by enforcing women's restriction to domestic space (32–42). For LASTESIS, patriarchal civil violence enabled by political society serves to control the distribution of bodies in space and thereby reinforce the sexualized division of labor upholding capitalism.

This highlights the importance of the performance's occupation of public space: the women who participate in this intervention are reconstituting who has this corporal distributive power (Urzúa Martínez 2019). As LASTESIS (2021b) argues in *Burn the Fear*, "We women and [sexual] dissidents erase the patriarchy's borders with our only territory: our bodies" (58). What is just as significant in the performance, however, is the use of the first-person singular (it was not *my* fault, nor where *I* was, nor how *I* was dressed). The performance eschews the formation of a singular, coherent, collective *we* in favor of a multitude of *selves*.[10] LASTESIS's performance does not create a community of women and sexual dissidents organized around a common essence, but rather choreographs and harmonizes a multitude.

A notable element of the performances I witnessed in Chile was the diversity in which participants dressed—there was no uniform (although certain elements like the green bandana, a symbol of the pro-choice movement, were encouraged) but a wide variety of apparels, bodily expressions, fashions, and body arts. The meaning of the shared message recited during "A Rapist in Your Path" was shaped by the subjects of enunciation (i.e., each participant), making the performance a kaleidoscope of meanings, experiences, and critiques rather than a univocal communiqué.[11] When they close the opening section of their manifesto by writing, "We women have been illegal immigrants. We are daughters of political refugees. We have been born and raised in exile" (LASTESIS 2021b: 11), LASTESIS are attempting to rethink the question of 'we,' of how to form a multiplicitous feminist collectivity. To rework the famous Zapatista slogan: LASTESIS imagines a feminism in which many feminisms fit.

Yet, as Martin Puchner (2005) argues, this has been the eternal tension of the literary form of the manifesto, regardless of content and authorial intent. The manifesto, he argues, seeks to install party discipline and authority while also permitting for flexibility and change. For Puchner, the classic function of the manifesto is "a declaration of the will of the head of state, monarch, or leader…the performative power of the manifesto was not only foundational but also authoritarian, commanding obedience, punishing perpetrators, and announcing judgments" (186–187), hence the difficulty to reform the communist party line after the publication of Marx and Engels's *Communist Manifesto*. As he concludes, the manifesto "replaces specters" of collective bodies "with the real thing" (25): the communist party in the case of Marx and Engels, the feminist social movement in the case of LASTESIS's *Burn the Fear*. In this sense, *the manifesto is always already a disciplinary literary form*, and one part of the history of this form is the attempt to evade this disciplinary mechanism while still holding on to its power to cohere and make real the imagined social body.

This strain between coordinating a multitude versus disciplining a unified collective can be seen through a basic unresolved tension at the heart of *Burn the Fear*: LASTESIS (2021b) convenes women and sexual dissidents—who they identify as "all those subjectivities that are recognized in the LGBTQIA+ community" (13)[12]—without analyzing the friction among those various social positions. For instance, returning to Judith Butler's "Merely Cultural," LASTESIS doesn't fully reflect on misogyny within queer male communities, trans- and homophobia within feminist communities (nor do they mention Federici's own transphobia[13]), and racism, xenophobia, and nationalism in all of those communities. That is, LASTESIS's envisioned harmonious coordination among women and sexual dissidents is by no means guaranteed, and their respective struggles are related but not equal. For instance, following Anca Parvelescu (2017), what would be said of Lee Edelman's radical rejection of heteronormativity that infamously ignores the queer theory of lesbians in its exclusive concern "with the figure of the queer man" (88), thereby implicitly reinforcing the sexual division of labor in which women are assigned the work of "reproductive labor" (89)? Or Federici's (2004) assumption of men's desire for access to women's bodies as one that ignores the experience of the queer man?

This is further problematized when race is taken into account. LASTESIS (2021b) acknowledges that their Federici-inspired theory of gender serving to divide the laboring class and to relegate women to a subclass must be supplemented by "the dimension of race" (53), but they never substantially engage such a theorization. They frequently appeal to the *figure* of the migrant, refugee, Black, and Indigenous woman, but they never consider the material conditions of existence that constitute their heterogeneous lives.[14] This is specifically notable in their *Feminist Anthology* (2021a). Although the anthology includes work by María Lugones, Mara Viveros Vigoya, and Chimamanda N. Adichie, as well as a note in the introduction that they wanted to include fragments from Angela Davis's *Women, Race, and Class*, they do not include any text originally written in a non-Western language. Feminism, it appears, is a Western phenomenon—the pre-World War II authors and artists included are by Mina Loy, Gertrude Stein, Gabriela Mistral[15], Artemisa Gentileschi, Elsa von Freytag, Mary Wollstonecraft, Olympe de Gouges, and Virginia Woolf—that must be reconfigured in response to questions of race and coloniality.

It is therefore noteworthy that they do not include feminist critiques of Western feminism by those like Gayatri Spivak (1999, 2003, 2012), Chandra Mohanty (2003), and Houria Bouteldja (2016). Bouteldja's theorization—European women's liberation was built on "the backs of the colonized,"[16] and feminism is "one of those exported European phenomena" (92) that serves to categorize "societies in which the feminist movement is nonexistent or marginal…as bearing a civilizational backwardness" (88–89), thereby making Western feminism a *colonial* ideology—is particularly important because she still insists that her position is one of "decolonial feminism" (8, 97). This doubly applies to the nationalism underlying France's dominant gay rights' movement insofar as it frequently paints 'coming out' for queer Muslims as necessitating the abandonment of their 'repressive' religion and entering into the Enlightened world of white French nationality (Mack 2017). In short, the discourses of feminism and queer liberation can be used to legitimize Islamophobia, coloniality, and racism.[17] LASTESIS reflects on how Western feminism often fails to include Black and Indigenous voices, but they do not sufficiently reflect on how feminism can enable continuing colonization, nor do they fully consider "the historical conditions" of colonialism "that have *enabled* feminism" in the West (Bouteldja 2016: 88). Yes, LASTESIS frames their 'we' as including the figural refugee, migrant, Black, and Indigenous woman—the point is not, I say this as emphatically as possible, is *not* that they are racist or colonialist—but what it means to include these women in their feminist collective is not entirely clear.

LASTESIS's activity convenes the oppressed and the leftovers of neoliberal heteropatriarchy by identifying how the State enables civil-society violence that disciplines women and sexual dissidents. In this sense, "A Rapist in Your Path" is a prefigurative coordination of post-patriarchal social relations, a striking ephemeral moment calling into existence the autonomous collective life of those oppressed and leftover by neoliberal heteropatriarchy. Nonetheless, it is unclear how social relations will be re-coordinated amongst those subjects. On the one hand, LASTESIS (2021b) accept this charge as they do not know what "comes after the patriarchy" (32). On the other hand, they desire to speak as a collective—they describe their performance as speaking "as [a] collective, in the street, in public space" (106) and they published a manifesto and an anthology.

If this reading appears overly critical, I'd like to conclude this section by noting that it is also a self-critique of *On the Chilean Social Explosion*. If this book sees itself as convening voices of the leftovers in an autonomous network, it is functionally (regardless of my intent) setting up a tentative cultural canon of the social explosion formed by: Daniela Catrileo, LASTESIS, Cheril Linett, the Catrileo+Carrión community, Danny Reveco, Pedro Lemebel, Tsonami, the CAC, Manuel Sanfuentes, and Ariel Dorfman. Like LASTESIS, this book presents itself as an autonomous coordination of social explosion voices, but implicitly constructs a social-explosion collective that valorizes certain voices and ignores others. The problematic identified in the work of LASTESIS is simultaneously a problematic of this very book, one that will be taken up again in the conclusion.

La Yeguada Latinoamericana

One of the more striking photos taken during the social explosion was of a group of women in pink tank-tops, boots, underwear, and horse tails—either pinned to the women's underwear or attached to inserted butt plugs—lying on the ground in the street. Between their flayed bodies was written on the pavement, "State of rebellion" ["*Estado de rebeldía*"]. A similar performance would be done at various times during October and November 2019 with these women posing during protests in front of barricades, occupying the street, and confronting police. Known as *La Yeguada Latinoamericana* [*The Latin American Herd of Mares*], the founder and leader of the performance, Cheril Linett (2020), describes the project as

> a performance project that I have created, developed, and directed since 2017, convening women and sexual dissidents to participate in actions in public space with the objective of subverting, criticizing, and challenging classist, patriarchal, colonial, and speciesist regimes…It is an invitation to disobey, together as women, the figures and institutions that represent order: the Pope, the church, the police and armed forces, citizenship [*la ciudadanía*], family, the State, and the homeland [*la patria*].
>
> (90)

In the midst of the social explosion, Cheril Linett was collectivizing the leftovers of Chile's neoliberal, colonial, patriarchal, and speciesist order by calling on them to reconstitute their subjectivity along trans-animal and feminist terms.[18]

La Yeguada Latinoamericana delves into the question of "what does it mean to be a woman?" (Linett 2020: 90–91) Linett reflects on how the hegemonic straight, white, male gaze "has positioned and qualified us women as inferior, mutilating our animality and instincts" (Linett, Concha, and Remmele 2018), a task that is partially accomplished by associating "sexually insubordinate [*insumisas*], indomitable women…with feminized animals" (93) such as the mare [*yegua*]. Linett appropriates that insult and constructs a feminine subjectivity around that "colloquial, pejorative, and speciesist term" (93), seeking "the embodiment of a non-human beast, a trans-species, trans-animal, hybrid, and mythological beast, body and machine at the same time" (95).

Linett links this anti-patriarchal and anti-anthropocentric resubjectivization to an economic critique, seeing the performance as a means to collectivize those exploited under capitalism. Linett insists on reading the horse as "a slave-labor force" (93), especially for mounted police, and celebrates "a new aesthetic and political imaginary: the metaphor of an equine revolution…against the police that enslave and instrumentalize horses" (94). She perceives the domination and taming of the mare as comparable to the patriarchal domination of the woman: capitalist production requires the State-enforced transformation of women and non-human animals into *docile bodies* (Hansen 2017). It is no surprise, then, that Foucault (1978a) describes the disciplinary process of subjectivization by using the horse metaphor of "dressage" (136).

For this reason, the transformation of the woman's human body into a hybrid through attaching a horse-tail that is simultaneously a butt plug is an autonomous reconfiguration of the feminine subject beyond capitalism—the focus on the pleasures of the anus is a rejection of the reproductionist definition of the woman in terms of the breasts and vulva (Linett 2020: 97)—and beyond the human/animal binary, instead seeking anti-capitalist, feminist, and anti-speciesist solidarity with enslaved non-human animals like the horse and an autonomous trans-species subjectivization and collectivization. The butt-plug horse-tail is a means to insurgently reconfigure the subject—she calls the performance's "sadomasochist eroticism" a "technology of the self" (95)—by reflecting on the interlocking fields of gender, species discourse, and capitalism.

In short, Linett's intervention is based on a critique of Western liberal humanism as an ideological foundation for patriarchy, capitalism, and speciesism. More theoretically, following Sylvia Wynter (2003), colonialism, patriarchy, and capitalism rest on "securing the well-being of our present ethnoclass (i.e., Western bourgeois) conception of human, Man, which overrepresents itself as if it were the human itself" (260). All those who do not fulfill the requirements of this definition—non-human animals, Linett's indomitable women, Black and Indigenous subjects, etc.—are therefore "the physical referent of...[non-Europeans'] irrational or subrational Human Other to its new 'descriptive statement' of Man as a political subject" (266). As such, following Zakiyyah Jackson (2020), the terror of patriarchal and racist violence is not so much "dehumanization but rather...the terror of liberal humanism's attempts at humanization" (47). If "[t]o overcome a competing model, Western humanism has historically harnessed the force of the state" (32), then 'humanization' is in fact the State violently disciplining all those so-called 'non-humans' embodying other modes of subjectivization and collectivization. Reflecting on this reality, Linett offers an alternative to the traditional political move of attempting to include 'dehumanized' women as 'fellow humans': the autonomous reconfiguration of the subject outside the bounds of the overrepresented human. Understanding the project as "an invitation, a call to operate as a herd [*operar en manada*]" (Linett 2020: 95), one can think of *La Yeguada Latinoamericana* as the collective autonomous reconfiguration of the subject by the leftovers of Western humanism.

Linett explicitly conceived of the Chilean social explosion as an insurrection of this herd in *La Yeguada Latinoamericana*'s November 2019 "Comunicado" (Linett 2019). Announcing, "Chile is ending, we are making it end," the communiqué reflects on the interlocking fields of neoliberalism (which only "gives us the *illusion* of liberty and autonomy"), feminism, and coloniality. The goal of the social explosion, according to this communiqué, is "to construct new courses [*rumbos*] and possibilities of existence." For Linett, the social explosion was a "*lumpen*, feminist, and dissident" revolt constituted by occupying the street with "our deformed, mutant, irate bodies," making the mobilization an "insurgency [that] emerges from the wildness as a herd [*salvajismo en manada*]." The social explosion was being reconfigured as an equine herd practice, "insurrectionary sisters that don't fit [*que no encajan*]." Far from being 'merely cultural,' Linett is imagining a novel form for coordinating social relations beyond capitalism, patriarchy, and anthropocentrism.

Yet my citations of Wynter and Jackson in dialogue with Linett should give the reader pause. Wynter (2003) argues that specifically *race*, "unlike gender," permitted the West "to reground its secularizing own on a newly projected human/subhuman distinction" (264). Jackson (2020) has further developed Wynter's hypothesis, insisting that for Enlightenment humanists, "'*the African*' does not symbolize '*the animal*'; '*the African*' *is* '*the animal*'" (14). This analysis thereby seems to offer a critique of Linett's performance: the indomitable white woman being called a horse is not equivalent to the scientific categorization of Black peoples as different species. Jackson's argument is particularly important since she insists that it is specifically Black women who are unrepresentable within Western humanism. Jackson forces us to ask whether Linett's project fails to adequately reflect on the racist—and not just patriarchal—deployment of species discourse.

It helps here to turn to a specific example in which white women are pejoratively referred to as horses to be trained by men: William Shakespeare's *The Taming of the Shrew* (Hartwig 1982). As Lynda Boose (1991) specifies, the association of women and horses is "an almost standard component of English folklore about unruly women" (199), and Shakespeare rehearses this association, representing the 'taming of the shrew,' Katherine, by her husband, Petruchio, as equivalent to a jockey training a horse. Petruchio even states when carrying Katherine away, "I will be master of what is mine own. / She is my goods, my chattels; she is my house, / My household-stuff, my field, my barn, / *My horse*, my ox, my ass, my anything..." [emphasis mine] (Shakespeare 2003: 118). Boose argues that Petruchio's attempt to tame his wife is part of a broader Elizabethan initiative to discipline women into proper behavior. If Federici focuses on witch hunts, Boose argues that a more common tactic was to punish the *scold*—Katherine is "Renown'd in Padua for her scolding tongue" (Shakespeare 2003: 81). If the "chief social offenses" ascribed to Elizabethan women were linked to "dominating one's husband," then the "veritable female offender of this era seems to be, in fact, the woman marked out as a 'scold' or 'shrew'" (Boose 1991: 184–185), meaning that "Kate is the archetypal scold whose crime against society is her refusal to accept the so-called natural order of patriarchal hierarchy" (192). Within *The Taming of the Shrew*, to be a woman-horse is to be subject to discipline due to rejecting dominant patriarchal social relations.

Boose further argues that a specific disciplinary technology was invented that reinforced the association of unruly women to horses: the scold's bridle. An iron muzzle attached to a metal apparatus encaging the head, the scold's bridle was reserved to punish women who dared to challenge patriarchal authority. It was, Boose insists, a tacit element underlying Shakespeare's representation of 'taming' Katherine: should she not accept Petruchio's more 'humane' domination, a more brutal punishment awaited her. Yet Boose (1991) notes something that is not fully explored in her article or, as far I have seen, in other research: the scold's bridle was later used in the Caribbean and the US South "to punish unruly slaves" (209–211). Like Federici, Boose links the experience of European women and enslaved West Africans insofar as both were violently coerced into performing unpaid labor for white men, and the scold's bridle transforming both into a 'horse' is evidence of this comparable experience.

Nonetheless, both Federici and Boose seem to overstate their case. For instance, Stephanie Jones-Rogers (2019) has noted the extent to which white women were slave-owners in the antebellum US South, "they were not passive bystanders [in slavery]. They were co-conspirators" (205). Many even managed to gain economic and social autonomy through their purchase and exploitation of enslaved people. As Jones-Rogers (2019) argues, "when formerly enslaved people talked about the control that their masters and mistresses exercised over them, they often accorded equal power to men and women" (xv). Both white women and enslaved Black people were subjected to dehumanization, but they do not occupy the same position within that species discourse.

This tension is apparently resolved by remembering, as Jackson insists, that the difference between 'human' and 'animal' has never been stable, as is expressed by scientific racists not being able to fully distinguish between a different 'race' and a different 'species.' At best they were forced to admit, as Josiah Nott (1854) did, that "*gradation* is the law" (417), meaning that, "the disaggregation of a conception of race as 'type' within a presumably shared humanity from the position of race *as* 'species' in a discontinuous (in)humanity, was never fully completed" (Jackson 2020: 171). For instance, many have also noted that in *The Taming of the Shrew* the horse metaphor is applied not only to Katherine but to Petruchio when he shows up drunk and dressed inappropriately to his wedding. He is a 'horse'—though *never* demeaned at the level of Katherine—insofar as he does not fulfill the requirements of a particular ethnoclass concept of Man. What Elspeth Graham (2021) offers is that Shakespeare tends to focus on a set of animals, including humans, "who need to be trained or educated into their proper mode of being" (183). Petruchio and Kate are both 'horses'—i.e., gradations of the non-human—insofar as they do not fulfill their roles within proper 'human' behavior.

Among these gradations of the human are significant differences between the dehumanization of white and Black subjects. Linett's hybridization with the horse speaks to just such racial differences. Within West Indian slave societies, the horse was primarily attached to white society, and enslaved Black people were banned from riding them (Lambert 2015: 625). Moreover, as Patricia Collins (2000) has noted, Black women are frequently associated with mules, not horses, with Zora Neale Hurston (1990), for instance, defining the Black woman as the "mule uh de world" (14).[19] Whereas "human women are less easily exploited," Collins (2000) concludes, mules "are living machines and can be treated as part of the machinery" (47). If the human/animal ontological distinction has always been more precisely a ladder of gradations in which the proper white Western bourgeois Man is overrepresented as the exemplar of the human, then both indomitable white women and Black subjects are 'non-human' but are located on distinct rungs of this ladder. Yet, similarly to Linett, Hurston transcends this pejorative non-human representation of Black femininity by imagining the mule/Black woman association as a mode of being that goes beyond "the genre of Man" (Bennett 2020: 129) and offering a trans-species mode of subjectivization.[20]

It seems that we have returned to the same problem we encountered with LASTESIS. Although Linett's intervention works to coordinate the insurrectionary activity of certain women and sexual dissidents, it struggles when it aspires to a broad-based collectivization that must take into account, for instance, the intellectual contributions of Black feminists. Black and Indigenous subjects and insubordinate women and queer subjects are all, to follow Ladelle McWhorter's (2010) phrasing, *enemies of the species* insofar as they threaten the reproduction of white supremacy and its attendant racialized and gendered mode of capitalist production; however, 'dehumanization' under Western liberal humanism is not a homogeneous experience. Racism—what Mbembe (2003) defines as "the distribution of human species into groups, the subdivision of the population into subgroups, and the establishment of a biological caesura between the ones and the others" (16–17)—and the patriarchal control of women and queer subjects—who are discursively transformed into non-humans when they reject the disciplinary command to perform the reproductive labor upholding capitalism—are related through the employment of anthropocentric species distinctions, but they are not equivalent.

Treated as an enclosed work, Linett's project leaves us divided. On the one hand, she is calling for the collectivization of all *enemies of the human species* (McWhorter 2010) whose mode of being does not fulfill the call to reproduce the coloniality of power and capitalism. In this way she seeks to reconstitute social relations based on the autonomous interrelationships between the leftovers of Western liberal humanism. On the other hand, her specifically *horse*-human hybrid based on the experience of a particular feminine subject excludes the historical conditions of existence and intellectual contributions of many Black feminists, at best making her performance based on an (institutionally validated) ignorance. If *La Yeguada Latinoamericana* as an individual's singular performance avoids this sticky issue, by calling on all enemies of the species to act as a herd Linett extends this metaphor to all subaltern bodies. Quite simply, would the social explosion imagined as the insurrection of Linett's equine herd have room for Hurston's mules?

Towards Affective Inter-communality

These intersecting questions of coloniality, race, feminism, and capitalism were being explored elsewhere during the social explosion. In December 2019, two members of the Catrileo+Carrión Community, Constanza Catrileo and Alejandra Carrión, undertook a Collaborative Art Residence, "Paleoduna: Vestigios y Tamices" ["Paleodune: Traces and Sieves"], in the small seaside town of Cartagena in central Chile. Initially planned prior to the social explosion, the residence sought to develop substantial links with the working-class neighborhood, Población José Arellano, in order to co-generate an artistic performance and presentation made in collaboration between residents and the visiting artists. During their stay, they worked with various artists, dance groups, social organizations, and the local municipal government to create a final performance in February 2020. In addition to their journal available online (Comunidad Catrileo+Carrión 2020), the entire Catrileo+Carrión community (in alphabetical order: Alejandra Carrión Lira, Manuel Carrión Lira, Antonio Catrileo Araya, and Constanza Catrileo Araya) along with other participants (Daniela Pailanca,

Selenna Guacucano Soto, and Filip Escudero Quiroz-Aminao) published a book in 2021, *Poyewün Nütramkan: Pikunmapu/Qullasuyu*, reflecting on their methods, objectives, and the relationship to the social explosion and COVID-19 pandemic.[21]

The publication reflects both the ongoing efforts of the Catrileo+Carrión Community that precede the social explosion as well as the formation of novel collective practices and formations as a result of the 2019 mobilizations. Regarding the former, the Catrileo+Carrión community is a diasporic Mapuche community (Antonio Catrileo and Manuel Carrión, for instance, were living in San Diego, USA, during the social explosion) that had been developing their methodologies, theoretical frameworks, and conclusions for years prior to the revolt.[22] The Catrileo+Carrión community had already established itself as a collective intellectual force dedicated to thinking through questions of sexuality, decoloniality, and interculturality. Regarding the latter, the authors of *Poyewün Nütramkan* frequently make reference to the group, *Jóvenes Indígenas Valparaíso* [Indigenous Youth of Valparaíso], an autonomous organization convened during the social explosion to create "a space to be recognized, to find one another, and to share their 'being Indigenous people of the city'" (Figueroa Irarrázabal and Calfucoy Gutierrez 2020).[23] This novel collectivity focused on intercultural dialogues among Indigenous youth from various nations—Mapuche, Aymara, Diaguita, Rapa Nui, and so on—who were living in the city of Valparaíso. The social explosion catalyzed the novel international and intercultural convergence of urban Indigenous youth.

As Constanza Catrileo and Alejandra Carrión outline, the basis of their residence in Cartagena was

> [to] rehearse our methodology and practice of *poyewün nütramkan*, that is, affective conversations that are developed after strengthening bonds and relationships. To practice affection among ourselves [*hacernos cariño*] with the word is the motor of our artistic practice that becomes also a rehearsal or desire to make community. In that sense, our practice and process of residency was crossed by the social revolt of 18 October 2019 and the outbreak of the COVID-19 pandemic.
>
> (*PN*: 7)

The model for such affective community-making was based on two related reflections. First, Antonio Catrileo remembered a moment from an earlier Collaborative Art Residence in Toltén and Neltume. Invited by Mapuche women from the community, they had the "uncomfortable" initial experience of the activity being exclusively among the men while the women prepared food in the kitchen. They were forced to reconsider "what could be our political power [*potencia*] today. We realized that the dimension of the conversations in the kitchen and *poyewün* [care] was where we also had a place, there in that space implicitly relegated to the women was playing out a way of doing politics very different from that of the men" (*PN*: 39–40). This affective space distinct from that of the masculine-dominated 'public sphere'—in single quotes because the women's space in the kitchen is just as public as that of the masculine table of dialogue—prefigures the re-coordination of social relations around *care* and *affect*, a politics building out from Mapuche women's theory and praxis. This experience implicitly opened up the possibility of a decolonial feminist coordination of social relations based around *poyewün* that organizes labor beyond capitalist accumulation.

Second, the Catrileo+Carrión community is "not heterosexual" (*PN*: 39). As Antonio Catrileo continues, when they went to live in Valparaíso for the first time, they were able to "freely live [their] sexuality" (*PN*: 39), but there was a failure among the LGBTIQ+ community of Valparaíso "to recognize Indigenous memories" (*PN*: 40). Once again, the double bind of the subaltern: to embrace the urban possibility to 'freely live one's sexuality' is to silence one's Indigenous memory, but to embrace the hegemonic Indigenous coordination of social relations—in which heterosexual men dominate activity in the 'public sphere'—is to silence one's counter-sexual life. We find ourselves returning to Judith Butler's "Merely Cultural": counter-sexual practice potentially—but not necessarily[24]—undermines the mode of social (re)production based on a gendered division of labor. The question thereby posed in *Poyewün Nütramkan* is: What is a politics built from Mapuche counter-sexual and women's affective practices of social reproduction? That is, what is a community-generating collaborative artist residence based on *poyewün* rather than the production of a work of art? Moving beyond the relating of culture to politics via hegemony (i.e., an artistic work serves to cohere a common conception of the world that is then disseminated across a community), the Catrileo+Carrión community explores how culture can catalyze collectivization through horizontal affective conversations and practices.

This speaks to an underlying aim of the group: to imagine social (re)production beyond heteronormative (re)productivity. They maintain affective practices frequently assigned to women as a political power, as Catrileo saw in Neltume and Toltén, but they reject the nuclear heterosexual family. In other words, they explore what politics affective praxis might permit when extended beyond the nuclear family. As Manuel Carrión outlines, the community seeks a practice of love permitting a "place of enunciation [that] is nourished on caring interchange and on the opening of an autonomous space of recognition of a communitarian sense that is constituted beyond or despite sanguinary ties. We are constellations, tides of dialogues" (*PN*: 87). In the end, the community seeks to *multiply* rather than reproduce, "We are a community that does not want to reproduce itself, but yes multiply itself through the affective interchange with other communities" (*PN*: 87). Affect is decoupled from its role in the social reproduction of labor in the circumscribed heteronormative nuclear family and becomes the foundation for intercultural and intercommunal linkages. Decolonially developing the counter-sexual critique of reproductivity (Edelman 2004), and in radical contrast to affect's traditional role of reinforcing intracommunal ties (i.e., the family, the nation, the race[25]), *poyewün* links together a pluriverse of communities and individuals in an archipelago[26] of care. For this reason, the book, *Poyewün Nütramkan*, "presents stories [*relatos*] without the necessity of establishing a discrete notion of community, or fixing the limits where one and the other start" (*PN*: 92). Indeed, the very authorship of *Poyewün Nütramkan* productively confuses the 'inner' members of the community and the 'outside' collaborators insofar as the publication is simultaneously of the Catrileo+Carrión community and of three authors who exceed strict 'membership' in that community.

Here, we finally return to the social-explosion organization, Indigenous Youth of Valparaíso, that is repeatedly mentioned in the publication. There is a particular emphasis in this group on the intercultural linkages *between* Indigenous nations. As Selenna Guacucano elaborates,

> this territory was shared with more communities...[A]fterwards you come to realize that this is a plurinational territory, not only inhabited by Quechua, Kollas, Aconcagua, Pikunche, but also Diaguitas and Aymara, and so it's much more complex...[For] me it's admirable that so many peoples have had to live together [*convivir*] because there had to be an interchange of language for understanding, and that we do not doubt, those of us who are part of Indigenous Youth of Valparaíso.
>
> (*PN*: 36)

What Guacucano is pointing to is how the social explosion opened *intercommunal exchange* among Indigenous nations conglomerated in Valparaíso, and how *Poyewün Nütramkan* elaborates a methodology to simultaneously theorize intercommunality/interculturality and enable the practice of interculturality through affective artistic praxis.

For this reason, it is largely unsurprising that the Catrileo+Carrión community refers to the social explosion as *Chileyem* ("Chile's over" in Mapudungun) insofar as they are seeking a recoordination of social relations beyond the nation-State known as Chile. In this way, the collaborative art residence in Cartagena was in some sense a prefigurative practice of those social relations,

> During the first few months of residence in Cartagena, we sought to guide our affective conversations towards empathy with the diversity of non-human existences that surround this sector; however, upon living through the social explosion in what we call *Chileyem*..., the meaning of our residence was diverted in attending to the human urgencies that were happening in multiple territories, where to do *poyewün nütramkan* was also a manner of organization, of communal work, of rearticulation of the social fabric.
>
> (*PN*: 9)

The imagined future coordination of social relations after Chile is over was being practiced in Cartagena during 2019 and 2020: the affective multiplication of social ties among individuals and communities using their diverse practices, epistemologies, and modes of care. In this small seaside town of Cartagena, an autonomous, feminist, decolonial, anti-capitalist, and intercultural world structured around affective conversations was being prefiguratively realized through an artist residence in a local working-class neighborhood.

At the same time that I was reading *Poyewün Nütramkan*, however, I had open a brief comment by Judith Butler (2019),

> neither vulnerability nor care can serve as the basis of a politics. I would surely like to be a better person and to strive to become that, in part by acknowledging my apparently profound and recurrent fallibility. But none of us should seek to be saints, if what that means is that we hoard all goodness for ourselves, expelling the flawed or destructive dimension of the human psyche to actors on the outside, those living in the region of the 'not me,' with whom we dis-identify.
>
> ("Postscript," par. 2)

Butler is pointing to a simple point: politics needs to account for interdependency among subjects and communities *even when they do not care about or for each other.* Beyond the local question of my relationships with those for whom I do not care, there is the question of being in interdependent relation with those who I do not know nor will I ever know. For instance, how can *poyewün nütramkan* account for what Butler identifies as our *global obligations*? When *poyewün nütramkan* is described as wanting to realize "collaborative experiences where we can generate empathy" (*PN*: 7), thereby making the open community of Cartagena formed specifically by "all those who collaborated and were part of the experience of the revolt that we lived in Cartagena" (*PN*: 92), how is it possible under that rubric to imagine not just the end of Chile but the rearticulation of social relations across that (formerly) national space, a space that includes those who did not collaborate and with whom one has no empathetic relation?

This political problem of affect is not limited to Chile, with James Joyce in *Ulysses* having already pondered this problematic in the context of decolonizing Ireland in the early twentieth century. Others have already noted that Joyce envisions municipal water infrastructure as a means to cohere the multiple communities inhabiting Dublin around a decolonial urbanism (Rubenstein 2010). Following Michael Rubenstein (2010), despite the desire of *Ulysses's* protagonist, Leopold Bloom, "for a city that is more like a family" (89)—i.e., the formation of social relations like those found in *Poyewün Nütramkan*—Joyce ultimately notes that decolonization requires the consideration of mundane non-affective tasks: paying taxes (indeed, contributing taxes to an *independent Ireland* is perhaps the ultimate definition of national decolonization), building public works, and so on. In the end, Rubenstein concludes, the decolonized autonomous construction of municipal water provision—not an ethics of care—becomes a means to generate intercommunal solidarity among those who we do not even know, much less care for.

Nonetheless, as I have argued elsewhere (Woods 2021a), Joyce also recognizes that there is *affective discord* among these various communities and individuals occupying decolonized Dublin, a discord that interrupts any attempt at intercommunal solidarity. In short, Joyce's *Ulysses* shows us the internal tension of a politics of care. On the one hand, autonomous politics is about coordinating horizontalist and cooperativist social relations that permit the flourishing of all life in dignity, regardless of whether or not we care for or about that life. This is a question of infrastructure and process, not empathy. On the other hand, not accounting for affect between and within communities and individuals guarantees the failure of that utopian longing embedded in autonomous politics. Regardless of the infrastructural success of decolonized Dublin's public works, anti-semitism directed at Leopold Bloom and Bloom's failure to empathize with the lasting affective effects of the Irish Potato Famine undermine any unification in an egalitarian water system (Ulin 2011).

In the end, the Catrileo+Carrión community left me wondering, what are our obligations to those with whom we have no affective relation? If capitalist alienation separates me from the producers of the commodities I use—for instance, I am writing this chapter on a computer built by someone I will never know and with whom I will never be able to share a kitchen while we prepare a meal and develop an actual affective relation—then how can I possibly imagine an ethics of care with regard to that person that is not merely a projection of my own values and affects? If this seems to be an unfair reading of the Catrileo+Carrión community, it is because it is ultimately a self-critique as well, for the same critique can be weighed against the close-reading methodology underlying this book—its openness, its *ethical care* for interdependence leaves untouched what Margaret Cohen calls 'the great unread,'[27] or what in the case of the social explosion would be the millions who took to the streets and whose own interventions remain untouched between the covers of this book.

Conclusion

Overlooking details, the argument of this chapter has been rather simple: the social explosion witnessed attempts to actualize the reconstitution of the collective political body of the territory today currently known as 'Chile' by autonomously imagining the re-coordination of social relations in a way that grants agency to a multiplicity of leftover communities and individuals. The social explosion was not an outburst of discontent without affirmative content; it was the explosion of the kaleidoscopic interrelations among autonomous subaltern communities and individuals. Moreover, it was not a revolt with distinct feminist, anti-neoliberal, and decolonial threads; instead, the social explosion was attempting to reconstitute the social body by placing each of these threads into profound dialogue. If we saw in chapter one how Danny Reveco illuminated the pluralism underlying the social explosion, LASTESIS, *La Yeguada Latinoamericana*, and the Catrileo+Carrión community were attempting to rigorously prefigure what a such a multiplicitous social body would actually be. In short, if the task of the CAC was to convene a collective in order to autonomously redefine water-society relations, the task of LASTESIS, *La Yeguada Latinoamericana*, and the Catrileo+Carrión community was to figure out what that convened collective actually was. Their response: the interwoven tapestry of all those leftovers under the neoliberal-heteropatriarchal-colonial Chilean State.

In this way, this chapter is undertaking two distinct theoretical tasks. First, the introduction discussed the tension between the post-hegemonic multitude of singularities and decolonial communality. The argument of this chapter has been that the social explosion attempted to synthesize these two strands by imagining a reality constituted by both singularities and communities in relation. For example, Constanza Catrileo was able to simultaneously be part of the Catrileo+Carrión community, multiply that community through affective relations with other communities and individuals, and be a member of LASTESIS's feminist multitude when she participated in the Cartagena performance of "A Rapist in Your Path" (a performance in which the final verse was performed in Mapudungun). Second, following Gramsci, Spivak (2005) has argued that any political collectivization requires the 'synecdochization' of the subject, in which individuals put aside differences in order to allow one part of their being "to stand for the whole" collective (480). Feminism, for instance, requires women to forget other elements of their subjectivities—class, sexual orientation, geography, race, and so on—in order to make political demands as a feminine collective. My argument in this chapter is that the social explosion imagined other modes of collectivization. Postmodern and autonomous thought has of course come up with various terms to imagine such a collectivity—multitude, swarm, rhizome, network, and so on—but in the social explosion we see people in the streets attempting to rigorously envision and practice such non-synecdochal collectivizations: communities in affective, intercultural relation; a multitude of women and sexual dissidents claiming public space; inter-species and anti-patriarchal hybridizations; and so on.

Nonetheless, these collectivizations all seemed to fall short. In the end, LASTESIS and Linett did require such synecdochization—the multitude of women was subjected to the manifesto and the anthology, and the trans-species insurgent did not fully take into account the intellectual contributions of some Black feminists under anthropocentric patriarchy—and the Catrileo+Carrión community's open, decolonial, feminist, and counter-sexual politics of care was limited in its scope. For this reason, if the reader will excuse a brief personal aside, this was the most difficult chapter of this book to write. The initial hypothesis of this chapter was that the isolation of leftovers illustrated in Daniela Catrileo's *Piñen* that was symptomatic of postmillennial Chile was being overcome by collectivizations induced by various cultural workers during the social explosion. That these collectivizations were incomplete was, I initially thought, negligible because their limitations were being actively worked out in the street in 2019–2020. For those participating, this was perhaps the most exciting part of the social explosion: it was a laboratory of political experimentation and imagination in which the autonomous formation of a horizontalist, intercultural, feminist, and decolonial reality was being collectively generated in real time. As I will discuss in further detail in the conclusion, this experimentation without a proper conclusion proved highly limiting with the onset of the COVID-19 pandemic in March 2020. The absence of a clear vision for collectivization proved devastating for radical politics when put under the pressures of a public health crisis. I therefore leave this chapter unfinished until the conclusion.

Notes

1 As Chibber (2013) argues, it is inconsequential who first imagines these racial and gender differences. Capitalist elites are more than happy to exploit and weaponize already existing differences. 'Define' in this instance signifies constructing institutional mechanisms, processes, and apparatuses that validate certain definitions.

2 "Historical conditions of existence" is common Marxist phrasing, not my own, that is usually attributed to *The Eighteenth Brumaire*. I thank Spivak (1999) for first bringing the valuable phrasing to my attention.

3 This is difficult for many to understand from the North Atlantic. 'Blackness' in Chile frequently refers to skin color and therefore includes dark-skinned Indigenous, South Asian, *mestizx*, middle-eastern, etc. persons. When referring to 'Black' as understood in the North Atlantic, many in Chile use the term 'Afrodescendant' [*afrodescendiente*]. As such, Carolina and Mel B are both 'Black,' but Carolina is Mapuche and Mel B is *afrodescendiente*.

4 Although all stories are told from a first-person perspective of a woman growing up on the periphery of Santiago, it is unclear if the same protagonist narrates all the stories.

5 Hence, Eve Tuck and K. Wayne Yang's (2012) definition of decolonization, "decolonization in the settler colonial context must involve the repatriation of land simultaneous to the recognition of how land and relations to land have always already been differently understood and enacted; that is, *all* of the land, and not just symbolically" (7). As they insist, equal political participation *within* Western-centered organizations of (re)production is not equal to decolonization.

6 This is the general date I have repeatedly seen referenced. In *Burn the Fear*, they also write, "20 November 2019, we convened women and dissidents to chant as a chorus [*corear*] with us a rapist in your path, in Plaza Aníbal Pinto, in Valparaíso" (LASTESIS 2021b: 39).

7 Lamadrid Alvarez and Benitt Navarrete (2019) give a brief history of the postmillennial Chilean feminist movement.

8 The organizational form of #NiUnaMenos has been covered by Urzúa Martínez (2019), Castro Riaño (2018), and Accossatto (2018).

9 In addition to the Ni Una Menos organization's communiqués, there is now a large set of theorizations of the significance of women's strike for thinking through the relationship between patriarchy and capitalism (Gago 2018, 2019; Gago et al. 2018; Gago, Malo, and Cavallero 2020).

10 The idea of "the multitude" is of course fully theorized by Hardt and Negri (2000, 2004) in order to find an alternative collective subject to "the people," "The people is somewhat that is one, having one will, and to whom one action may be attributed...The multitude is a multiplicity, a plane of singularities, and open set of relations, which is not homogeneous or identical with itself and bears an indistinct, inclusive relation to those outside of it" (Hardt and Negri 2000: 103).

11 For instance, the performance of the piece in India in the Bengali language served "to highlight the patriarchal violence that Modi's idea of Hindu Rashtra represents" (Daniyal 2020). That the piece is now being used to critique Hindu nationalism in South Asia shows the kaleidoscopic effect of the performance.

12 This is to ignore that "LGBTIQ+ categories" can serve as colonial ideologies within Mapuche counter-sexual communities, meaning that many counter-sexual Mapuche subjects seek to enunciate "another sexuality distinct from LGBTIQ+ categories" (Catrileo 2019: 128).

13 See Knudson (2020).

14 This is a recurring theme in literature on the women's strike as well (Filigrana 2020).

15 The only non-European author included in the pre-WWII context, Mistral's poetry still nonetheless supports a white supremacist (and, at times, arguably patriarchal) project (Fiol-Matta 2002; Pratt 1994).

16 As Spivak (2003) notes in her reading of *A Room of One's Own*, Virginia Woolf was already aware of this dilemma. It is notable that LASTESIS do not include this fragment from *A Room of One's Own* in their anthology.

17 Of course, as shown in the work of Maria Lugones (2010), the opposite can also be true: the repackaging of heteropatriarchy as decolonial liberation as happens, for instance, when Indigenous counter-sexualities are critiqued as 'Western' influence.

18 The reader is also highly encouraged to see the collection of photographs of and essays on *La Yeguada Latinoamericana* edited by aliwen and Lucy Quezada (2021).

19 Stacey Patton (2011) has reviewed various discussions of this connection of Black womanhood to the figure of the mule.

20 There are plenty of instances of horse/Black human (and, more specifically, Black woman) hybrids, especially during social movements (Bennett 2020; Howell and Taves 2021). There is also of course the long history of male and female Black cowboys (Glasrud and Searles 2016). Moreover, Daniela Catrileo (2018) has discussed potential decolonial undercurrents to Linett's performance from a Mapuche perspective. My point is that Black women's relationship to the horse and white (and *mestiza* and Indigenous) women's relationship to the horse are distinct, a difference not fully taken into account by Linett.

21 As they state in the title page of the book, in line with many of the autonomous small-press productions analyzed by Rabasa (2019), "This book can be reproduced and circulated always and when its authors are mentioned: Colectivo Cuerpo Mumo, PAIM Cartagena, Patio Ferreiro y Comunidad Catrileo+Carrión." Authorship is applied due to existing citation standards, but their open collectivization challenges such ideas of authorship. As such, I will site the book as *PN* here, and all authors will be listed in the works cited.

22 They have published two other books (*Yikalay pu zomo lafkenmapu* and *Poyewün witral: Bitácora de la comunidad de tejedoras de neltume*) and edited a collection

(*Torcer la palabra: Escrituras obrera-feministas*), in addition to making multiple videos, art installations, and interviews.

23 The thinking of this group can be found in a series of six podcasts, *¿Origi-KE?*, that they made during the COVID-19 pandemic.

24 I do not want to make an argument with regard to whether counter-sexual practice interrupts Mapuche social reproduction. As Antonio Catrileo (2019) has argued *much* more extensively elsewhere, counter-sexual practices (ones that do not abide by the representative contours of Western LGBTIQ+ identities) were a part of Mapuche life prior to colonization. Whether this transformation of social reproduction is a symptom of the *coloniality of gender* (Lugones 2010) is outside the scope of this book. I insist that my claim is very specific: the Catrileo+Carrión community's counter-sexual practice undermined *this particular mode of social (re)production* as found in Toltén and Neltume in the twenty-first century.

25 The relationship between the reproduction of the family, the reproduction of the nation, and the reproduction of race is a central part of the poetic work of Gabriela Mistral (Fiol-Matta 2002).

26 This idea of an archipelago of communities is of course from Glissant (1997); however, Antonio Catrileo (2019) has himself developed this concept, hence my use of it here.

27 This is of course thanks to Moretti's (2000) development of this concept.

5 On Myth

While walking through Santiago on 7 March 2020, I was confronted with a protest poster plastered on walls at various points across the city quoting a line from "Los perturbados entre lilas" by Alejandra Pizarnik: "My only country is my memory and it does not have hymns" ["*Mi único país es mi memoria y no tiene himnos*"]. With this phrasing, the poster articulated a disjuncture between official nationality ("hymns") and a dissenting memory ("my memory *does not have hymns*") that served as a cultural grounding on which to reconstruct collective relations with the past ("*my only country* is my memory").[1] In this way, the poster repeats the basic thesis of this book: the social explosion represents the bursting forth of leftover cultural formations, practices, and concepts against a dominant elite Chilean culture. In this particular case, memory was to act as the new cultural foundation against the "hymns" of nationality.[2] Building off the analysis of this protest poster, this chapter explores how subaltern historiographical practices during the social explosion served to cohere a novel autonomous collectivity that challenged the dominance of Chilean neoliberalism. In this way, the social explosion can be understood as the subaltern cultural reconstitution of Chilean nationality.

The poster is also marked by a paradox. The phrase "my only country is my memory" insists simultaneously on the individual autonomy of memory—by being *my* memory it evades the hegemonic bonds of nationality—and on its collective nature insofar as memory forms a country. In other words, the poster begs the question: How can one claim the singularity of their individual memory—a singularity that allows for dissent from official nationality—and at the same time discuss its capacity to form a coherent collective subject ("my country") (Ricoeur 2004: 96)? One resolution to this problem is provided by Maurice Halbwachs: the concept of *collective memory*. Halbwachs's basic thesis is simple: "to remember, we need others" (Apfelbaum 2010; Ricouer 2004: 120). By sharing common memories within a group, one not only reminds oneself that they are part of a community and remembers "by situating himself [sic] within the viewpoint of one or several groups and one or several currents of collective thought" (Halbwachs 1980:

DOI: 10.4324/9781003224594-6

33)—that is, memory is "socially conditioned" (Erll 2012: 18)—but, additionally, a collective memory and corollary community is formed around this remembering-in-common. The result is not that collective memory embodies some romantic notion of the "spirit of the people" with a "set of recollections attributable to some overarching group mind," but rather that collective memory is constituted by the circulation of a set of cultural "practices or material artifacts" through active participation by those who share that collective memory (Klein 2000: 135–136). "My memory" is "my country" insofar as my individual participation in a set of cultural practices, alongside the participation by all other citizens in "my country," fortify the collective articulation of the past of 'our' community. In this way, participating in a given collective memory demonstrates that one who remembers also belongs to that group; collective memory plays a substantial role in the formation of a collective identity (Erll 2012).

This chapter argues that myths are one cultural practice through which a community establishes and fortifies its collective memory.[3] This is not a common understanding within literary and social-movement studies. Since the publication of Roland Barthes's *Mythologies* in 1957, post-World War II theory from the North Atlantic has tended to take a critical view of myth, seeing it as a way for a ruling class to *naturalize* the social relations in which they are dominant; myth is a narrative structure that transforms a political and historical reality into a naturalized image of that reality, thereby essentializing a contingent and socially constructed world as inevitable and immutable (Barthes 2013; Lincoln 1999; McCutcheon 2000; Nancy 1991; Nancy and Lacoue-Labarthe 1990; Sandoval 2000).

Similarly, but from the perspective of insurgent classes rather than the ruling class, social-movement scholars have argued that activists use myth in order to imaginatively reconcile "elements which, in the real historical or social world, cannot be integrated" (Wieviorka 2009: 107). In this theorization, myth *reifies* the thinking and praxis of activist groups, effectively cementing their unity but precluding the possibility of taking outside perspectives into account (Wieviorka 2009: 109). Others counter this understanding by theorizing that any insurgent collective is always already mythic insofar as only myth can "suture" together "dislocated elements" into a coherent worldview that unites a collectivity, "Thus, the effectiveness of myth is essentially hegemonic: it involves forming a new objectivity by means of the rearticulation of the dislocated elements" (Laclau 1990: 61). On the one hand, myth dangerously naturalizes rebels' social vision; on the other hand, any rebellion is impossible without a unifying narrative (i.e., a myth).

These social-movement theorizations of myth are largely based on a reading of Georges Sorel's (1999 [1908]) theorization of the connection between myth and insurgent proletariat violence. For Sorel, myth is "a body of images capable of evoking instinctively all the sentiments which correspond to the different manifestations of the war undertaken by socialism against modern society" (118). A myth effectively unites insurgents

> in a coordinated picture and, by bringing them together, gives to each one of them its maximum intensity; appealing to their painful memories of particular conflicts, it colours with an intense life all the details of the composition presented to consciousness
>
> (118).

What post-Sorelian myth-based theorizations of "social-movement unity" (Shantz 2000) frequently miss, however, is that Sorel insists that such myths are *individualistic*, with each revolutionary "marching with as much fervor as possible, each acting on his own account, and hardly troubling to subordinate his conduct to a carefully drawn up overall plan" (Sorel 1999: 242). Myth is not the basis for hegemony or a reified collective will; it is the dynamic and decentralized discourse of a revolutionary multitude that is employed on an individual basis but links together insurgents in a discursive web that mobilizes each rebel in moments of insurrection. In this way, postmodern anarchist social-movements' use of myth like the Zapatistas and Tute Bianche that reflect on diversity, play, and individuality are more akin to Sorel's initial idea than the insistence on myth's unity-generating power (Graeber 2009; Wu Ming 2002).

Troublingly, however, these anarchist theorizations of myth's function in social movements largely leave unclear myth's structural definition. They answer what myth *does*, not what it *is*. CrimethInc's (2001) distinction between myth and history is an extreme example of this theoretical hollowness. Against the "anti-subjective" "dead hand" of "objective" history "guiding and controlling as if from the grave" with its claiming of "the official Truth about the past," CrimethInc imagines a myth that "belongs to everyone, as it is made and remade by everyone," such as when punk's past is made imminently "*present* every time a punk band plays and…recaptures the ageless, timeless frenzy that makes punk rock matter in the first place" (111–115). While the differing effects and functions of myth as a multiplicitous discourse versus history as a frozen object are clear, it is entirely unclear how to *structurally* distinguish the two as narratives. Why is a punk band making present a certain past *structurally* different than a history book? Indeed, why a lively *historical* discussion of a revolution in a classroom cannot also 'recapture the ageless, timeless frenzy' that makes revolution matter is unknown. These anarchists' (tacitly) Sorelian theories hint at the possibility that myth may provide a narrative foundation for polycentrically linking together multiplicitous autonomous social movements, but it is unclear what myth structurally is.

Silvia Rivera Cusicanqui provides us with just such a robust structural definition through an analysis of the relationship between myth and twentieth-century Indigenous Aymara decolonial rebellions in Bolivia:

myth is a narrative structure constitutive of collective memory that coheres a community through its dynamic recursive intra-community telling, revising, retelling, and transmitting to future generations. As she writes, myth "reworks [*reelabora*] the collective memory of a colonized people...in a (post)colonial situation: the central Andes in the twentieth century from the broader background dating back to the anticolonial struggles of the sixteenth century" (Rivera 2012: 389). By retelling, reworking, and recodifying myths, Aymara subjects both reproduce the collective memory of decolonial struggles dating back to the sixteenth century and dynamically re-write those myths in order to mobilize activists in response to the demands and contingencies of present events.[4] A myth's significance is not in the 'authentic' and/or 'original' myth, but rather in the popular inter-generational process of narrative re-codification (Iles Johnston 2018). Collective memory is not contained in *the* myth, but rather in the collective process in which individuals participate in a variety of ways that is constantly and dynamically reshaping a communal relationship to the past from within the present. In this way, myth as an inter-generational narrative structure rooted in collective memory can function as a grassroots historiographical practice that transmits social-movement memory to new generations, "feeding the vision of autonomous historical process and the hope for recuperating control over one's historical destiny" (Rivera 1987: 59). In short, one might understand Rivera as providing a more rigorous structural discussion of Sorelian theory and a concrete grounding—i.e., collective memory—on which to understand myth.

Returning to the Chilean social explosion, the implication of this theoretical introduction is that this poster from March 2020 was speaking towards how Sorelian myth was linking together protestors with collective memory as its foundation. The "country" of the social explosion was based on "my memories" providing the content for collective myths being shared within that community. In this way, I argue in this chapter, myths in which the social explosion was narratively codified from within a post-dictatorship grassroots collective memory served as an autonomous cultural and historiographical foundation for an oppositional communality that could then be leveraged to challenge elite Chileans' domination of the nation's geopolitical space.

More precisely, I argue that social explosion myths based in a collective memory offered a narrative and historiographical technique with which to fortify a grassroots nationality that had been suppressed by dictatorship-era political repression and by the installation of a globalized neoliberal marketplace starting in the late 1970s. In this way, this chapter is simultaneously a development of and rejoinder to all previous chapters. On the one hand, the use of myth for the unification of a pre-dictatorship grassroots nationality demonstrates once again that neoliberalism represented "dominance without hegemony" in Chile. Social explosion myths embody alternative cultural foundations that had been initially suppressed during the 1970s but forcefully returned in 2019 to challenge the globalized cultural foundations of neoliberal dominance. On the other hand, despite the multiplicitous character of the mythical discourse, insurgent myths during the social explosion took on a definitive *national* character that could not accommodate the thinking of, for instance, migrants whose collective memories and myths ran adjacent to those mobilizing many protestors. That is, if a general trend of the social explosion represents the subaltern fighting to become a legitimate and autonomous voice within social relations—not trying to subordinate the ruling class to their worldview, but demanding the capacity to substantially participate in the co-generation of a shared pluriversal geopolitical space—this other wing of the social explosion presented an alternative: the refoundation of the Chilean nation according to a distinct grassroots sociocultural vision.

After discussing how a grassroots nationality was initially developed by cultural workers in the mid-twentieth century, I will then outline how neoliberalism suppressed that national culture. Subsequently, I will analyze how popular sectors preserved their national culture by embedding it in various myths based in a shared collective memory. Although this gave the impression that this nationality had been successfully eliminated and replaced with a neoliberal hegemony, I argue that in fact it had only been suppressed by neoliberalism. Lastly I discuss how this subterranean collective memory fed the social explosion[5] and manifested itself in a series of myths—the Baquedano torture center, the romanticization of figures like Víctor Jara and Gladys Marín, *negro matapacos*, and so on—that served as socio-political foundations for a contestatory nationality. I conclude, however, that this imaginary was limited insofar as its boundaries were strictly national in character. In contrast, for instance, to Lemebel's capacity to weave together peripheralized queer subjects of Santiago, Chilean neoliberal high culture, and pop culture from the United States, this grassroots nationality limited the possibility for international coalitions and alliances with the various immigrant communities living in Chile. Myth proved powerful insofar as it glued together the subaltern into an identifiable, coherent, and singular collectivity, but was weak insofar as it undermined any possibility for international solidarity.

How Neoliberalism Became Hegemonic

To understand the significance of postmillennial collective memory for the social explosion, it helps to first review the cultural history of twentieth-century Chile. Prior to the dictatorship, cultural production in Chile was largely structured around the process of fostering, unifying, and cohering the "imagined community" of a national space (Anderson 2006; Moreiras 2001, 2016).[6] For instance, during this era we see the publication of works like Gabriela Mistral's *Poema de Chile* (2013 [1967]) and Pablo Neruda's "Canto General de Chile" in his *Canto General* (1989 [1950]) that sought to manufacture a unified collective national imagination out of the individual elements of Chilean geography and social life. Beyond these canonical examples, Bernardo Subercaseaux (2007) has demonstrated that much early twentieth-century Chilean literature was marked by an elite integrationist mission that attempted to "rescue cultural particularities… with the objective of reinserting [them] in the narrative of the nation" (7–8). This top-down relationship in which elite authors fashioned a singular nationality out of the disparate elements of Chilean life is exemplified in a 1924 comment by the Chilean avant-garde poet, Vicente Huidobro (2000), "My highest desire is to create a country...If you left me 20 years with my beloved Chile solely in my hands, you would see what beautiful poem I would make" (50).

It should also be noted, however, that another national culture was simultaneously generated that emerged from the grassroots. Within the field of Chilean folklore, for example, this twentieth-century nationality initially germinated with the intellectual and musical work of Margot Loyola and Violeta Parra who collected music from "avenues little explored in the traditional [Chilean] song" (Contreras Román 2016: 206) in order to amplify the voices, music, and cultural practices of Chile's leftovers, "the farmer of the central zone, the Indigenous subject of the south and north, the fisherman of the Island of Chiloé" (Contreras Román 2016: 210; Ruiz 2006; Torres 2004). As Fabio Salas Zúñiga (2003) argues, this bottom-up study of folklore would eventually synthesize with rock music from the North Atlantic in order to form the popular cultural movement of the "New Chilean Song" with singers like Víctor Jara (discussed in more detail later in this chapter) and Patricio Manns as well as groups like Quilapayún, Illapu, and Inti-Illimani (who played a concert at Dignity Plaza during the social explosion on 13 December 2019).

This national popular culture would subsequently become a "cultural ally" of the Chilean left during the 1960s and 70s, brandishing their campaigns with "an authentic sound of songs and rhythms *that was embodied in collective memory*" (Salas Zúñiga 2003: 75) [emphasis mine]. Within this interpretation of mid-twentieth-century Chilean popular culture as an instrument to cohere and reproduce a collective memory that unified a popular nationality in defiance of elite national integrationism, one can understand the socialist administration of Salvador Allende, the socialist president of Chile just prior to the 1973 military coup. It is often forgotten in English-speaking contexts that Allende was the culmination of a national developmentalist agenda that had reigned in Chile since the 1930s with presidents like Pedro Aguirre Cerda and Eduardo Frei Montalva, a progressive nationalism that was bolstered by this emerging grassroots popular culture. The significance of Allende, then, is not only that Chile was seeking a peaceful, non-violent path towards socialism, but rather that he embodied the utopian hopes of the bottom-up nationality based in the work of Violeta Parra, Víctor Jara, and many others.[7]

This collective project of unifying the Chilean nation would subsequently fall apart not so much with the coup of 11 September 1973[8] as due to Pinochet's embrace of neoliberalism (Bernedo 2013; Collier and Sater 2004: 365–366; Moreiras 2001, 2016). In addition to specific policy decisions linked especially to privatization and deregulation,[9] Chilean neoliberalism was characterized by a shift in hegemony: the dominant drive to generate a coherent national culture was replaced by the segmentation of the social landscape into discrete packages to be understood in terms of economic optimization in the global marketplace (Rumié Rojo 2019; Tironi and Barandiaran 2015). The previous collective project of generating "harmony among the elements that composed the nation" (Moulian 1997: 27) was exchanged with a "daily culture...penetrated by the symbolism of consumption" thereby placing "the individual...above the group"—neoliberalism witnessed the collapse of the collective strategies of the nation in favor of isolated individual strategies of the consumer (Moulian 1997: 105–106). As a result, in neoliberal Chile we find on "equal footing Che and the Simpsons, Violeta Parra and Madonna" (Cuadra 2003: 17) and the popular culture of the local market is replaced by the "trans-class" character of the mall occupied by multinational brand stores (Moulian 1997: 111). With neoliberalism, Chileans were "transformed ideologically from citizens into consumers" (Cuadra 2003: 106).

This shift from a national to a globalized neoliberal project was hailed by some as creating an egalitarian level cultural field in which all consumers had access to the same materials, even if they had differing purchasing power. Andy Warhol's (1975) famous commentary in the US context demonstrates this utopian view:

> ...the richest consumers buy essentially the same things as the poorest. You can be watching TV and see Coca-Cola, and you can know that the President drinks Coke, Liz Taylor drinks Coke, and just think, you can drink Coke, too. A Coke is a Coke and no amount of money can get you a better Coke than the one the bum on the corner is drinking
> (100–101).

This theorization of egalitarian progress under neoliberalization has been used to explain why the post-dictatorship democratic government continued the neoliberal political-economic model generated by the dictatorship as well as to explain how they built consensus around that model (Moulian 1997). According to this theorization, to return to the framework of Ranajit Guha (1998), the only difference between dictatorship and post-dictatorship Chilean neoliberalism is a shift in domination from one of *coercion*, in which neoliberalism was instituted through the barrel of the gun (Klein 2007), to one of *persuasion*, in which a majority of the Chilean population seemingly embraced the system of values in which it was accepted that globalized neoliberal commercialization should dominate the organization of the political economy and social landscape. The Chilean population had apparently been persuaded by the following logic: by tearing asunder the collective project of national development and constructing a new neoliberal socio-political landscape, the citizen-cum-consumer now had access to a more diversified and egalitarian marketplace of commodities as well as new avenues for individual economic development and upward social mobility.

Despite this celebratory ideologization, this new neoliberal culture was anything but beneficent. As Timothy Clark (2018) argues, and as discussed in Chapter 1, Chilean neoliberalization created a new capitalist elite sponsored by a novel State formation. In this sense, the neoliberal discourse of upward mobility (against the previous discourse of national development), individual freedom (against the previous logic of social responsibility), personal taste and branding (against the previous discourse of a shared popular culture), and egalitarian pop culture (against the previous discourse of popular cultures) served as an ideological rhetoric that legitimized social disparities produced under neoliberalism and undermined the national cultural project that preceded it.[10]

What I want to argue in the next sections, however, is that the previous national imaginary was not eliminated by neoliberalization, it was only suppressed. Instead, the cultural practices that reproduced such a national imaginary had to take covert forms such as myth. In fact, various myths developed during the social explosion testify to a long-standing powerful national imaginary bubbling beneath the surface of neoliberalism that burst to the forefront in October 2019. The collective memory of Chile's leftovers—the claim that "my only country is my memory and it does not have hymns"—as embodied in various myths served as a national cultural form that contested neoliberal hegemony.

...And How Myth Countered that Neoliberal Hegemony

For many, the trajectory of the historical memory of the dictatorship's brutalities mirror the advance of neoliberalism. The Pinochet dictatorship has long held a reputation for its glaring abuses of human rights including the torture and imprisonment of citizens for political purposes. Following the dictatorship, two Truth and Reconciliation Commissions—the National Commission on Political Imprisonment and Torture's [*Comisión Nacional sobre Prisión Política y Tortura*] (CNPPT) "Rettig Report" of 1991 and "Valech Report" of 2004[11]—were put together in order to address and redress these atrocities.[12] The goal of these reports was to end the "culture of silence about torture that slowly extended across the country" (CNPPT 2004: 17), to firmly establish the factuality of the political violence waged against individuals during the dictatorship, and "to complete, in the best manner possible, the reparation and justice that the country owes to those [tortured and killed], in order to advance along the always difficult and necessary path of re-encounter and reconciliation among Chileans" (CNPPT 2004: 17). In the end, the commissions worked towards "official recognition" (CNPPT 2004: 46) of torture by evaluating any and all individual cases between 1973 and 1989 in order to enable reconciliation among Chileans as well as to reintegrate those tortured into the social fabric of the nation.

Initially, many hoped that these Truth and Reconciliation Reports would provide an institutional mechanism to bring justice to those who had committed such atrocities during the 1970s and 1980s, hopes that were soon dashed as the commissions "seal[ed] off…judicial consequences" for those State officials who gave their testimony, thereby focusing on the sharing of truth (Collins and Hau 2016, "Truth Recovery," par. 7). Moreover, the focus of the reports was directed at analyses of torture against the individual body—the Valech Report, for instance, was designed to bring together the individual testimonies of "persons who suffered privation of freedom and torture for political reasons"[13] (CNPPT 2004: 21)—and not in terms of how it served to further a specific political project. In other words, the reports ignored that, as Tomás Moulian (1997) argues, torture under the dictatorship was more precisely the exercise of collective terror, the goal of which was "to be able to govern without discussion, without convincing, without sharing power" (192). By focusing on individuals' testimonies, such political dimensions of torture were erased. Álvaro Cuadra (2003) made this diagnosis perhaps most bluntly, "Pinochet is not being judged on political foundations but rather in the name of *ethical foundations*; that which is aired out in his case refers to *crimes against humanity*" (76). Quite simply, the Rettig and Valech Reports never link the exercise of torture to the political project of installing neoliberalism through the barrel of the gun. In the end, as Anna-Emilia Hietanen (2007) concludes, the State's reports aimed to produce a hegemonic collective memory of dictatorship-era political violence, one in which the exercise of terror was depoliticized and rebranded as the systematic torture of individual bodies, thereby leaving neoliberalism's connections to State repression unquestioned.

Already in the 1980s, however, new cultural and literary narratives were emerging that sought to "split from hegemonic narratives" and to reconfigure "words hostile to the slogan of official truth" (Richard 1994: 25). This challenge to the official history of torture would be furthered in the 2000s with the publication of literary works like Nona Fernández's *Mapocho* (2002), which destabilizes official national history by appealing to the collective memory of those who form that history's "residues": "homosexuals, the Indigenous, women" (Opazo 2004: 42; Rojas 2015; Valenzuela Prado 2018). If the Rettig and Valech Reports sought to create a new post-dictatorship hegemonic historical memory, alternative collective memories began creating spaces of conceptual dissent.

Although some studies of the memory of violence insisted that such political dimensions of torture had been lost on the broader Chilean population (Moulian 1997: 31), Katherine Hite, Cath Collins, and Alfredo

Joignant (2013b) later argued that this initial pronouncement was made too soon: it is not until the 2010s that "'countermemories' of the dictatorship began to make themselves heard" (244). Indeed, by the 2010s new grassroots claims for justice like the *funa*—"street-based denunciations of former agents at their homes and workplaces, carried out since the mid-2000s by flash mobs summoned through social networking" (Collins and Hau 2016, "Proportionality of Sentencing," par. 2)—had emerged that contested the depoliticized hegemonic collective memory proffered by the Truth and Reconciliation Commissions. Moreover, as Ana Deutsch (2007: 264) puts it, those communities whose countermemories of torture had been silenced under the hegemonic collective memory of the State reports created "myths and legends" in order to "reconstruct" that past in their own terms. In other words, new postmillennial narratives started to emerge that reproduced and maintained alternative understandings of dictatorship-era torture.

These countermemories did not appear out of nowhere. During the 2000s, groups like the Union of Ex-Political Prisoners [*Unión de Ex-Presos Políticos*] and the Historical Memory Collective [*Colectivo de Memoria Histórica*] began collectively and consciously organizing counter-narratives to those offered by the State. The Historical Memory Collective's examination of the collective torture of working-class Santiago neighborhoods is particularly notable in this regard. In some way, their report, *Torture in Santiago Working-Class Neighborhoods [Poblaciones], 1973–1990*, was a (still incomplete) bottom-up alternative to the official Valech and Rettig reports. The Collective's chief conclusion is that torture was practiced not only against individuals, but against social, collective, and territorial bodies—they focus on the mass repression of working-class neighborhoods in Santiago—for the purpose of eradicating

> the spirit of struggle, democracy, and participation that had taken root in the popular masses since the first labor social movements at the beginning of the twentieth century...Without torture, the implementation of the neoliberal model, based in the violation of economic, social, and cultural rights would have been impossible
>
> (Colectivo de Memoria Histórica 2005: 16).

Against the Rettig and Valech Reports, the Historical Memory Collective shifts the focus from the systematic exercise of torture against individuals to how torture was a shared experience among working-class communities and neighborhoods and "applied by the elites who held power" (Colectivo de Memoria Histórica 2005: 65) for the purposes of installing the political project of neoliberalism. As they note, these communities were targeted not for individuals' particular political interventions (though this did of course happen as well) but because those communities in themselves were seen as "potential enemies to the political, social, cultural, and economic model that the dictatorship sought to impose" (22). Torture sought to discipline not only individual dissidents but leftovers as a collective and territorial body. As they conclude, through mass-based torture tactics like raids [*allanamientos*] of neighborhoods, "working-class Santiago neighborhoods in their totality acquired the character of a prison" (165). The Historical Memory Collective's work served to generate a collective countermemory in which torture was not a discrete event experienced by certain individuals that could be collected in a State report, but rather an all-encompassing environment of violence in which certain populations were living that served to install the new neoliberal social landscape.

The Historical Memory Collective was therefore not just offering further perspective on the torture experienced during the dictatorship, they were developing a collective memory that served to cohere a political critique of neoliberalism. Indeed, the Historical Memory Collective founded its alternative report on a major blind spot of the 2004 Valech Report: it did not include testimony from "persons deprived of freedom in public protests" or "temporal retentions carried out during raids [*allanamientos*]...or another similar form of collective or indiscriminate control of the population" (CNPPT 2004: 22). To recognize these acts, the Historical Memory Collective argues, would require a re-theorization of torture not just as an expression of systemic corruption weighed against individual bodies that violated human rights and ethical foundations, but rather in terms of an instrument of political discipline utilized by the elite against the collective subaltern body and that body's territories, a body that through its very existence threatened the stability and integrity of the neoliberal social order. Whereas the recomposition of Chilean collective memory by the Rettig and Valech reports conceptually decoupled the neoliberal political economy from torture, the Historical Memory Collective composed a dissenting collective memory in which the foundation of Chilean neoliberalism was built on the torture of the collective subaltern body.

The Historical Memory Collective's focus on raids [*allanamientos*] and arrests during public protests is particularly notable. In the wake of the dictatorship, the Chilean state undertook massive reform that sought to reorganize the police as a modern institution that executed civil duties rather than political functions (Oviedo 2007; Vallejos Muñoz 2019). Mass raids [*allanamientos*] and the imprisonment of persons during public protests, however, challenge precisely this clean division between political repression and civic policing. To put it in question form: Does the disciplining of working-class neighborhoods for the sake of the functioning of the neoliberal socio-economic order (i.e., the purpose of the mass raids [*allanamientos*] according to the Historical Memory Collective) constitute a civic duty or political repression? What about arresting protestors who erect barricades—and therefore prevent the smooth mobility of bodies and goods that is necessary for the operation of the economy—as was done during the social explosion? The Historical Memory Collective's focus on mass raids and arrests during public protests illuminates that the political functions of the police during the dictatorship were in fact civil duties—to install an everyday order of social life, which, in this particular case, was structured around neoliberalism—and that the post-dictatorship civil duties of the police themselves hold political functions—to maintain and regulate that neoliberal social life installed during the dictatorship.[14] The cultural work performed by groups like the Historical Memory Collective thereby serve a specific end: to generate a grassroots collective memory of the relationship between policing, political repression, and neoliberalism.

In this way, the poster that I saw in March 2020, "My only country is my memory and it does not have hymns," was part and parcel of this general post-dictatorship trajectory that witnessed an *autonomous repoliticization* of collective memory during the 2000s and 2010s. This poster was not the only evidence that the work by groups like the Historical Memory Collective had informed protestors' discourse during the social explosion. For instance, during the first weeks of the social explosion a rumor started circulating that Chilean police had transformed the Baquedano metro station, located underneath Dignity Plaza (formerly Plaza Italia) at the center of Santiago's protests, into a torture center. In addition to this story widely circulating in daily conversations, there is a wealth of examples of people who wrote about it: the member of the Chilean Communist Party and the Chilean Chamber of Deputies, Camila Rojas, tweeted, "in the Baquedano Station precinct one finds blood and handcuffs" (El Mostrador 23 October 2019); a video circulated around social media claiming to record screams of torture victims rising from the Baquedano station; and the police cleaning up the station at 3:00AM after the accusations were initially circulated was quickly interpreted by some as proof of a torture center and evidence of a cover up (@Carabdechile 2019; Gamba 2019). Months after the fact, the story was still circulating among protestors.[15] Additionally, this was not the only instance in which a police precinct was represented as a torture center, with information emerging that officers at the precinct in the Santiago neighborhood of Peñalolén were "crucifying" arrested protestors (Villarroel 2019).[16] By framing police violence in terms of a torture center, protestors were responding to State repression using the language and discourse of the collective memory fostered by groups like the Historical Memory Collective (Figure 5.1).

The critic may object that such a connection of collective memory to the discourse of the Baquedano torture center is unsubstantial: the police *were* torturing protestors during the social explosion, and therefore the denunciations by protestors were more precisely a reflection of fact, not an expression of a collective memory. Recognizing this objection, we can look at graffiti captured by Carolina Cisneros on 28 October 2019 at the entrance of the Baquedano metro station: someone had spray-painted "1973" on the wall

Figure 5.1 Graffiti at the entrance of Baquedano station, "they torture here".
Source: Photo by Maxwell Woods, 25 October 2019.

with an arrow pointing down into the underground station (Cisternas, Loncón, and Klenner 2020: 20–21). Nearly a year later, the group, the Millennial Nucleus of the Arts, Performativity, and Activism [*Núcleo Milenio Artes, Performatividad y Activismo*], released a collection of brief retrospective responses by Chilean citizens to elements of the social explosion including a set of reflections on this "1973" graffiti at Baquedano station (Cisternas, Loncón, and Klenner 2020: 20–29). Many contributors reflected on the historical continuity between dictatorship and post-dictatorship governance as well as a collective memory of torture that dissented from the official word of the Chilean State's reports. As Pascale Bonnefoy noted, "That graffiti of '1973' in the Baquedano subway would not have existed if the civil governments had intervened, refined and reformed the Chilean police when they should have done it, in 1990" (25). More abstractly, Juan Diego Bonilla writes,

> The graffiti of 1973 in a photo from 2019. A denunciation of the future that we thought was going to be better, but which turned out to still exist in the present. Times cross. The past influences the future and the

> future influences the past...The distinction between past, present and future seems to be an illusion
>
> (29).

This graffiti and these writings testify to how the dominant periodization of recent Chilean history within the official history of State reports—national development (1938–1973), dictatorship repression (1973–1989), neoliberalization (1980s), post-dictatorship neoliberal consensus (1990-present)—was countered by a contestatory collective memory with a different periodization: dictatorial imposition of neoliberalism followed by the maintenance of that neoliberalism by a police force guaranteeing its smooth operation. This "1973" graffiti combined with the discourse surrounding the tag is evidence of how the experience of the social explosion was being expressed in the terms of a contestatory collective memory.

For others, the Baquedano torture center was one more piece of "fake news" given that the claim was ostensibly disproven by Chile's National Institute of Human Rights (Ayala 2019b). To be sure, in the days after 18 October 2019 unsubstantiated rumors circulated throughout the country: the workers of Chile's state-owned oil corporation (ENAP) were going to go on strike, thereby limiting access to the transportation of basic goods and to personal mobility (a rumor that provoked extremely long lines at many local gas stations for the first few days of the social explosion); the Chilean State was going to cut off water to particularly mobilized communities in order to suppress the movement; banks were going to freeze accounts in fear of a bank run and supermarkets were going to run out of food due to lack of viable transportation routes as a result of barricades (leading to long lines at ATMs and supermarkets on 21 October 2019, the first Monday after the beginning of the social explosion); police had started raiding houses of activists and were using live ammunition; and so on. Various rumors started circulating among upper classes as well: the social explosion was a communist plot by infiltrators from Venezuela and Cuba[17]; activists were organizing marches in order to invade upper-class neighborhoods; protestors were raiding and pillaging houses of the wealthy; people with blond hair were specifically being targeted with violence; anarchists were threatening to burn down private schools perceived as the abodes of rich children; and so on. That these rumors turned out to be false was quickly used by many to denounce the perceived excesses of the social explosion. According to this interpretation, the Baquedano torture center was a *myth* in the sense that it was merely fake news, a consequence of leftist imaginations run wild.

What an analysis of the trajectory of the historical memory of the dictatorship demonstrates, however, is that it may be better to see the story as a *collective myth* in the sense of one of those "myths and legends" of the leftovers analyzed by Ana Deutsch, "from which a good part of their history had been reconstructed" in defiance of the official historical memory of the State. By focusing on those detained during protests, on the intimidation of collective insurrection, and on the territorial element of torture (i.e., all elements of torture under the dictatorship that were not fully acknowledged in the Truth and Reconciliation Reports but that were and are remembered in Chilean collective memory as embodied in artifacts like the Historical Memory Collective's report), the myth of the Baquedano torture center highlighted that torture works not only to target individual political agents but to discipline the collective subaltern body. The story of the Baquedano torture center, regardless of its factuality[18], is founded from within a collective memory emerging from (at least) the dictatorship—and one can trace this collective memory back even further to the early twentieth century when the failure of the military to violently repress strikes led to the militarization of the police in order to complete the suppression of working-class discontent (Aguila Zúñiga and Maldonado Prieto 1996: 78–79)—in which torture serves to fragment grassroots solidarity. Yes, the narrative of Baquedano station being transformed into a torture center is a myth; yet it is a myth not because it is 'fake news' but rather because it narratively codifies the Chilean social explosion from within a grassroots collective memory and thereby opposes the depoliticizing logic of neoliberalism with the collective imaginary nurtured by remembering in common.

The Myths of the Social Explosion

What I am pointing to is that the myth of the Baquedano torture center is evidence of a robust grassroots Chilean nationality organized around a collective memory that contests the hegemony of Chile's official historical memory. The simple graffiti of "1973" with an arrow pointing down into the interior of the Baquedano subway station requires a profound familiarity with this alternative narrative of the recent national past, including knowledge of: the significance of the 1973 coup, the brutalities of the dictatorship, the political persecution of protestors that went undiscussed in the official Truth and Reconciliation Reports, the transition to democracy that did not impart judicial consequences on the agents of repression, and the claim that recent Chilean history is defined by the continuity between dictatorship and post-dictatorship regimes (in contrast to official history's claims of a clear break between authoritarianism and liberal democracy). The claim that the Baquedano subway station had been transformed into a torture center, that in its dark depths one returned to "1973," is based on a profound and intimate knowledge of Chilean national past articulated in a collective memory that contests official history and the dominant neoliberal social order.

Moreover, the Baquedano torture center is not the only instance of myth-making embodying a grassroots collective memory during the social explosion. Most famous, perhaps, are *pareman* (see Chapter 6) and *negro matapacos* ("Cop-killing black dog"). *Negro matapacos* was a black, stray dog who lived on the streets near the center of the 2011 student protests and was famous for being simultaneously extremely tender and friendly with students and antagonistic towards police.[19] During the social explosion, the dog became a shared symbol for resistance and communality in the face of State violence. His face appeared on bandanas and t-shirts, statues and mosaics were made in his honor, slogans with his name appeared in marches, and Michel Bonnefoy and Celeste Merino (2020) in the midst of the social explosion published a comic book recounting the story of the dog. In other words, *negro matapacos* became a way of creating a historical trajectory of resistance to State violence stemming from the 2011 student protests and continuing to the present day via the collective practice of re-telling and re-imagining the mythical figure of this dog. The myth of *negro matapacos* constructs an autonomously imagined historical line that connects the social explosion to previous student protests.

Beyond these new mythical figures, the social explosion has also been occupied by the consistent re-codification of a variety of Chile's national popular cultural heroes. Arguably most prominently were the central presence during protests of images of Víctor Jara—the left-wing folk singer of the "New Chilean Song" from the 1960s and 1970s who was murdered by the military in the wake of the 1973 coup—and Gladys Marín—a famous Chilean Communist politician and activist from her youth in the 1960s until her death in 2005.[20] For instance, images of Jara's face and remembrances of his death at the hands of the Pinochet regime quickly populated urban spaces across Chile. Additionally, his song, "The Right to Live in Peace," was one of the central anthems of the social explosion, with thousands gathering with guitars and their voices outside the Chilean National Library in Santiago on 25 October 2019 to collectively sing the folk song. From within the social explosion, the figure of Jara was reshaped into an expression of the social mobilizations; his call for the right to live in peace became a poetic phrasing of the demand for dignity lying at the heart of the movement. The popular cultural figures that had formed the foundations of the unified grassroots Chilean nationality prior to the coup were central mythical referents for those of the social explosion.

The same can be said of the use of the image of Gladys Marín in the lead up to the march on International Women's Day, 8 March 2020. Attended by nearly 2 million women in Santiago alone and tens of thousands in other cities across the country, one commonly shared advertisement for the march had a photo of Marín smiling and looking off to the right with a message printed underneath, "Fight like Gladys."[21] Marín's longer hair and clothing making her image feminine-presenting, the use of an older photo from the years preceding the coup, and its employment in order to advertise for a feminist march speak to how the social explosion was re-narrating its historical foundations as a feminist-oriented appropriation of the working-class leftist Chilean tradition using figures who were part of that tradition but often marginalized.[22] In a swift narrative and imaginary move, the International Women's Day protest was reconstructed as the continuation of a working-class tradition of feminism emerging from the leftovers of Chile and embodied in figures like a smiling Gladys Marín during an era when a socialist government was democratically elected. In the image, Gladys Marín is not a bureaucrat within a political party moving forward a well-established political programme based in Marxist State politics[23]—though it should be noted that posters with this image and phrase were often distributed by and included the logo of the organization where Marín started her political career, "Communist Youth of Chile" [*Juventudes Comunistas de Chile*]—but an individual woman engaged in a social struggle founded in a working-class feminism. The central message was not, 'Join the Communist Party,' it was 'Fight like Gladys.'

Through these processes of myth-making—the narrative of the Baquedano torture center, *negro matapacos*, the reworking of the images of Gladys Marín and Víctor Jara, and so on—the protestors effectively presented their collective memory dating back (at least) to the 1960s as a well-established communal relationship with Chile's national past. To return to the claim of dignity as the cry of 'here we are!' (Holloway 1998), this is the historiographical equivalent to that cry: the presentation of the grassroots national collectivity formed in the social explosion as something that not only *is* but *has been* for decades. In this way, the use of myth during the social explosion fulfills Sorel's understanding of myth with collective memory at its foundation. That is, these myths are not meant as a means to maintain relations of power, as Barthes would have it, but rather as a means of establishing a dissenting national *being* in the face of State violence which denies that being's existence. Through the myths of the Baquedano torture center, Gladys Marín, and Victor Jara, the social explosion was articulated as the declaration of 'here we are!' by those collectively tortured by the Chilean elite and pushing towards a new sociality built around a working-class feminism and the clamor for the right to live in peace.

The Tensions at the Heart of the Social Explosion

The presence of such a national imaginary should come as a surprise given that, as already discussed, one popular narrative of post-dictatorship Chilean history argued that neoliberalization and political repression during the dictatorship had successfully weakened the national imaginary, replacing the hegemonic discourse of the nation with that of the globalized marketplace. Pedro Lemebel (Chapter 2) is evidence that such logic of the globalized marketplace had taken root even within subaltern communities, though Lemebel's success is that he re-shaped that neoliberal discourse for and from the position of the leftovers, constructing a contestatory subaltern discourse from within the neoliberal landscape. For instance, instead of speaking of a distinct and identifiable popular Chilean culture, Lemebel speaks of Madonna of San Camilo singing Madonna songs without understanding the English and of "reiterations of the same infinite image" of Madonna (Madonna of San Camilo; the *gringa* Madonna; the classical

Madonna; etc.) torn from images of pop magazines. If on the one hand the celebration of Lemebel as a cultural hero points to how the insurgent imaginary during the social explosion was reconfiguring neoliberal culture from the bottom up, on the other hand the presence of collective practices, narratives, and images founded in a contestatory collective memory spoke to the resurgence of the utopian hopes of the pre-dictatorship national collective projects embodied in voices like Violeta Parra and Víctor Jara.

As a result, the social explosion was being pulled in two different directions: the resurgence of the mission to cohere a national collective project *versus* the breaking apart of nationality itself in order to make room for new modes of living in common. To oversimplify, the question of the social explosion is the following: Is it the revolution of Pedro Lemebel or of Violeta Parra? The revolution of Reveco and FáBRiKa's pluriversal margins or of a grassroots nationality unified by a collective memory? The revolution of multiple diginit*ies* and feminism*s* or the vindication of a united pre-dictatorship nationality[24]? And if it's the revolution of both, how were their differences resolved within the imaginary of activists?

This tension can be seen in the cultural politics of collective memory of the Mapuche myths that frequently circulated among protestors during the social explosion. For instance, during the International Women's Day march, many shared the myth of the *trawünko*—a *ngen*[25] (spiritual Mapuche being) who inhabits the rivers of Chilloé—as a mythical rapist in order to redefine Chilean feminism in a way that recognizes Mapuche cultural traditions. In this way, feminist activists were reigniting the grassroots mission of figures like Violeta Parra to join together a popular nationality—in this case, a nationality founded on the shared experience of gender violence across women's communities—from the individual fragments of Chilean social life. As Jaime Cuyanao recounts, however, the myth of the *trawünko* was in fact generated after the arrival of Catholic priests during the colonization of the continent when more and more women became pregnant but refused to identify the father; the *trawünko* myth is a narrative recodification of the collective memory of the rape of Mapuche women by colonizing priests (@JaimeCuyanao 2020). Cuyanao's comments tacitly identify conflicting mythical logics: the attempt to construct a national Chilean identity founded on joining together cultural practices of various communities *versus* the attempt to decolonially explode Chilean nationality itself by narratively recodifying the colonial violence waged against Indigenous communities from within a Mapuche collective memory.

The apparent resolution to this tension was in the appeal to the concept of plurinationality. Prior to the social explosion, and following the footsteps of other Latin American countries like the Plurinational State of Bolivia, Indigenous intellectuals within the geopolitical space dominated by the nation-State of Chile had outlined what a new constitution would mean for Indigenous nations and what a plurinational constitution would look like (Moraga 2016; Namuncura 2016). As Luis Cortés (2016) explains, "Chile is not only of Chileans and, to that end, the new Constitution must contain strong plurinational components like the concept of 'peoples' [*pueblos*] and 'diversities'" (132). The concept of plurinationality was even a central part of some debates in the 2013 Chilean presidential campaign (Provoste 2016: 141). Another strand of thinking outlined by Fernando Pairicán (2016), however, sees plurinationality as a means to "crack open the homogeneous Republic in order to give space to a project of radical democracy that has as a possible horizon a plurinational society...in order to continue creating an autonomous consciousness" (112–113). Plurinationality itself is evidence of a friction regarding Chilean nationality at the heart of the social explosion: Was it a resurgence of the project of composing a nationality constituted by uniting discrete leftover communities, or was it an assault on Chilean nationality itself in order to empower other forms of community building (for example, autonomous Indigenous communality)?

In either case, the thinking of the social explosion was largely based on a bounded imaginary or set of imaginaries that ignores what today constitutes more than 6 percent of the Chilean population: immigrants. The vocabulary and discourse of the collective memory or collective memories that fed the social explosion—whether that be autonomist collective memories seeking to explode Chilean nationality or a recomposed nationality based on gluing together multiple collective memories into a coherent singular collective memory—required a profound familiarity with how the nation's past was articulated within leftover communities, a familiarity that was not guaranteed for those foreign to those communities. More precisely, the myths that fed the social explosion reproduced a troubling tendency of subaltern collective memory: they frequently limit the possibility for those who do not share those collective memories (i.e., 'foreigners') to participate in defining the identity and social order of that community bonded together through sharing memories in common (Woods 2021a). That is, the national or bounded plurinational collective memory of the social explosion could not make substantial room for the cultures of the hundreds of thousands of immigrants from Venezuela, Haiti, Peru, China, and so on. One of the central rallying cries of the social explosion, "*Chile despertó!*" ["*Chile has awoken*!"], the constant presence of Mapuche and Chilean flags, and the use of Spanish, Indigenous, and even English languages (but only rarely or never Haitian Creole, Chinese, or Portuguese) in chants and posters all speak to an underlying nationalism within the mobilizations.[26] Even Pairican's vision of plurinationality, for instance, requires a bounded set of nations that compose that plurinationality, and Haitian nationality, for instance, was never offered to be included in that new plurinational State.

To ward off misunderstandings, the claim here is *not* that the social explosion is xenophobic. As an immigrant in Chile—but by no means subaltern (I am a white US emigrant of the professional middle class) and with an extremely different immigrant experience from many arriving from Haiti, Venezuela, and other countries that have fed the recent waves of immigration to Chile—never once did I experience hostility towards 'foreigners,' and anti-xenophobia was frequently explicitly mentioned in calls for marches. That said, many specifically immigrant-based concerns—the indignity of the immigration process in Chile, immigrants having to camp outside government offices overnight in order to receive a meeting to have a single form stamped by an overburdened immigration system, having to wait sometimes over two years to find out if you have received a visa only to discover that you received one that lasts less than a month, the fear that an immigrant's mere presence at a protest was technically grounds for deportation under the abusive foreign resident laws installed by the dictatorship, difficulties finding work in a political economy built on networking and contacts, and so on—were not fully addressed within the protestors' discourse. In the various lists of demands that circulated throughout the social explosion, reformation of the immigration system was almost never mentioned. That is, calls for anti-xenophobia and "migratory" feminism (to quote one poster's definition of the feminism of the International Women's Day march) are to fundamentally misunderstand that the absence of discrimination against migrants is not equal to migratory justice (Sheller 2018) nor is it to embrace the socio-cultural and political imaginaries of those immigrants (Woods 2019). That, for instance, the immigrant may participate in different collective memories with different myths—collective memories and myths that are just as legitimate and autonomous as those emerging from within Chilean plurinationality—was not substantially acknowledged during the social protests.

Conclusion

This chapter has argued that the social explosion was enabled by a robust contestatory collective memory reproduced, reinforced, and maintained by sharing various myths: the Baquedano torture center, visual re-codifications of Víctor Jara and Gladys Marín, folktales like *negro matapacos* and *pareman*, and so on. The culture of the social explosion was at least partially marked by the resurgence of a grassroots nationality previously generated and popularized by cultural heroes like Violeta Parra. In this way, the social explosion demonstrates two more general theses. First, neoliberalization did *not* completely fragment all communities, but more precisely suppressed such communality so that it had to be reproduced in covert forms of collective memory like myth. The social explosion is evidence of such communal forms based on collective memory bursting forth to make claims for power. Second, as has been repeatedly demonstrated by others, "Collective memories are both foundational to and constitutive of collective political identities" (Hite, Collins, and Joignant 2013a: 2). Collective memory fed the contestatory politics of the social explosion.

As a result, however, the culture of the social explosion remains stro
national in character, limiting the possibility for planetary (or even

international) collaboration, dialogue, and organization. If the myths of the social explosion effectively empower leftover Chilean communities—where "Chilean" is understood as the rearticulation of the signifier that refers to the multiplicitous totality of communities that compose the geopolitical space frequently today called "Chile"—it disempowers other subaltern immigrant communities living within this space, not to mention the possibility for a broad-based internationalist front. This remains my harshest critique of the social explosion to date. Though it represents a serious and novel mode of feminist, decolonial, environmentalist, and anti-capitalist organizing by and for the subaltern, it fails to seriously address questions of mobility justice and migrant organization. The point here is not that migrants and internationalism did not play a role in the social explosion. (As an immigrant who was holding conversations in Chile, the US, and Germany during the social explosion, I am living evidence that that is not the case.) The claim is that these issues of immigration did not hold a central place in the discourse, and the use of collective memory as an alternative cultural foundation is at least partially responsible.

More profoundly, a tension emerged in the culture of the social explosion between two diverging poles. On the one hand is the attempt to break apart Chilean nationality in order to make room for new modes of communal organization and self-definition. Here, we find autonomist decolonial organizing as well as the attempt to reconfigure the globalized neoliberal landscape according to the demands of the subaltern as is the case in the adoption of Pedro Lemebel and Los Prisioneros, whose appeal to North Atlantic New Wave music can be interpreted as a rejection of the Chilean popular culture that had preceded it (e.g., Víctor Jara) and an embrace of the offerings of the globalized marketplace (Salas Zúñiga 2003). On the other hand is the attempt to re-empower a grassroots national community united through collective memory. Here, we find the myth of the Baquedano torture center, *negro matapacos*, and the ubiquitous presence of representations of cultural heroes like Víctor Jara and Gladys Marín.

We can say, in other words, that an unresolved tension lies at the core of the social explosion. On the one hand, the fight for dignity, Lemebel's reconfigured neoliberal landscape, the use of the graffiti mural, the feminist multitudes organized by LASTESIS and Cheril Linett, and so on functionally appealed to the co-generation of a shared pluriversal geopolitical space that recognizes the multiplicity of the Chilean socio-political landscape as well as the various differentiated subaltern communities that were vying for empowerment during the social explosion. This wing of the social explosion explicitly eschewed the political tactic of challenging the State with a ngular, unified, counter-hegemonic proposal, instead favoring a diversity ivities coming together in mutual solidarity. On the other hand, a oots nationalism emerged during the social explosion that llectivities based on a collective memory of State re- ing of the social explosion had its benefits—most obviously, it presented a more coherent idea and definition of the collective that was fighting for power in the streets—but it was also marked by an insularity as a result of its strictly defined boundaries. In contrast to Reveco's and FáBRiKa's call, "BE MARGINAL / BE A HEROINE / BE A HERO," this alternative vision embodied in various myths called on the protestor to "BE CHILEAN." One cannot help but ask: was Chile over, as Reveco, Linett, and the Catrileo+Carrión community claimed, or had Chile awoken (*Chile despertó*)?

Notes

1 The debates and tensions between discourses of history and memory are too extensive to list. The central debates are summarized by Klein (2000). The foundational texts of this debate are still often those of Pierre Nora (1989, 1996–1998) and Maurice Halbwachs (1980). Interested readers are also encouraged to see the work of Astrid Erll (2008; Erll and Nünning 2008); Jeffrey Olick, Vered Vinitzky-Seroussi, and Daniel Levy (2011); and Susannah Radstone and Bill Schwarz (2010).

2 I recall one other moment from the social explosion when one night police drove a caravan of police cars through the center of Valparaíso while blaring the official Chilean police hymn over loudspeakers.

3 A review of basic European theorizations of the relationship between collective memory and myth can be found in Astrid Erll (2012). Jan Assmann's (2011) work has been especially influential in this debate. Of course, this is not the *only* theorization of myth. For a survey of common theories of myth see Segal (2004).

4 Though I focus on Rivera's article that specifically talks about myth, the relationship between decoloniality, myth, and collective memory appears at various moments throughout her career (Rivera 1987, 2010a, 2010b, 2012).

5 After writing this chapter, I had the honor of reading Manuela Badilla's (2021) article also exploring the relationship between collective memory and the social explosion. We take two different paths, but are addressing the same theme.

6 The attendant political form of the *developmentalist State* (i.e., a strong, central government directing the development of the nation) has been outlined by Manuel Riesco (2011) among many others. Indeed, the thesis of this section—a national Chilean imaginary was fragmented into a globalized marketplace of commodities under neoliberalism—is perhaps exemplified most simply by the Chilean nationalization of copper during the 1960s and 1970s and neoliberalism's subsequent privatization and sale to foreign multinationals of copper rights (Caputo and Galarce 2011).

7 This history of Allende and the progressive national developmentalism preceding Allende has been covered by Taylor (2006), Moulian (1997), Salas Zúñiga (2003), and many others.

8 It should be noted, however, that Pinochet did successfully wipe out the entire infrastructure of cultural production tied to the "New Chilean Song" (Sala Zúñiga 2003).

9 Social scientists have extensively catalogued the details of Chilean neoliberal policy and ideology (de la Barra 2011; Harvey 2005; Klein 2007; Taylor 2006).

10 This relationship between postmodernism and neoliberalization is at this point well known given David Harvey (1990) and Fredric Jameson's (1991) canonical works on the question.

11 This commission was reopened in 2010 to address more cases.

12 A full history of these reports can be found in Hite, Collins, and Joignant (2013a). The politics of memory in Chile during the post-dictatorship era has a full bibliography at this point (Lazzara 2006; Stern 2010; Winn, Stern, Lorenz, and Marchesi 2014). My argument follows research that analyzes how this memory of political violence shifted during the 2010s, where political commemoration "re-presents or reinterprets particularly controversial figures for the new movement" (Collins and Hau 2016; Hite and Collins 2009: 392).
13 This was in one way a step up from the Rettig Report which only discussed those who had been murdered by the dictatorship.
14 This theorization of policing is thanks to Reiner (1992), Lea (2002), Walters (2007), and Bloembergen (2011).
15 For instance, on 4 May 2020, the popular Instagram account, @portadasonada, shared a video of the re-opening of the Baquedano Metro station with the following caption, "With a contingent of police, a few transfers, and very few passengers, the Santiago Metro reopened Baquedano station. The place where people were detained, were shot at, and were tortured."
16 A judge dismissed the specific claim in 2020, but concluded that other harassment had occurred (El mostrador 2020).
17 More embarrassingly was the official State report that identified so-called 'foreign influences' on the social explosion that included K-Pop, the pop singer Mon Laferte, and the comedian Paola Molina (Ayala 2019a).
18 I want to insist: I am making no comment on the factuality of the Baquedano torture center. As Sorel already notes, this factuality is insignificant. I am analyzing the discourse surrounding the story of the torture center.
19 The facts of story, while widely known colloquially among protestors, are summarized in a 2013 documentary made about the dog, *Matapaco* (En Marcha 2013).
20 For more on the life of Gladys Marín, see Marín (1999a, 1999b, 2002).
21 This of course was not the only photo of Marín shared with this message. Other posters included an image of her being dragged away by State forces while trying to speak from a balcony.
22 Allende's regime, for example, has widely been noted for its *machismo*, only rarely including women's voices in its decision-making processes (Franceschet 2005; Munoz 1999).
23 For a contextualization of Marín's work as a communist, see Bravo Vargas (2010).
24 This interpretation of the social explosion as the vindication of Allende's political project is made by Ariel Dorfman in *Chile: Juventud Rebelde*.
25 A fuller definition is found in Antonio Catrileo (2019: 49).
26 As of the start of quarantining measures in response to the COVID-19 pandemic, I had seen a total of one poster written in Haitian Creole. That said, I look forward to future research analyzing the role of Haitian immigrants in the social explosion.

6 On the Middle Class

In January 2020, I presented an early draft of Chapter 2 to a group of researchers in Leipzig, Germany. During the question and answer session, I was asked (paraphrasing from memory) why I had not considered the reaction and contribution of the middle class to the social explosion. With my focus on the subaltern, on the leftovers of hegemonic Chilean nationality, the questioner implied, I had ignored those communities in the middle, so to speak, who nonetheless suffered under the inequities of neoliberalism, patriarchy, colonialism, and environmental exploitation. What about these folks who were neither subaltern nor elite?

The questioner was not without reason. Many argued during the social explosion that inequality had actually *decreased* in Chile during the twenty-first century, leading to a dramatic expansion of the middle class. Ricardo Gonzalez and Carmen Le Foulon Morán (2020) summarize this position in their reflections on the social explosion (quoted at length to exemplify the optimistic perception of postmillennial Chile held by many):

> In terms of GDP per capita, Chile had a very successful performance over the last thirty years. In contrast to other countries from the region, the economic progress in Chile did not experience major setbacks over the last three decades, turning it into the medium-size country that has shortened the most its distance to the average OECD country in terms of GDP per capita. There has been progress in the social front as well. Life expectancy at birth increased, child mortality decreased, and poverty levels dropped sharply, placing Chile in the highest position within Latin America. Life satisfaction and happiness levels have increased over time. In fact, year after year, Chile has been the happiest country in South America, according to the World Happiness Report, although it lost this position in 2019.
>
> (228)

Nonetheless, Gonzalez and Le Foulon continue, despite how "economic progress and upward mobility contributed to enlarge the size of the middle class" the "current institutional framework" of the Chilean State was not

DOI: 10.4324/9781003224594-7

able to fulfill the "increasing short- and long-term expectations about the satisfaction of social needs" (228). In the end, this led to a growing *perception* of political parties "as elite-driven and out of touch of citizens concerns" (228) as well as an increase in "perceptions of inequality" despite the fact that the "ratio of justified inequality" was consistently decreasing (230–231).

Ignoring the condescending language of "perceptions of inequality"—as if those taking their first steps in upward mobility cannot recognize material reality, and the experts are needed to step in and educate the masses about the truth of the socio-political landscape—as well as how they side-step the basic issue that moving from extreme poverty to basic poverty (or, as I will detail shortly, what they would call the lower middle class) is still to be in poverty, the underlying thesis of Gonzalez and Le Foulon, as well as my interrogator, does need to be recognized: What of the middle class during the social explosion? With the open conflict between Chile's leftovers and elite, middle-class individuals seemed to have a serious choice to make. Would they side with the elite in hope for continuing their upward social and class mobility, leaving the leftovers in their dust? Or would they side with the leftovers and posit a radical bottom-up challenge to Chilean elites' domination? In other words, a middle-class oriented supplement to Chapters 1–5 is necessary.

In response to this question, the argument of this chapter is largely double. First, the so-called middle class, a class identity that will be deconstructed in the next section, will come to be extremely important with respect to how the social explosion is resolved. Given that they constitute the majority of the Chilean population, with whom they align will likely determine the outcome of the mobilizations. Second, I argue that it is, at this moment in August 2021 when I am writing this chapter, unclear as to how the middle class will respond in the long run to the social explosion. Although there is a strong movement by many in the middle class to align themselves with the leftovers of Chile, another substantial middle-class group nonetheless seeks to strengthen their representation within the existing Chilean socio-cultural and political system and open up new lines for social mobility.

I make this argument through a close analysis of two authors: Manuel Sanfuentes Vio, a poet of the Valparaíso area who released a poem about one of those mythical folk heroes of the social explosion (*pareman*) described in Chapter 5, and Ariel Dorfman, a Chilean exile and former cultural advisor to Salvador Allende who wrote a series of essays on the social explosion in late 2019 and 2020. Sanfuentes and Dorfman, I offer, represent two distinct responses. First, Sanfuentes recognized that the subaltern insurgency was functionally challenging the middle class's system of values, and to put himself into solidarity with the leftovers required deconstructing that middle-class socio-cultural paradigm. Second, Dorfman sought to synthesize middle-class aspirations with the recognition of the wretchedness to which the leftovers had been relegated. In effect, Dorfman's position of greater inclusivity and the expansion of middle-class cultural production to the subaltern is a functionally conservative one that seeks to preserve the integrity of the middle-class socio-cultural paradigm.

The Middle Class

A theory is quickly emerging that the social explosion can be explained as a response by a rising middle class that has rejected the elitist political frameworks determining the post-dictatorship Chilean socio-political landscape and that additionally seeks to reconfigure State apparatuses in a manner that reflects middle-class needs and desires. The social explosion, according to this narrative, is a consequence of a mismatch between the growing power of a previously weak middle class and a neoliberal State that was not designed to represent that social grouping. Moreover, it is almost guaranteed that a corresponding historical narrative will quickly emerge that will proceed something like the following. After the transition to democracy, a moderate Pink Tide in Chile represented by Michelle Bachelet (and preceded by center-left Ricardo Lagos) led to the accelerated growth of a burgeoning middle class. When this postmillennial left-wing program failed to live up to its promises of economic ascendancy and equality, however, the middle class sided with the right-wing neoliberal rhetoric of Sebastián Piñera in 2017 only to then become disillusioned again in 2019, this time leading to radical and confrontational direct action in the streets. In this narrative, a new State with 'true representativity' for the middle class was the ultimate end of the social explosion.[1]

Those pushing this narrative of the middle class will likely refer to a survey conducted by the Center of Public Studies [Centro de Estudios Públicos, CEP] in December 2019 that shows that only 19 percent of Chileans supported barricades—despite my focus on this phenomenon in Chapter 1—and only 9 percent supported looting as a protest tactic (Encuesta CEP 2019: 39). Barricades, this argument runs, were a radical element of the protests that were tolerated by a majority—59 percent insisted that Chilean police should never "use force against a violent protestor," 70 percent that they should never "use tear gas," and 81 percent that they should never "fire rubber bullets or buck shot" (Encuesta CEP 2019: 40)—but are not representative of the social explosion in general. The 'true' voice of the people, this narrative may argue, runs somewhere between the barricades and the police, seeking reforms of an unjust political-economic system or even wanting the end of the neoliberal model but generally accepting of the basic political form of the Chilean State. The social explosion, this argument runs, was a middle-class phenomenon.

This argument follows a common claim by 2019 that Chile was primarily a middle-class country. Writing only months before the social explosion for the independent neoliberal Chilean think tank, Liberty and Development, María Paz Arzola and Catalina Larraín (2019) defined the middle class as "those houses whose total income is between 1.5 and 6 times the poverty line," with the "lower middle class" as that between 1.5 and 3 times (about $800–$1,600USD monthly for a four-person home), the "middle class" as that between 3 and 4.5 times ($1,600–$2,400USD), and "upper middle class" as that between 4.5 and 6 times ($2,400–$3,200USD). Under this definition, they note, the middle class "has considerably increased since 2006–2017, from 43.2 percent of the population to 65.4 percent" (10). By defining class nominally in terms of income, they were able to conclude that "during the last decades Chile has been transformed into an emerging middle-class country, leaving behind—although not completely—poverty" (10).

Yet this clean distinction between the Chilean middle class and the subaltern, between those rising the ranks of social mobility and those who up until October 2019 had apparently "accept[ed] wretchedness as normality" (Spivak 2012: 280) (I remind the reader here that the majority of those protesting in at least Dignity Plaza had not previously participated in social movements), is not entirely clear. According to Arzola and Larraín's own statistics, the lower-middle class constitutes the vast majority, 63.1 percent of the middle class to be exact and 42.5 percent of the total population of Chile. They even admit that "the lower middle class finds itself closer to vulnerable homes than to the rest of those who belong to the middle class" (13). Quite simply, the distinction between poor and middle class is not as strict as it appears in their paper, and the majority of those in the so-called middle class have more in common with those considered in poverty than those categorized as the upper echelons of their own class.[2] If belonging to a class in some sense implies that "all units…within a given class should be more like each other than like units in other classes" (Wright 1985: 137), it is not entirely clear what justifies their definition.

This speaks to the broader issue that the Chilean middle class has no recognizable identity. As Emmanuelle Barozet and Vicente Espinoza wrote in 2016, the Chilean "middle classes comprise a heterogeneous set of social groups" (98) that lack "common social identities" (98). Furthermore, despite emerging representative voices in Chilean politics, the middle class frequently does not have

> clear channels of expression in traditional representation systems. A suspicion about their proclivity to support populist movements emerges, bringing to the present a classical threat to political stability in Latin America...As a Christian Democrat congressman interviewed in 2006 put it, these 'barbarians,' who show no interest in politics or state action, could be open to risky political projects.
>
> (110–111)

In the end, Barozet and Espinoza conclude,

> the situation that is of most concern is that of the emerging middle-lower classes, which border low-income manual workers, who do not

> have their own representation channels and who are not represented in the new electoral system. Thus, in the event of an economic crisis, as a group, they may be available for projects defying the current representation system.
>
> (115)

To clarify their argument for our purposes: Barozet and Espinoza argue that the middle class is a largely incoherent social grouping without representation in the Chilean State. Therefore, a new political party or representative system is needed in order to cohere this middle class and subsequently give voice to their needs in the State. The failure to do so, they were already noting in 2016, will likely result in massive disillusion with the Chilean political model and insurgent political action *especially among the so-called lower-middle class*. In this way, Barozet and Espinoza were implicitly arguing for the reconfiguration of Chilean liberal politics in a manner that cohered the middle class into a representative body that could articulate its demands within more inclusive State apparatuses.[3]

Recognizing Barozet and Espinoza's implicit argument—the middle class currently does not have a unified representative voice within Chilean politics, and cultural and political work is necessary to cohere that group into a collective subject—one could arrive to a diverging conclusion: the lower-middle class could either side with the upper-middle and upper classes in a bid for continued upward socio-economic mobility, or this class could reject the offerings of these groups and side with the leftovers. In other words, what remains to be seen is whether the lower-middle class, which constitutes 42.5 percent of the Chilean population, will side with the subaltern or the elite. Will they seek to be included in a reconfigured Chilean hegemony that recognizes their voice, or will they see their collective destiny as in concert with the leftovers of Chile and contest that hegemony itself?

What I am pointing to is what Erik Olin Wright (1985, 1997, 2015) calls the *contradictory class location* of the middle class. Working within the Marxist tradition, Wright's analysis is founded on a rejection of the definition of class in terms of nominal income, insisting that is defined in *relational* terms, "classes are definable only in terms of their relations to other classes" (Wright 1985: 34). More precisely, class is defined in terms of *exploitation*, "the acquisition of economic benefits from the laboring activity of those who are dominated" (Wright 2015: 10). In this way, the working class is not defined by making less money than capitalists, although this is the case under normal conditions, but rather by being excluded "from access to certain productive resources…[which then] generates material advantage to exploiters because it enables them to appropriate the labor effort of the exploited" (84). Or in Marx's particularly polemic language, capitalists own the means of production and workers have nothing to sell but their labor. "Working class" is defined by sharing these historical conditions of existence in real conflict with capital, not by their income.

More directly, as Ana Dinerstein (2015: 205–206) points out, the redefinition of class around *income* (e.g., redefining the working class as the lower middle class) serves to "hide the struggle" that produces the class locations generating those identities. Class identities are not measurements of one's purchasing power, but are rather a consequence of real relations of production and the antagonistic interests arising from those relations. The working class is not defined in absolute terms of how much money they make, but in relational terms of their material interests being in conflict with those who own the means of production. One's class position is determined by class struggle. Arzola and Larraín's nominal definition of class therefore has a tacit political function: it obscures the relational aspect of class that generates the antagonistic interests underlying class locations.

What is especially of interest to Wright (2015), however, are those who are in between the workers and the capitalists: the middle class composed of small-business owners, careerists, professionals, and so on (104). What is the class location, for instance, of a manager who is simultaneously a wage-earner and oversees the labor of others? Of a small-business owner who has no or very few employees? Wright argues that they occupy *contradictory class locations* insofar as "they partake of both sides of" the conflicting interests of workers and capitalists. For instance, a small employer may have a lower income than a worker and "have specific immediate interests opposed to large capitalists when those large capitalists compete with them"; however, it is not the case that "they have any fundamental interests that are necessarily opposed" to those large capitalists (Wright 1985: 53). Indeed, they may even benefit from weakening the collective power of the working class. Class is defined by one's location within class relations, which in capitalism are defined by exploitation, and the middle class is defined by their contradictory location within those relations.

What is important with respect to the middle class, then, are *the political alliances* that they forge (Wright 1985: 124–125) and whether they side with workers or capitalists. What I am implying, in other words, is that a foundational question of the middle class during social explosion is of *political articulation* and not just material reality. Even Marx argued for the importance of political articulation in *The 18th Brumaire of Louis Bonaparte* (Cowling and Martin 2002). If the topic of this work of Marx is ostensibly a detailed political history of the 1848 uprisings in France and their aftermath, the book more theoretically is concerned with the representativity of various French political bodies and formations that emerged over the course of 1848–1851. For instance, Marx talks about the "social republic" pushed forth by the proletariat that was "drowned in [their] blood" in June 1848 (Marx 2002: 95); the "democratic republic" headed by the petit bourgeoisie but which "fizzle[d] out on 13 June 1849" (95); and the "parliamentary republic" (95) of the bourgeoisie proper that was undone by the rise of Louis Napoleon, who generated his base from the peasants and the "dregs, refuse and scum of all classes" (63). Later in this work Marx even develops a full calendar outlining the peculiar and particular social and political groupings and shifts that emerged with almost every coming month during the turbulent years of 1848–1851.

In other words, despite having a reputation for being a class determinist, Marx is highly sensitive in *The 18th Brumaire* to how political groupings are artificial constructions generated by uniting multiple social groups into a singular, coherent collective that can compete for institutional recognition within a given territory (Martin 2002). It is in this way that we can read the following oft-cited section of Marx's work:

> In so far as millions of families get a living under economic conditions of existence that divide their mode of life, their interests and their culture from those of other classes and counterpose them as enemies, they form a class. In so far as there is merely a local interconnection amongst peasant proprietors, the similarity of their interests produces no community, no national linkage and no political organisation, they do not form a class. They are therefore incapable of asserting their class interests in their own name, whether through a parliament or constitutional convention. They cannot represent themselves, they must be represented.
>
> (Marx 2002: 100–101)

Marx here notes that what is important is not just that certain groups share "economic conditions of existence that divide their mode of life," but additionally that they generate a sense of community through mutual interaction with one another. What is essential is not just material reality, but a political and social articulation that coheres a group or groups (Price 2002). Expanding this argument, one can say that *culture* plays a significant role in any revolution insofar as it is cultural identities, practices, artifacts, and values that generate a unity of national connections that can subsequently be expressed in a unity of political organization and interest. As Bob Jessop (2002) puts it, Marx here "is more concerned with the discursive limitations on the representation of class interests...than [he] is with the organisational forms in and through which they might be advanced" (182).[4]

What Marx is pointing to is what many analysts of Gramsci already note, "Classes cannot be defined *sociologically*, but precisely only insofar as they have and propagate a 'vision of the world' with which they fight the 'war of position' and the struggle for hegemony that traverses every society" (Liguori 2015b: 155). That is, to describe a 'class' is not only a clinical description of historical conditions of existence (class in itself), it is to call into existence a collective subject who can then consciously fight for material gains as a group (class for itself). This is precisely the point of Marx and Engels's *Communist Manifesto*: to call into being the proletariat as a coherent collective political being (Puchner 2005). Similarly, to describe a 'middle class' is simultaneously to call them into being as a political actor. More provocatively, the middle class (or any class for that matter) does not exist—each and every class is a conceptual invention that serves to unify a given grouping based on their location within relations of production (i.e. "unity of interests") and organized around shared "national linkage." Barozet and Espinoza's analysis of the Chilean situation implies that the middle class does not exist for itself and therefore cannot represent itself, meaning that the cultural task is to conceptually unify this group in a coherent manner so that it can represent itself in the State. In this way, class analysis serves to generate conceptual tools of unification for a given cultural-political grouping.

Under this theorization, Arzola and Larraín's description of the Chilean middle class only a few months before the social explosion served three purposes. First, to obscure the class relations underlying one's class position (i.e., they argue that one is middle class because of their income, not because of their contradictory class location). Second, to configure the Chilean middle class as expanding (i.e., they argue that the income of the "lower class," not the working class, is growing). Third, based on this expansion, to insist on the desirability of the actually existing neoliberal political-economic model in Chile. The ostensibly objective analysis of Arzola and Larraín in fact serves conservative political ends. Wright's theorization posits an alternative: the middle class is defined by being pulled in two different directions with regard to their class interests—i.e., income in itself is insignificant here, being more precisely an effect of the organization of class relations—meaning that the conceptual cohering of this group that enables their political expression is whether they side with workers, side with capitalists, or attempt to mark out their own intermediate position.

The question to ask of the social explosion, then, is what was the culture of the so-called middle class that was being generated during the later months of 2019 and the early months of 2020? Were middle-class cultural workers trying to reconfigure the hegemonic culture enabling the existing Chilean State, thereby working towards the inclusion of a new voice in the State that represents the middle class among the elite? Or, were they putting themselves into solidarity with Chile's leftovers? Additionally, in either case, did they see themselves as the new leaders of the novel political articulations that were emerging in the social explosion, or perhaps were they working towards novel horizontal relations among variated groupings that were being yoked together in the cultural crucible of mobilizations in the street? How did the middle class deal with their contradictory class location? In the following section, I discuss two middle-class responses to the social explosion.

The Middle-Class Intellectual

Aligning with the Leftovers

One reading of the social explosion is that those of the so-called lower-middle class sided with—or at the very least tolerated—the insurgency of

Chilean leftovers. This is demonstrated by the already stated fact that 57 percent of the Chilean population opposed any form of police force against "violent protestors." Chile seems to have repeated the same situation identified by Eamonn McCann (2018) with regard to Northern Irish Catholic perceptions of insurgent violence at the very beginning of what eventually became the Troubles,

> Commentators reported—and they may have been right—that only a minority of Catholics actively supported violence. Occasionally someone...would come into the middle of a riot, box the hooligans' ears and tell them to get the hell out of it and let people live in peace. But for all that, the hooligans were the sons and daughters of the area, and however much their activities may have been regretted or condemned there could be no question of any section of the people backing the army *against* them.

To rework McCann's argument from the context of the Chilean social explosion, there was without a doubt profound disagreements amongst those at protests with respect to barricades. For instance, I remember watching a hooded protestor attempting to uproot a street sign for a barricade who was then approached by another protestor who scolded them for this act. The two protestors maintained a heated discussion for about five minutes, with bystanders coming to the aid of one side or the other at certain times. Finally, the hooded protestor decided not to uproot that particular street sign. This was not an uncommon event. Nonetheless, I also have no doubt that the dissenting protestor would never side with the police against the hooded protestor. Recognizing such internal disagreements, it appears that the majority of mobilized citizens knew on which side of the barricade their allegiances lay.[5]

In other words, it appears that the social explosion represented the formation of a substantial cultural, social, and political body in which the leftovers of Chile had considerable agency but were not its unique members. Indeed, almost every artist discussed in this book holds a university degree and is by no means a 'pure' subaltern. The CAC is exemplary in this regard. The coordinator was by no means a subaltern organization, with some participants holding advanced degrees, teaching at universities, and having, to the contrast of the subaltern, "access to the lines of mobility within a society" (Spivak 2012: 209). Nonetheless, as was discussed in the previous chapter, their aim was the delivery of power directly to the people; they recognized and attempted to empower the agency of the leftovers, they did not try to speak for the mobilizations. In this way, the CAC is in large part testimony to the fact that the social explosion was not about greater inclusion within the Chilean representative system, but was evidence of the empowerment of a more radical discourse in which the leftovers of Chile, together with the lower-middle classes and other allies, had generated a novel social and political formation that challenged Chilean politics as such.

The CAC, however, was not unique in this regard. During the social explosion, a small Chilean press noted mostly for their limited distribution of works of poetry, *Al fragor*, released two editions of what they named *Malecón* [*Boardwalk*], a highly politicized broadsheet including poetry and images that reflected on the social explosion. I want to focus on one work in particular from the first issue of *Malecón*, "*Paraman*" ["Stop-Man/Paraman"], by Manuel Sanfuentes Vio, in which the author poetically represents a mythical folk hero of the social explosion: *pareman* (stop-man). An anonymous hooded protestor who used a stop-sign as a shield to protect his body against the violent advances of police forces, *pareman* was a symbolic embodiment of protestors' demand that the Chilean State "stop" abusing the subaltern. In this way, *pareman* was part of the emerging mythology of the social explosion that I described more fully in Chapter 5.

Sanfuentes was born on 20 April 1970 in Viña del Mar. He later attended the School of Architecture at the Pontifical Catholic University of Valparaíso in order to become a designer. This school is particularly known for how it relates architecture, design, and urbanism to the practice of poetry (Pendleton-Jullian 1996), a cultural practice embraced by Sanfuentes leading to him becoming a poet by the time he finished his undergraduate degree. More recent studies of this school's cultural practices, however, have noted how their poetry is frequently interested in putting into relation the elite literary culture of Latin America that has enabled patriarchal, capitalist, and colonial ruling classes across the continent with various subaltern classes. In the little interest Sanfuentes's work has generated in critical discussions, his work has been understood within this lens: someone who has inherited a particular elite poetic culture and placing that culture into dialogue with subaltern communities (Woods 2020b).[6]

His social explosion poem, "*Paraman*,"[7] repeats this general tendency, attempting to place an elite poetic discourse into dialogue with the popular cultural formations of the leftovers. I quote the poem here in full:

robusto del genio sin rostro,	[robust of the genius without a face,]
sus ojos debilitan el miedo,	[his eyes weaken fear,]
entre sus brazos,	[between his arms,]
el escudo de ilión	[Ilion's shield]
en su pecho desnudo,	[on his naked chest,]
descorazonado	[disheartened]
sangre deliberada,	[deliberate blood,]
el deseo intangible de su cuerpo	[the intangible desire of his body]
sin heridas,	[without wounds,]
la minucia de sus músculos,	[the minutiae of his muscles]

evadiendo las piedras del infierno	[evading the stones from hell]
y el raro aire de la paradoja	[the strange air of the paradox]
dividida la señal,	[divided the signal,]
para	[stops]
e inflama su heroísmo	[and inflames his heroism]
en la delicia extraordinaria	[in the extraordinary delight]
al margen del abandono,	[on the margin of abandon]
sus omóplatos descollan	[his shoulder blades stand out]
como una belleza desmarcada,	[like an unmarked beauty]
y sus miembros suponen	[and his members suppose]
antigua existencia	[ancient existence]
y de nuevo,	[and again,]
vana excitación del arquetipo,	[vain excitation of the archetype,]
posible coyuntura	[possible conjuncture]
que golpea la pulcritud del tránsito	[that hits the neatness of transit]
y su coronación	[and his coronation]

The narrative of Sanfuentes's "*Paraman*" can be summarized rather simply as the artful description of this folk figure of the social explosion in a flowery literary discourse followed by the "coronation" of that subaltern hero as the new 'king' of Chile. On the face of it, the underlying motivation of the poem is the recognition that the leftovers of Chile have been 'crowned' as the new rulers of the geopolitical space previously governed by the elites of the Chilean State.

Despite this narrative, Sanfuentes's poem cannot be said to be in alignment with the subaltern, if we understand alignment in the sense of basing one's discourse from within a shared socio-cultural paradigm. Instead, by clothing *pareman*'s body in a high-cultural nobility via the language of "heroism," "stones from hell," "Ilium's shield" (a Homeric reference), and so on, Sanfuentes's poem registers a disjunction between two such paradigms: the use of high-cultural mythical references from classical Greek culture *versus* the emerging popular mythology of the social explosion. This tension between high-cultural literary references and the popular myth of *pareman* is further exemplified in the collision between Sanfuentes's highly detailed corporal description that raises the protestor to the level of an ancient Greek mythical hero and the anonymity of the actual *pareman*. For not only is the actual *pareman* literally anonymous insofar as he is hooded, but his clothing is nondescript and mass-produced (non-brand sweatpants, Calvin Klein underwear, a black t-shirt with an unidentifiable graphic covering his face, and old white Nikes). In contrast to *pareman*'s existence as a mythical protestor decked in mass-produced commodities that surpass his defining unique characteristics—one more example of the subaltern appropriating and reworking the products of the neoliberal marketplace for their own purposes—Sanfuentes focuses on his particular distinguishing individual qualities.

Sanfuentes's Homeric references are particularly significant insofar as there is a long tradition in Latin America of using classical Greek and Roman references in order to glorify and appropriate subaltern resistance from within the socio-cultural paradigm of the ruling class. For instance, colonial-era chronicles frequently described Indigenous resistance in terms of Greek and Roman warriors in order to critique the injustices of the conquest while simultaneously legitimizing colonial rule. This was precisely the thesis of John Beverley (1993) almost three decades ago: celebrations of Indigenous decolonial resistance using Greek and Roman myth were still nonetheless colonial insofar as they centered the thinking and culture of European paradigms over and above Indigenous ones. If in Latin America, as Beverley argues, "State forms and functions are products of a centralization and/or monopolization of certain types of intellectual labor, among them the exercise of literacy and the production and dissemination of written discourse" (57), then poetic production has an imminently political function by valorizing certain types of written discourse over and above all others. By valorizing a Eurocentric writing paradigm populated by Greek and Roman myth, then, elite settler-colonial subjects legitimized their position as the ruling class insofar as they had privileged mastery over those cultural forms. As such, whether or not authors using Greco-Roman mythical figures in their poetry sympathize with the subaltern is insignificant: the simple insistence on Greek and Roman mythical references reinforces the hegemony of a poetic paradigm enabling the ruling class's political dominance.

Sanfuentes's poem, however, departs from this hegemonic elite use of poetic language and structure in the final two stanzas. After identifying the tension between the subaltern on "the margin of abandon" and the reinterpretation of this figure as "supposing ancient existence," Sanfuentes notes that this is "once again, [the] vain excitation of the archetype." Quite explicitly, he identifies the poetic conceit of including the subaltern in an already existing elite cultural discourse as "in vain"; the last two stanzas serve to undermine the very cultural project of the first four. Against recasting *pareman* in the language and poetic structure of the ruling class, Sanfuentes concludes by noting a "possible conjuncture that hits the neatness of transit and his coronation." I am suggesting, in other words, that against an immediate reading of the poem as the "coronation" of *pareman* as the new mythical leader of Chile, Sanfuentes is actively critiquing the poetic act of representationally doing such a coronation from within an elite cultural paradigm. The poetic act of crowning *pareman* within the cultural paradigms of the elite is shown to be merely a "vain excitation of the archetype."

Sanfuentes's poem thereby walks a very careful tightrope. Announcing the ascendancy to power of those struggling in the streets by describing the "coronation" of *pareman* using a language tied to classical nobility, he immediately registers and struggles with the fact that such a socio-cultural paradigm no longer serves its purpose because the very image and myth of *pareman* are testimony to that paradigm's delegitimation. In other words, "*Paraman*" is a poem of crisis attempting to recognize the agency, power, and culture of the leftovers but in so doing coming to the revelation that the representational tools at one's disposal are inadequate to such a task. In short, I am pointing to Sanfuentes's poem as evidence of a burgeoning attempt to create interclass forms of solidarity that recognize and struggle with questions of difference. Sanfuentes explicitly rejects the attempt to include *pareman* in the ruling class's representational configurations, instead exploring how those elite configurations need to be realigned in order to account for the new mythical figures emerging in the streets. He does not have an answer as to what this emerging socio-cultural paradigm will look like, but his poem represents a determined attempt to reconfigure lines of allegiance in order to mark the diffuse contours of a newly emerging, internally diverse collective. Sanfuentes's poem is a product of high-cultural poetic forms being put into horizontal dialogue with the cultural forms and discourses of the subaltern.

Politically, one might argue that Sanfuentes's work reflects the difficulty of the radical autonomous politics of the social explosion. He explicitly rejects the attempt to integrate the subaltern into the hegemonic cultural paradigm that enables the existing ruling class's domination—he is evidence of the middle class entering into solidarity with the subaltern—and thereby separates from State politics in order to nurture alternative spaces of collective discussion and organization. Nonetheless, his poem makes evident that it is still not entirely clear what the result of that dialogue will be. In other words, his poem functionally supports the act of the middle class abandoning the elite politics of the State in order to enter into those political forms like the *cabildo* that serve to generate contestatory political formations and decision-making processes, but, like the CAC, Sanfuentes offers no solutions—his poem is one of crisis, of looking towards reconfiguring political alignments and articulations based on the bottom-up interclass alliances that were emerging during the social explosion.

Raising Up the Leftovers

I close with a rather pessimistic view. Whereas Sanfuentes's poetry represents the possibility for the social explosion to be an insurgent moment led by and for the leftovers of Chile that then enters into dialogue with the middle classes and the elite—who accept the 'coronation' of the subaltern—another line of thought is quickly emerging that seeks to recenter the social explosion around the middle class. In this line of thinking, I want to argue, the social explosion represents the possibility to reconfigure the Chilean social landscape in a way that bolsters the stability of the middle class and opens up new lines of mobility for the 'leftovers' to enter into the middle class. In doing so, however, this thought still nevertheless privileges a Chilean middle-class identity over and against the insurgent collectivities that formed the leftovers of the social explosion: working-class women, Indigenous communities, those living in the "sacrifice zones" of Chile, and so on.

This middle-class vision is found in the various essays and articles published by Ariel Dorfman during the social explosion.[8] Dorfman is perhaps most well known for having been a cultural advisor of the Salvador Allende socialist administration (being one of the few to have escaped death at the hands of Pinochet), being exiled during the dictatorship, and having written the play, *Death and a Maiden* (1991), describing the lingering traumatic effects of the violence of the Pinochet regime. During the social explosion, he published a series of essays in *The New York Review of Books, The New York Times*, *The Nation*, and independently. I refer to Dorfman in this final section for two reasons. First, his work functionally—regardless of intent—appeals to middle-class integrationism. It is evidence of an emerging conservative force on the left that will neutralize the radical position of the subaltern, stealing what they have done in the streets to bolster the stability of the middle class. Second, to the contrary of many such integrationists who dismissed subaltern insurrectionism as a chaotic and destructive tendency of the '*lumpen*'—an often dismissive phrase that the CEP survey referred to earlier explicitly uses—Dorfman is seriously struggling with the tension between middle-class cultural values and the emerging subaltern voice that threatens that socio-cultural paradigm. That is, I do not wish to polemically critique Dorfman. Instead, I want to see his work as an opportunity to once again refocus on the agents of the social explosion: Chile's leftovers.

His essays published in *The New York Review of Books* and *The Nation* are perhaps most notable for how they grapple with recognizing the pain, difficulties, and struggles of the leftovers of Chile while simultaneously being suspicious of the destructive and destabilizing effects of the protests. Dorfman's (2020a) *New York Review of Books* piece, "Chile: Notes from a Revolt," is telling in this regard. The essay opens with a discussion of the statue of General Manuel Baquedano at Dignity Plaza. Prior to the social explosion, this Plaza was well-known in Santiago for being the dividing line between wealthier areas to the east and poorer areas to the west. Dorfman notes the potent symbolism of this general who faced west from the plaza,

> I realized at some point [in my youth] how symbolic it was that General Baquedano was facing the disadvantaged areas of Santiago, as if to resist the hordes that might someday be tempted to cross the line dividing the rich from those who were less fortunate.

Furthermore, this is not simply a class divide given that this division between the elite and the leftovers "has marked the history of this country ever since the Spanish conquistadors dislodged the original native inhabitants from their ancestral homes." As Dorfman continues, by choosing this plaza as a central protest site, protestors "shatter[ed], symbolically and spatially, the border between the two Chiles...a deliberately transgressive way of declaring that in order for a new country to be born, the old boundaries and myths need to be demolished." Dorfman argues that the social explosion is the eruption of subaltern collective organizing against the Chilean elite and, against many arguments limited to a critique of neoliberalism, connects the mobilizations' anti-capitalism to decolonial organizing of Indigenous communities.

Dorfman's (2020a) response is therefore one primarily of sympathy. Nonetheless, reflecting on how the discontent of the social explosion is a consequence of 30 years of post-dictatorship neoliberal, colonial, and patriarchal governance, he insists,

> it is imperative for Chile to work out a solution that is not individual but collective…If everyone in office or with power is suspect, who is to lead us out of the labyrinth? The popular uprising that has shaken Chile to its core has not, so far, provided sufficient answers.

Dorfman was consistent in this regard: responding to protestors who bluntly told him that "they did not intend to tone down their militancy," he admitted, "I was hesitant to raise my reservations about their tactics."[9] He would even go so far as to claim that the "movement was being hijacked by delinquents and narcotraffickers." In the end, Dorfman expresses worry that the "fury" of the activists

> may be on the verge of devouring them. Their anger may inspire them in their battles…[but] such rage is not the best counselor when it comes to making allies for the difficult negotiations required to ensure a transition to fuller democracy and bring the structural reform the country needs.

On its surface, Dorfman seems to be repeating the discourse of most liberal and leftist English news media outlets: the discontent of the leftovers is entirely legitimate, yet their "fury" and "rage" lacks any affirmative articulation. Yet to the contrast of these outlets—and the reason why I want to highlight Dorfman's position in this chapter—he remains "cautiously optimistic" (Dorfman 2020a) with regard to the potential for the social explosion to generate its own resolutions to the problems that had been laid out in the streets during 2019–2020. Dorfman mirrored these liberal outlets' skepticism about the protestors' militancy and anarchism, but remained a sympathetic voice firmly on the side of those lighting barricades in the streets (perhaps one more of those who would have responded to a survey that they do not support looting and barricades but opposed any police force used against "violent protestors").

Dorfman's writing during this period was highly self-conscious that perhaps, as he put it in that same *New York Review of Books* piece, "it may be that I am missing the point" (Dorfman 2020a). Indeed, it may be rather confusing for the readers of this book and Dorfman's essays to note that we largely examine the same *corpus* of materials—speaking with protestors, tracking the news, and so on—but have arrived at starkly differing conclusions. He explicitly celebrates, just as I have, that during the social explosion "Chile [experienced] an extraordinary outburst of creativity" (Dorfman 2020a): the rediscovery of Víctor Jara, LASTESIS's "A Rapist in Your Path," the murals across Chile, the myth of *negro matapacos*, and so on. Dorfman identifies and celebrates many of the same cultural products discussed in this book. Why, then, have we arrived at what appear to be contradictory conclusions, with Dorfman doubting that the social explosion "provided sufficient answers" and myself insisting that the social explosion was offering a novel affirmative autonomous mode of coordinating social relations?

An answer to this question might be found in an essay, "Confronting the Pandemic in a Time of Revolt: Voices from Chile," written by Dorfman (2020d) for *The Nation* in April 2020, after the end of the social explosion as a result of the institution of quarantining measures in response to the COVID-19 pandemic. His essay attempts to outline a potential cultural foundation for a renovated post-social-explosion Chilean society through a comparative analysis of two Chilean novels: *Martín Rivas* (1862) by Alberto Blest and *Patas de Perro* [*Feet of a Dog*] (1965) by Carlos Droguett. As Dorfman (2020d) summarizes, Blest's novel presents the idea of a bourgeois culture "bring[ing] civilization to the least educated classes of society." *Martín Rivas*, Dorfman concludes, embodies the middle-class values of meritocracy and upward class mobility that are the cultural keystones of a "free-market, laissez-faire worldview." Dorfman admits that throughout his life he has been highly skeptical of the novel insofar as Chile is in fact marked by brutal economic and social inequalities, especially in regard to education, health care, and the pension system. In this reading that he maintained during most of his life, *Martín Rivas* serves as ideological support for the Chilean ruling classes.

Against this celebratory vision of a culture that enables the current elitist politics of Chile, Dorfman (2020d), similar to my own analysis, identifies various "literary incursions expos[ing] a submerged country that did not believe that the road to liberation depended on imitating the conventional Martín Rivas archetype." He further argues that "the one who best exemplifies a fierce and unbending rejection of [Blest's] vision of what Chile should be is Carlos Droguett," most powerfully in his novel, *Patas de perro*, about a leftover boy named Bobi living Santiago's peripheral neighborhoods who is born with the feet of a dog—a metaphorical embodiment of how he is literally treated like a dog within Chilean society. In Dorfman's analysis,

> Refusing to submit to society's way of dealing with him (he won't join a circus, will not put himself on display, will not market his divergence from the norm, will escape from an insane asylum where his murder is being planned), Bobi represents everything that official Chile has suppressed.
>
> (Dorfman 2020d)

In our terminology, Bobi is the embodiment of the leftovers of Chile, an image created by Droguett in 1965 that still serves to understand the post-millennial cultural dynamics of Chilean power relations. Dorfman (2020d) even goes so far as to contend that one might understand the social explosion as "thousands of inadvertent emulators of Bobi...rising up and demanding recognition, that their countercultural voices be appreciated and their strangeness and desires be given legitimacy and respect." If *Martín Rivas* represents the values of bourgeois capitalist respectability and upward class mobility, Bobi represents the leftovers of that political model who in late 2019 would rise up in defiance.

Dorfman (2020d) imagined the resolution of the social explosion as finding a balance between Rivas and Bobi. On the one hand, without the "radical interrogation of established reality and societal norms" provoked by the insurrectionary actions of the "disciples" of Bobi, "there is no likelihood of significant change." On the other hand, such "anarchic insurrection against all forms of authority does not provide a blueprint for how, in concrete political terms, such real change might be implemented." Against the anarchism of the Bobis of Chile, it is necessary, Dorfman argues, to include "followers of decent, hard-working, liberal Martín Rivas" in order to form a "long-lasting response to the challenges posed by the protests."

If Dorfman (2020d) was "uncertain" during the social explosion whether such a coalition could be formed, he argues optimistically that perhaps the COVID-19 pandemic would force all social actors to form "some sort of social pact," concluding that this public health crisis may have "ended up creating the conditions for a marriage between Martín Rivas, with his moderate bourgeois dreams, and Bobi, with his implacable dog legs." By demobilizing the leftovers of Chile, Dorfman seems to conclude, a level-headed conversation between Rivas and Bobi may provide a novel avenue for a future social pact for Chile that offers a way out of the conflict of the social explosion.

Dorfman's reading of Droguett, however, seems to overlook two elements of the novel. First, in the middle of the novel, the Communist Party approaches Bobi in order to encourage him to become a member and their cultural symbol.[10] As one character of the novel summarizes, the party wants to use Bobi

> as if he were a flag or testimony. They [the communists] weren't bad, they were violent, with the violence accumulated of misery, of abandon, of the shamelessness enthroned [*desvergüenza entronizada*] in the city since time immemorial, the communists industrialized that, coldly administered it.
>
> (Droguett 1965: 176)

In effect, the communists were "scientifically, technically exploiting human suffering, [they] aren't bad, [they] aren't good, [they're] technicians" (176), and for that reason they sought to have Bobi "loaned" (176) since "Bobi is much more eloquent than them, than their grand speakers, than their lofty poets, than their dark and disheveled novelists: Bobi is the best poem" (177).

Droguett's novel speaks explicitly against having Bobi being inserted in an already existing politics that gives affirmative form to the suffering experienced on a human level by the leftovers. Droguett's critique is not just of the Communist Party in particular, but of a general political disposition that sees the subaltern as raw information to be scientifically exploited for the technical construction of a new political formation. To return to Dorfman's own language, Droguett explicitly rejects the possibility of putting Bobi into dialogue with Martín Rivas in order to transform Bobi's "anarchic insurrection" into "a blueprint for how, in concrete political terms, such real change might be implemented." Droguett refuses to allow Bobi's suffering and insurrection to be "industrialized" and "coldly administered."

Secondly, and perhaps more significantly, Droguett hints at an affirmative politics emerging directly from Bobi. Late in the novel, a "multitude" (267) gathers in the street led by Bobi. The list of who is in the streets following Bobi is a long enumeration of the leftovers of Chile during the twentieth century:

> they came from far away...from the first massacres of workers in Iquique, in Valparaíso, in Lonquimay...shouts, lively, long live the working class, long live the copper and saltpeter miners, long live the communist party, down with the oligarchy, down with reaction, kill the rich, kill the bankers, kill the industrialists, long live the worker in their workshop, long live the rancher in the depths of the desert, long live the tuberculosis patient in the depths of their hospital bed...children were walking alongside crying, dogs that were going along barking dogs dogs dogs and then I saw them, the blind man Horacio and Bobi.
>
> (263–264)

Despite the mention of the Communist Party in this initial march discourse ("long live the communist party"), that political allegiance would quickly disappear in the insurrection, "walking without hurry, without fleeing from the many years before,...without voices that proclaimed their abandon, without discourses that highlighted their misery, without posters, phrases, slogans, microphones, speakers, deputies" (266). Here, in the pages of *Patas de perro*, we see in 1965 a prefigured image of the Chilean social explosion. This list of the subaltern who had abandoned the techno-scientific logic of the Communist Party (and all party politics for that matter, "without voices that proclaimed their abandon, without discourses that highlighted their misery, without posters, phrases, slogans, microphones, speakers, deputies") for an autonomous multiplicitous insurrectionary discourse was what the social explosion would eventually become.

This alternative politics based on a set of alternative insurrectionary socio-cultural relations emerging directly from leftovers like Bobi, what the narrator of *Patas de perro* calls "canine civilization" (243), is what seems to be missed in Dorfman's analysis. The foundations of the socio-cultural revolution he envisions in his essay for *The Nation* is primarily governed by integrating the reality of the leftovers embodied in the figure of Bobi into the already existing literary canon of Chile—he names over a dozen authors who would be included in a typical seminar on twentieth-century Chilean literature including (listed in order of appearance) Pablo Neruda, Gabriela Mistral, Volodia Teitelboim, María Luisa Bombal, Pía Barros, Nicanor Parra, José Donoso, Antonio Skármeta, Manuel Rojas, Diamela Eltit, and Raúl Zurita. Dorfman wants to maintain the values of the literary world in which he received his formation, but now seeks to integrate the subaltern into that world. The blueprint for the new post-social-explosion Chilean society will be based on the values of that canon, but it must design using the materials at hand: the Bobis of Chile. Dorfman functionally resolves the contradictory class location of the middle class by cohering that social grouping around a set of cultural values, and then seeking to integrate the leftovers into that culture.

Dorfman seems to miss that the subaltern during the social explosion was attempting to develop an autonomous politics with a novel reconfiguration of social relations. The *cabildos*, the CAC delivering water-society relations directly to the community, Danny Reveco imagining the barricade as a means to illuminate the autonomous communal relations being developed behind the front line (the *ollas comunes*, Mapuche communality, the first-aid teams, and so on), Lemebel's public space of public transport in the anal city, and so on were already providing a novel blueprint for a renewed Chilean society. Dorfman may therefore be understood to be driving a compromise between the counter-revolution—the elite politicians of Chile attempting to repress the social explosion as pure violence and their aspirational middle-class allies—and the radical politics of the protestors by attempting to integrate the protestors' material reality into the framework of the dominant socio-cultural foundations of the Chilean landscape. If Sanfuentes attempted to open a dialogue between the cultural foundations of the middle class and the leftovers—the basis of a potential bottom-up coalition—Dorfman imagines the solution to the social explosion as the integration of the leftovers into the middle class. Two distinct resolutions to the contradictory class location of the middle class.

Conclusion

The so-called middle class has remained largely unrepresented in neoliberal Chilean politics, making this social collective, as Barozet and Espinoza argue, a potentially destabilizing force in the Chilean socio-political landscape. One might understand the social explosion as the middle class, that social body with a *contradictory class location*, siding with the leftovers of Chile to challenge an elitist neoliberal governance structure in which they had no representation. More precisely, if, as Victor Hugo (1992) eloquently summarizes in *Les Misérables*, "an insurrection breaking out is an idea passing its examination before the people" (1071), the social explosion might be conceptualized as the social ideas of the leftovers of Chile "passing its examination" before the so-called middle class. What remains to be seen is not only whether this idea will be suppressed by the Chilean elite, but how the middle class decides to interact in the long run with this idea passing before its eyes.

This chapter has principally argued that there was no consensus with regard to middle-class responses to the politics of the leftovers during the social explosion, a reflection of the unstable identity of this class as discussed by Barozet and Espinoza. On the one hand, visions like those of Manuel Sanfuentes emphasize how those who had received their cultural formation from within 'high culture' were attempting to put themselves into direct relation with the socio-cultural forms and cultural practices developed by the leftovers in the streets during the social explosion. Rather than integrating the subaltern into the cultural forms of the Chilean elite (e.g., Greco-Roman myth), Sanfuentes put that latter culture into conversation with the popular culture of the subaltern (e.g., *pareman*). On the other hand, sympathetic voices like Ariel Dorfman saw the grievances of the leftovers as legitimate, but theorized that they needed the structuring power of the middle- and upper-class socio-cultural forms that had been developed during the nineteenth and twentieth centuries, in the process ignoring that the subaltern were developing their own cultural forms that enabled a different mode of politics.

Much of this book has been centered around noting the central conflict between the elite and the leftovers in Chile as expressed during the social explosion. I have argued that coherent subaltern socio-cultural foundations—though with their own internal tensions like those between reconfiguring the globalized neoliberal marketplace from the bottom up versus the resurgence of a grassroots nationality—challenged the dominance of elite socio-political figures, ideas, and governance structures. If, as Marx and Engels (1974) famously argue in *The German Ideology*, "The ideas of the ruling class are in every epoch the ruling ideas, i.e. the class which is the ruling *material* force of society, is at the same time its ruling *intellectual* force" (64), then the social explosion is an instance in which Chilean leftovers were challenging those ideas with their own, challenging the ruling class as the "ruling intellectual force." What remained largely outside of this discussion were those who remained in between, so to speak: the middle class with their contradictory class location. Whether the political articulation that will emerge from the social explosion is one in which the middle class (especially the so-called lower-middle class) aligns with the leftovers or aligns with the elite in a bid for upward social mobility was not answered in the limited space of the five months between October 2019 and March 2020.

Notes

1 For the basic outline of the Pink Tide (as well as its supposed 'ebb') see Chodor (2015); North and Clark (2018), and Gonzalez (2019). I am implicitly following John Beverley's (2011) argument about the Pink Tide that it represented the subaltern "becoming the state," thereby requiring a total transformation of State apparatuses, "The challenge that confronts the [pink tide] if it is to move forward rather than recede is to generate, first, the idea and, second, the institutional forms of a different state, a state that would, under the conditions of globalization, embody and express the egalitarian, democratic, multicultural, and multiethnic character of the 'people': a people-state, or a state *of* the people" (125). I differ from Beverley insofar as the social explosion was proposing what he may call an "ultraleftist" (123) position: an alternative and autonomous mode of organizing social relations outside of the State. In this way, I am following Macarena Gomez-Barris's (2018) call to push us "beyond the pink tide" and outside State-based politics to see other possibilities for coordinating social relations.

2 This critique of the concept of the Chilean middle class is done much more profoundly by Fundación Sol (Durán and Kremerman 2017, 2019, 2020; González 2020; Sáez 2019). Indeed, Marco Kremerman was warning of the instability of the concept of the "middle class" already in 2004. Their work engages methodological techniques that are, quite simply, beyond my own capacities. Readers interested in this discussion are highly recommended to visit their work.

3 Emmanuelle Barozet in 2017 wrote a series of five articles (2017a, 2017b, 2017c, 2017d, 2017e) on the middle class and on how new political parties and coalitions like *Frente Amplio* (see Chapter 1) might potentially represent them. Her work on the problems of defining the "middle class" and their representation in the Chilean State is at the heart of my discussion in this chapter.

4 As is likely obvious for those who are familiar with the work, this reading of Marx is *highly* indebted to Spivak's (1999) own reading of *The 18th Brumaire*. I don't cite her in individual phrases since this entire discussion is dependent upon a citation of her work.

5 I am once again siding with Gayatri Spivak (2003) here: social science analysis struggles with such questions of deep, theoretical reflection on the part of participants. A survey asking if you support a barricade cannot tell you why or why not, what 'support' means in this case, if that support is conditional, if opposition to the barricade signifies opposition to those lighting the barricades, whether your lack of support for a barricade still nonetheless acknowledges its necessity, and so on. As has been a consistent refrain throughout this book, the social explosion demonstrates the need to take seriously the theoretical, cultural, and epistemological frameworks of the Chilean leftovers and not to treat them as 'case studies' and 'native informants' to be contained within the figures of empirical surveys.

6 This is *an* element of Sanfuentes's work but by no means the only or even the principal one. For instance, his poetic work, *Noli me tangere*, published in the midst of the social explosion (though written before), is a work of love poetry.

7 There is a play on words here. Although referencing "pareman," Sanfuentes intentionally spells the name, "paraman," where 'para' is used in the sense of the prefix meaning beside or closely related to (paramilitary, paralegal, etc.). In the title, Sanfuentes refers to the tension between actuality (*pare*man, the real person in the street) and representation (paraman, the representation beside or closely related to the actual person). He is carrying *pare*man into a nearby para-space.

8 In addition to the two essays closely analyzed in this section, see also Dorfman (2020b, 2020c, 2020e).

9 Dorfman would subsequently say that he was worried that he had "forfeited that right [to critique the protestors] when I left Chile." Such an unjust critique of Dorfman (as well as other exiles), I insist, would be symptomatic of the nationalism critiqued in Chapter 5 and the conclusion.

10 There is a relative paucity of research on this work, with discussions of the novel usually being a mere piece embedded in more general discussions. Four exceptions consulted while developing my own reading of Droguett are Rocío Rodríguez Ferrer (2011), Marcelo Navarro (2017), Francisco Serratos (2019), and Gloria Favi (2014). Favi's work was particularly helpful.

Conclusion

On (Re)Constitution

The thesis of this book is rather simple: the Chilean social explosion in the last months of 2019 and early months of 2020 marked an uprising of the nation's leftovers as they claimed their presence in a Chilean socio-political landscape that was designed to deny them any institutionally validated agency. Their various interdependent collectivities ordered around collective memory, values like dignity, and the claiming of public spaces like public transport challenged the dominance of neoliberal, patriarchal, and settler-colonial governance while offering new autonomous modes of coordinating social relations. In contrast to many readings that see the social explosion as an eruption of discontent that subsequently had to be organized into a blueprint for social relations—a blueprint that would eventually be embodied in the debates of writing a new constitution—the social explosion was already offering nascent novel cultural formations.

The central question asked of us participating in the Chilean social explosion was how to autonomously coordinate social relations in a horizontalist manner that annihilated the heteropatriarchal, neoliberal, and settler colonial Chilean State. As such, the task of the social explosion was to imagine a feminist, cooperativist, and decolonial collectivization of Chile's leftovers. In short, we had to respond to the following question: *How can we live together in a non-hierarchical way that responds to feminist, decolonial, environmentalist, and anti-capitalist demands for dignity?* There were, of course, tensions and contradictions within the imaginari(es) of the social explosion, and much of this book is dedicated to highlighting them. That said, these modes of collectivization and autonomous organization were all organized around responding to this same problematic of envisioning a mode of collectivization that recognized difference and the interlocking threads of multiple social struggles. LASTESIS, Cheril Linett, the Catrileo+Carrión community, Danny Reveco, the CAC, the Water Assembly, the evasion movement, and Manuel Sanfuentes were all functionally asking the same question: What does a post-patriarchal, post-hegemonic, post-State, post-colonial, post-neoliberal world constituted by interdependent autonomous collectivities look like?

DOI: 10.4324/9781003224594-8

That the social explosion has been accused of lacking adequate answers to this problematic (see Chapters 1 and 6) is therefore rather curious. For instance, the Paris Commune of 1871 was similarly, "a working laboratory of political inventions, improvised on the spot or hobbled together out of past scenarios and phrases, reconfigured as need be, and fed by desires awakened in the popular reunions" (Ross 2015: 11), yet the Commune is not critiqued to the same extent as the Chilean social explosion with regard to the failure to imagine a fully fleshed out concrete political system. Yes, the social explosion like the Paris Commune had not yet worked out in detail an alternative political system—and I will critique this limitation here in the conclusion—but it was more properly the collective effort to reconstitute our political imaginaries and to imagine new possibilities for living in common in a more egalitarian manner beyond the structural restrictions imposed by the neoliberal, patriarchal, and settler-colonial State. It is therefore unsurprising that no clear resolution was immediately available given that the social explosion was the previously unforeseen and never-before-experienced divine opening in which to imagine how to live together in those brief moments in 2019–2020 when the law had been ephemerally suspended behind the barricade.

This problematic was under debate when the social explosion was put to its premature end in March 2020 with the implementation of quarantining measures to fight the COVID-19 pandemic. Although resurgences of social explosion discontent would occur throughout 2020—most notably, in July 2020 social mobilizations successfully demanded the return of privatized pension funds so that citizens might use that money to survive during the extended economic recession caused by the pandemic—the spread of COVID-19 proved to be a *deus ex machina* functionally demobilizing Chilean society. The tensions and contradictions of the social explosion were not unresolved because they were unresolvable; they were unresolved because their resolution through discussion and struggle in the streets was cut short by external forces.

As I write this conclusion in August 2021, many are currently looking towards discussions about the new constitution as the potential resolution to the unrest of the social explosion. On 25 October 2020, a national plebiscite was held determining that Chile would write a new constitution over the next two years, after which the Chilean population would vote again to see whether they preferred this new constitution or the constitution already in place from 1980. Many hope that a new Chilean social contract will emerge with this new constitution that responds to the demands of the leftovers.

When this new constitutional process was offered by politicians in November 2019, many activists I knew heavily critiqued it, saying that it was 'cooking up' a reactionary response that would serve to maintain the privileged positions of those in power. This constitutional process, they argued, was a deception that gave the image of acquiescing to the demands of those in the street, but which actually ripped agency out of the hands of the leftovers and placed it safely once again into the hands of politicians. I was initially skeptical of this view. It seems, however, that they were not without reason. The constitutional convention was organized in such a way that it functionally guaranteed that many of the politicians who the social explosion had been ruthlessly critiquing would be the ones who would write the new constitution. Moreover, there are no guarantees in this new writing process that the advances and work done by the *cabildos* across Chile would be taken into account. The work by groups like CAC to insist on the delivery of power directly to the people was being torn asunder by this constitutional process. The cancellation of the "Water Action" by the COVID-19 pandemic therefore serves as a prescient metaphor for the social explosion: with communities attempting to seize the power of self-determination, a public health catastrophe interrupted this process and demobilized this grassroots political and cultural rebellion.

This book therefore concludes on a note of cautious pessimism (to the contrary of Dorfman's cautious optimism). The current unfolding of the constitutional process hints that many of the radical ideas of Chile's leftovers during the social explosion will be left in the dust. Many of the demands by Chile's leftovers are likely to be forgotten in the emerging narrative of insurrection, governmental response (plebiscite), the writing of a new constitution, and the possible re-constitution of Chilean society (should the new constitution be accepted by the Chilean populace). The bursting forth of subaltern collectivizations will be eclipsed, once again, by debates in government offices far away from the struggles that had occurred in the streets.

Post-social Explosion, Migration, and Border Closure

This conclusion is apparently contradicted by a simple fact: the elections of constitution writers in May 2021 witnessed the massive support of independents who had no ties to political parties and many of whom had initially emerged as political voices as a result of their participation in the streets during the social explosion. One example of this non-party political organizing was the formation in 2020 of the "List of the People," a coalition of various independent candidates, many of whom became known as a result of their contribution to the social explosion, who campaigned together on little to no funds, and whose main support in their bid to become constitutional writers was grassroots mutual solidarity networks. They were initially successful, with 25 of the 155 convention writers being from the List of the People (in addition to another 30 unassociated independents).

The eminent goal of the List of the People as of August 2021 is to organize a multiplicitous coalition that does not unify as a political party. As they state explicitly on their website, "Because we are not [the political] parties, nor do we want to be one…each candidate will be chosen in a Grand People's Primary, in which all can present themselves fulfilling certain minimum requirements." Nonetheless, it is unclear what structurally differentiates the List of the People from a political party. They do not have a list of policy positions, but they do have a "Declaration of Principles" that each candidate must sign; they do not have a party hierarchy and leadership, but they do have a select list of candidates and accept the hierarchical reality of the State; they argue for a "horizontal" "space of collective work," but they do not demonstrate how such horizontality is maintained when there are specific and particular voices that are elected to the constitutional convention. In short, they ran into the same problem as Occupy insofar as they were pushing towards a new way of doing politics, but it was not clear what distinguished them from a "nascent political party" (Dean 2012: 60; Green 2015). It appears that the List of the People is trying to circle the square: how to destroy political parties in a political system that structurally—regardless of intent—generates such party forms. They are taking the multiplicity, horizontality, and bottom-up character of the social explosion and trying to make it work from within a hierarchical State structure.

This is why Chapter 4 was critical (perhaps overly critical) of LASTESIS, *La Yeguada Latinoamericana*, and the Catrileo+Carrión community. The initial hypothesis of that chapter was that these were particularly compelling articulations of the social-explosion imaginary to be celebrated—indeed, to this day my alignment with the social explosion is based on continuing support of these projects—but were individual threads of the movement that were being dynamically and actively woven together with other threads in the streets. Each thread of the social explosion was being supplemented by other voices, practices, and perspectives, meaning that their individual limitations were insignificant in relation to the overarching tapestry of the mobilizations. For instance, I did not initially plan on discussing how Linett did not fully integrate the intellectual contributions of some Black feminists to trans-species subjectivization and collectivization, because I saw Black women claiming space in the streets.[1] And I did not discuss in Chapter 1 how Reveco's representation of the social explosion in the tradition of street art did not employ, for example, the Quechua and Aymara visual culture dating back to Guaman Poma de Ayala (Adorno 2000) which still informs decolonial thought like that of Silvia Rivera Cusicanqui[2] (2018), because I knew Indigenous Youth of Valparaíso were insisting on Aymara re-existence. With dozens of assemblies, marches, concerts, performances, exhibitions, community meals, and so on occurring daily in Valparaíso alone—not to mention the rest of the country—the limits of one voice seemed rather insignificant. My hypothesis, which I still maintain, is that should the social explosion have been able to run its course, the detailed form of this tapestry would have been autonomously worked out in interventions, assemblies, *cabildos*, marches, murals, graffiti, occupations of public spaces, and so on. In the end, these autonomist threads may have lost out to the grassroots nationalism examined in Chapter 5; however, I did not see the lack of a perfected and refined vision of collectivization as a severe obstacle because that collectivization was being actively and autonomously developed.

With the onset of the COVID-19 pandemic, however, the social explosion took a different turn: because there was as of yet no clear understanding of what autonomous, multiplicitous collectivity was actually being offered, many were quick to accept and revise the already existing political structure at hand under a public-health emergency. COVID-19 guaranteed that nationalism won out over autonomous collectivization. More precisely, the failure to fully work out what co-existence would be after 'Chile's over' meant that under a public-health emergency many reverted to a fully fleshed out project while still trying to maintain the social-explosion's political-cultural foundations. The emergence of the List of the People is not evidence of the success of the social explosion, it is evidence of the social explosion being cut short, a symptom of the contradictory attempt to encourage multiplicity, horizontality, and decentralization while maintaining the existence of the State. Whether the List of the People is an enduring political force or a flash in the pan (and given the multiple scandals rocking the coalition in August 2021, the latter seems to be much more probable) is irrelevant to my argument: their existence is based on a contradiction.

This thesis is demonstrated by looking at an extremely common demand by many in Chile during the first year and a half of the COVID-19 pandemic: the closure of national borders to prevent the arrival of virus variants. For instance, a 30 June 2021 survey found that 93 percent of respondents supported the total closure of national borders (El Mostrador 2021). Moreover, the Chilean College of Doctors [*Colegio Médico de Chile*] (2021) offered a counter-plan to the Chilean government's response to the pandemic that advocated a total closure of national borders and that was highly popular among those on the left. The response by many in Chile during the COVID-19 pandemic was not, 'Chile's over,' but rather called for the exercise of State sovereignty by reinforcing strict control over movement into and out of the national territory. Regardless of the critiques of individual policies within the State system, what was frequently sought during the COVID-19 pandemic was to increase the power of the national Chilean State.

The justification of this reinforcement of State power by many who less than two years earlier had been critiquing the State form itself was justified largely based on the perception of the purpose of international travel: leisure and vacations for the wealthy. This perception is not unjustified. As discussed in Chapters 1 and 5, neoliberalism's undermining of working-class national solidarity via the multinationalization of business enterprises made globalization as such appear as an elite endeavor. As Don Kalb (2012) argues, contemporary globalization is largely driven by neoliberal capital's undermining of national sovereignty in order to open labor to greater exploitation. In this way, international mobility becomes a symbol of how globalization benefits the elite but places the national working class in danger. Closing borders became a means for certain leftovers to affirm their presence, to demand their right to life in the face of an elite internationalization that saw their lives as disposable.

Such a position, however, ignores the population on whom such a State policy would have the greatest effect: working-class migrants. Working-class migrants, especially undocumented migrants, greatly suffered in Chile during the pandemic with journalists reporting an increase in xenophobia as well as accusations that migrants were responsible for the arrival of the virus (Hererra 2021). Perhaps most notoriously, there was a *cacerolazo* in Iquique in September 2020 against the arrival of undocumented migrants to the city who were blamed for the rise in coronavirus cases (CNNChile 2020). In fact, even the regional Medical College of Iquique partially blamed the continuation of the pandemic on undocumented migrants,

> The lack of rigorous control on our border with Bolivia is making [the arrival of undocumented migrants] a fact that is becoming a custom. Each time that people illegally enter our population of Tarapacá [a city on the border with Bolivia] there runs a health risk...The entrance of new persons to the region increases the possibility that the virus expands and generates new outbreaks.
>
> (Colegio Médico Iquique 2020)

Regardless of the public health benefits of closing borders and regardless of the College's insistence on giving vaccines to all migrants (independent of their documentation status), it is hard not to read this communication as nationalist xenophobia. This heightened xenophobia should be largely unsurprising given the Chilean government's increasingly anti-immigrant policies in the years preceding the pandemic: 45 percent of all exportations between 2010 and 2020 occurred in the last two years (Hererra 2021), and the government passed a new migration law that sought to restrict migrants' capacity to enter Chile, one that will likely lead to greater precarity in migrants' lives (Thayer 2021).

The Chilean left is ostensibly far removed from this discourse, explicitly opposing xenophobia, increased deportations, and the new migration law. Nonetheless, migratory justice was absent in their discussions of border closures. Even beyond the Iquique regional office's declaration, the Chilean College of Doctors counter-plan, for instance, never mentions migrants once, despite the College's demands for the total closure of borders, nor does it offer to reach out to migrant social organizations in the future. Regardless of their ostensible opposition to explicit xenophobia, much of the Chilean left during the pandemic was enabling right-wing Chilean xenophobia by invisibilizing migrant struggles. More frankly, there seems to be a general ignorance of migrants' conditions of existence as not only those who suffer a certain form of discrimination and not only those who "exist because there is a border"; instead, "borders exist because, from the point of view of the State regime, it is necessary to maintain the migrant person under control and hypervigilance in order to avoid their mobility since it represents a problem" (Handerson 2020: 32).

More precisely, this element of the Chilean left seemed to ignore a basic reality: the closure of borders did not serve to protect the working class in general, it served to protect the Chilean national working class in particular at the cost of the migrant working class. To understand such an idea, it is necessary to understand the general theory of the relationship between capitalism and migration. These theories usually return to Marx's theorization of "surplus population," wherein he argues that, in addition to being necessary to immediately fill certain emerging labor roles on demand, a reserve army of labor is instrumentalized to put "downward pressure on wages and stym[y] political organization of the 'normal' laboring classes" (Rajaram 2018: 630). National borders aid in this endeavor, as capital under such a multinational system is able to construct *nationalized* and *racialized* reserve armies to whom labor can be outsourced or who can be called upon to migrate to the metropole (Farris 2019). As Reece Jones (2016) puts it, "Boundaries create discontinuities that can be exploited, and corporations use the multiple labor pools to increase profits" (132).

As Pastora Filigrana (2020) outlines through an analysis of Moroccan agricultural workers immigrating to Spain, the strengthening of borders receives support from both capital and the national working class but for two separate reasons. Whereas workers seek to reduce capital's access to a reserve labor army and thereby to increase the national working classes' collective power, capital is much better aware of what will happen: migration will continue in a clandestine form meaning that migrants will now be in a much more legally and economically precarious position and therefore more exploitable. Strengthened borders effectively create a highly precarious labor force that is available as a hyper-exploitable surplus population.

This position became clear in Chile in July 2021 when the Ministry of Agriculture began pushing for the "secure ingress" of migrants in order to work on farms due to a labor shortage (EMOL 2021). The likely consequence of such hypothetical policy would be the creation of a precarious migrant labor force whose presence in Chile is dependent on accepting the terms and conditions of their employers since all other migration options have been closed.[3] The closure of borders may be an inconvenience for many of the Chilean elite, but working-class migrants will ultimately pay the price for this policy, being subject to greater control by the State and by their employers who are now both fully legitimized to treat migrants as a disposable labor force insofar as a xenophobic right explicitly supports such treatment and the left has largely invisibilized migrant lives.

The obvious critique of this argument is that protecting borders during the pandemic was done for public-health reasons, not for economic ones. Ignoring the explicit xenophobia of the Iquique regional office of the College of Doctors that betrays any such clean distinction, many in Chile, including the national College of Doctors (2021: 4), frequently pointed at the successes of New Zealand's 2020–2021 responses to the pandemic and the importance of the closure of borders in that response. Yet it is becoming clearer in early

2021 that the New Zealand Labour Party may attempt to use that power to push through immigration reform that will drastically reduce the number of immigrants allowed in the country, a reform that they have been pushing since 2017 (McMillan and Gibbons 2020). Indeed, the closure of borders is enabled by an economic populism that targets specifically "low-skilled workers," meaning that immigration reform seeks to permit the entrance of only those in "the mega-rich category" (McClure 2021; McMillan and Gibbons 2020). In a July 2021 speech, the New Zealand tourism minister, Stuart Nash, went so far as to bluntly state that COVID-19 "presents once-in-a-generation opportunity to change…the way we manage immigration" (SCOOP 2021). As he would put it elsewhere, "Let me be clear. The government is looking to shift the balance away from low-skilled work, towards attracting high-skilled migrants and addressing genuine skills shortages" (McClure 2021). It is unclear how this should be read other than as xenophobic and classist ideology opportunistically taking advantage of global catastrophe. By using the pandemic to close borders, the New Zealand Labour Party functionally resolved a series of political dilemmas that had hounded them since the 2017 election: (1) appease the nationalist constituency of the New Zealand First party with whom the Labour Party formed a coalition in 2017 (McMillan and Gibbons 2020), (2) find a scapegoat for its political failures to improve housing and infrastructure by blaming "pressure…on housing and infrastructure" on "our reliance on migrant labour—particularly temporary migrant labour" (McClure 2021), and (3) avoid the legitimate critiques of xenophobia from the left by using State powers acquired for public health reasons.

New Zealand is not alone. The pandemic has permitted many politicians to obtain "extraordinary powers in order to take measures that affect migrants, *justified for reasons of public health and the protection of their co-nationals*" (Castro Neira 2020). This is a growing common conclusion with regard to State-based reactions to the COVID-19 pandemic: borders will likely become strengthened, and politicians will quickly use their new powers to enforce xenophobic, anti-migrant legislation (Ikotun, Akhigbe, and Okunade 2021; Radil, Castan Pinos, and Ptak 2021). In short, "Practically all governments in [the Western Hemisphere] have fortified their anti-immigrant policies" using powers gained during the pandemic (Castro Neira 2020: 58). Indeed, border closures are not only an attack on "the right to free movement and refuge," but are increasing a "hyper-nationalist [reinforcement of] the image of the foreigner as a 'public burden' or as the incarnation of the virus, elements that intensify xenophobia and racism" (Álvarez Velasco 2020: 11). During the pandemic, all countries of the Western Hemisphere "sought to limit to the maximum extent possible international movement of people and to prevent border crossing" thereby intensifying "the precarity of the life" of migrants and affecting "the right to asylum and refuge" (Domenech 2020: 18). As all of these studies insist, this was in itself nothing new given that governments over the past decade have been generating more and more xenophobic and anti-immigrant legislation that effectively creates greater precarity in the life of migrants. In general, "illegalized migrants and asylum seekers have suffered diverse impediments or remained directly excluded from any State support" (Domenech 2020: 21). Chile participated in the global offensive against migrants.

I am not arguing that participants in the social explosion embraced xenophobia during the COVID-19 pandemic, I'm saying that they did not even consider migrants. The College of Doctors did not recommend barring migration, they did not even mention migration. Again, *this* is the definition of the subaltern: not those who are oppressed within a society, but those who have no recognizable identity. In the push to close borders, the effect that such a policy would have on working-class migrants was not even considered. In short, in the tension found in the social explosion between the multiplicitousness of Chapters 1–4 versus the nationalism of Chapter 5, it seems that nationalism won out in the pandemic wake of the social explosion. The open intercultural collectivization of the Catrileo+Carrión community based on affect was sidelined in favor of closed borders. This is why this book has slowly turned more critical between its initial conception during the social explosion and today: the failure to actualize a clear vision of what such autonomous social relations among the leftovers would actually be meant that under a crisis many reverted to nationalist protectionism.

Who Are We, and How Many?

To oversimplify, I am repeating a conclusion already developed by Raquel Gutiérrez Aguilar in the analysis of autonomous rebellion in Bolivia in the late 1990s and early 2000s in her book, *Los ritmos de Pachakuti* (2008). Many have focused on her celebration of "the communitarian-popular proposal" which reformulated "the relationship between government and society, reconfiguring and renegotiating the spaces of autonomy and the deconcentration of power as a fundamental strategy to reorganize the *State relation*, understood as an agreement of admissible co-living [*pacto de convivencia admisible*]" (345). Furthermore, she argues that it is "during moments of rupture from the ordinary, of mobilization and uprising," that a new "*type of collective subjectivity*" emerges that offers "communal possibilities" and "*utopian horizons*" (22). It has been the argument of this book that the same was seen during the Chilean social explosion, although with different sociocultural foundations than that of Bolivia.

What goes little mentioned in many discussions of Gutiérrez Aguilar's work, however, is that she concludes that activists never formulated "any acceptable and generalizable proposal for the reconfiguration of a non-State-based agreement of multiplicitous co-living [*pacto de convivencia multiple*]" (348). Though she mentions the successes of the Constitutional Assembly as well as local assemblies, she insists that the lingering question was that of configuring "an open 'we,' neither 'national' nor 'State-based,' that permits and reinforces cooperation" (360). These closing words of Gutiérrez Aguilar's book (they appear on the penultimate page) are little discussed, but they are perhaps, as the Chilean social explosion demonstrates, her most important insight. There remains the question of asking who 'we' in the streets are, of asking, to return to Spivak's (2003) phrasing, 'How many are we?'

As I've argued throughout this book, many during the social explosion were in agreement: we were in fact many we's. Yet this merely postpones the problem by now calling on us to ask who are the we's that are included and what brings them together (i.e., what is the we formed by the combination of the we's). At its heights, the social explosion seemed to be pushing towards such a novel conceptualization of collectivization: the kaleidoscopic feminism of LASTESIS's "A Rapist In Your Path," Danny Reveco's mural depicting a congregation of marginalities, Catrileo+Carrión's affective intercommunality, Pedro Lemebel's public transport as a public space becoming embodied in the evasion movement, Manuel Sanfuentes's cross-class poetry, Cheril Linett's trans-species subjectivization, and so on. Nonetheless, as I argued, these never cohered into a clear mode of collectivization. The social explosion might be understood as the attempt to resolve this problematic, but no one did so adequately.

I must fully admit that this is not a critique of *them*, so much as a self-reflection on and self-critique of the collective processes in which *we* were participating. If the explicitly pro-migrant positions (which I personally supported at the time and support today) of Reveco, Lemebel, the CAC, LASTESIS, Linett, and the Catrileo+Carrión community seemed so clear to me in 2019, by 2021 I had to take seriously the question: Why was this not being reflected in popular responses to the pandemic? My answer was that, as Gutiérrez Aguilar warns, the question remains of how to configure an open, non-national 'we' that coordinates social relations beyond the State. I decided to be particularly pointed in my critiques in order to more insistently point to this problematic. This was the same reason why Gramsci worried about letting "spontaneous movements" run their course autonomously: "declining to give them a conscious leadership and raise them to a higher level by inserting them into politics" effectively "opened the way to reaction, to Fascism" (Liguori 2015b: 63). This was also what Marx discovered with the *lumpenproletariat* turning to Louis-Napoléon Bonaparte, and this is what I found when many who had participated in the social explosion turned during the COVID-19 pandemic to calling for giving the State new, exceptional powers that would primarily punish working-class migrants. Like the activists discussed by Gutiérrez Aguilar, we failed to offer a clear political solution and it should therefore be no surprise that under public-health threat many turned to instrumentalizing already existing State apparatuses.

That said, a political solution was slowly starting to emerge near the close of the social explosion. Mirroring ideas dating back to council communism

(Ness and Azzellini 2011a; van der Linden 2004), the social explosion was hinting at a mode of social coordination based on orchestrating the polycentric and decentralized cooperation of a horizontalist network of autonomous assemblies, *cabildos*, and community organizations. Indeed, the social explosion might be seen as a step forward from council communism insofar as the latter's vision has been hounded by its myopic focus on male waged labor at the cost of other social struggles and their entwinements (Ness and Azzellini 2011b; van der Linden 2004). This comparison is doubly justified given that council communism has frequently struggled with its relationship to party politics when revolution was not a possibility, a tension that we see once again with the formation of coalitions like the List of the People (van der Linden 2004; Wallis 2011).

Nonetheless, the details of this large-scale cooperativist proposal had not been worked out by March 2020. As Donny Gluckstein (2011) argues through a survey of European workers' councils, without a robust "self-conscious understanding of the revolutionary potential of the council, its very strength—grassroots democracy—will tend to reflect reformism and stay within the bounds of capitalist society" (46). Like the Chilean social explosion, council communism never developed "a systematic analysis of the concept of [political] form" (Bonnet 2011: 79). The Chilean social explosion was working towards such an understanding, but, cut short by the COVID-19 pandemic, it reverted to the reformism mentioned by Gluckstein.

In fact, the constitutional convention—regardless of whether or not the constitution is eventually approved—can in many ways been seen as a compromise between the call for such total decentralization and the existing Chilean State. Perhaps the best expression of this compromise came from Elisa Loncón, the Mapuche linguist and academic who became the president of the constitutional convention. In her opening speech as president of the convention, she insisted that the process would be one of *founding a new Chile*, "plural, multilingual, with all cultures, with all peoples, with all women, with all the territories. That is our dream to write a new Constitution." The writing of the new explicitly plurinational constitution was dedicated to representing all those leftovers of the Chilean nation-State: "for the rights of our Indigenous nations, for the rights of the peripheral regions, for the rights of Mother Earth, for the rights to water, for the rights of women, for the rights of children" (Ferrer 2021). This would be reinforced in an op-ed written by Loncón (2021) in which she described the constitution-writing process as,

> a task of all the peoples of Chile and Wallmapu, since we are all inevitably tied together, we diverse peoples who inhabit this country with a shared history, although it is fundamental to say that this history has shadowy nooks [*recovecos claroscuros*], memories that circulate against the grain of [*a contrapelo de*] official stories.

Loncón is explicitly conceiving the constitutional convention as an assembly of leftovers struggling to coordinate autonomous demands.

The point here is not to see the constitutional convention as the culminating apex of the social explosion. There is a problematic tendency noted by the Subaltern Studies Group for State-based projects to appropriate popular struggles, seeing their institutionalized expression (i.e., the constitutional convention) as the 'proper' political resolution of insurrection (Guha 1988). In this sense, the constitutional convention runs into the same problematic outlined in the introduction with respect to the Pink Tide: it is trying to take a horizontalist, decentralized, autonomous politics and make it work within hierarchical, centralized, institutionalized politics. Even if Loncón and the rest of her allies in the convention are successful, the multiplicitous social order they are institutionalizing will still be one written by a select(ed) cadre and then approved by the popular sovereign when eligible voters vote again in 2022.

To give just two limitations of this constitutional process: the convention's list of peoples included in their plurinationality will always be insufficient—for instance, the convention rejected the proposed inclusion of Black Chileans as another nation within the plurinational tapestry of Chile (a fact that Loncón was trying to rectify as of August 2021 given her meetings with representatives of the *afrochilenx* movement)—and this vision of plurinationality cannot adequately account for migrants. Regarding the latter, not only is there the obvious problem that the constitution is only approved by those citizens who it legitimizes as having full political rights—for instance, undocumented immigrants do not have a voice in this process—but the idea of plurinationality as defined by Loncón does not include people who belong to no nation or stateless communities, an issue that I have discussed elsewhere (Woods 2020a).[4] The point here is not that Loncón or the discourse of plurinationality is xenophobic. In fact, in a survey answered by most constitution writers, Loncón explicitly states that she wishes to include migrant issues in the new constitution. The issue is that these migrants as well as Black Chileans are not capable of representing themselves in the constitutional convention.[5] More simply, Loncón is highly aware that the 'we' with which she speaks is an internally divided 'we'—hence her insistence on speaking to and about peripheral regions, Indigenous nations, women, and so on—but it is still unclear how to form a truly open 'we' that does not close in on itself. Yes, Loncón is pushing towards plurinationality, but such multiplicity is still a circumscribed 'we.'

Many are currently in the process of asking what the results of the social explosion are and/or will be. I hope the reader has understood from this book that this is the wrong question: the social explosion was autonomously activating a new way of doing politics. The importance of the social explosion was not in what it *will have accomplished*, it was in *what it was actively doing*. Nonetheless, what it was doing (e.g., the limitations discussed in Chapters 4 and 5) as well as the articulation of post-social-explosion politics during the

COVID-19 pandemic and the constitutional convention require us to more seriously consider Gutiérrez Aguilar's (2008) critique at the end of *Los ritmos de Pachakuti* cited above. The future task for autonomous politics is to resolve how to conceive an open and multiplicitous collectivization.

Notes

1 For instance, on 25 October 2019 I saw a Black woman in Santiago as part of an anti-racist bloc holding up a sign reading, "I am afrochilena and I want an anti-racist country."

2 I mention Rivera Cusicanqui here because Reveco informed me that he attended a series of her seminars; he is informed of her work.

3 The actual (highly unlikely) implementation of this policy is beside the point: I am speaking of the underlying discourse and logic motivating policy positions.

4 Furthermore, two texts on plurinationality in Chile were published by the publisher, Pehuén, in the lead up to the constitutional convention (Pairicán 2020, 2021).

5 In response to this limitation, some migrant social organizations such as the National Coordinator of Migrants participated in hearings at the convention.

Bibliography

Abedrapo Bustos, Eduardo, Germán Correa Díaz, Sergio González Tagle, and Sergio Solís Mateluna. 2000. *Política y plan de transporte urbano para Santiago 2000–2010.* Santiago: Comite Asesor del Ministro de Obras Públicas, Transportes y Telecomunicaciones.

Accossatto, Romina. 2018. "Movimientos feministas en la era digital. Las estrategias comunicacionales del movimiento *Ni Una Menos*." *Encuentros* 6, no. 8: 117–136.

Adkimvn. 2011. "Menoko ñi mongen." *Youtube*, 24 June. https://www.youtube.com/watch?v=NPuKv7ORw2Q&feature=youtu.be.

Adorno, Rolena. 2000. *Guaman Poma: Writing and Resistance in Colonial Peru.* Austin: University of Texas Press.

Agosín, Marjorie. 1996. *Tapestries of Hope, Threads of Love: The Arpillera Movement in Chile, 1974–1994*, translated by Celeste Kostopulos-Cooperman. Albuquerque: University of New Mexico Press.

Aguila Zúñiga, Ernesto and Carlos Maldonado Prieto. 1996. "Orden público en el Chile del siglo XX: trayectoría de una policía militarizada." In *Justicia en la calle: ensayos sobre policía en América Latina*, edited by Peter Waldman, 73–98. Medellín: Konrad Adenauer Stiftung.

Albán Achinte, Adolfo. 2008. "¿Interculturalidad sin decolonialidad? Colonialidades circulantes y prácticas de re-existencia." In *Diversidad, interculturalidad y construcción de ciudad*, edited by Wilmer Willa and Arturo Grueso, 64–96. Bogotá: Universidad Pedagógica Nacional/Alcaldía Mayor.

Albán Achinte, Adolfo. 2013. *Más allá de la razón hay un mundo de colores: Modernidades, colonialidades y reexistencia.* Santiago de Cuba: Casa del Caribe y Editorial Oriente.

Albert, Catalina and Tamara Köhler. 2020. "Yo me organizo en la plaza: las cientos de asambleas que surgieron tras el estallido social." *CIPER*, 14 February. https://www.ciperchile.cl/2020/02/14/yo-me-organizo-en-la-plaza-las-cientos-de-asambleas-que-surgieron-tras-el-estallido-social/

Albertani, Claudio. 2011. "'Flores Salvajes'. Reflexiones sobre el principio de autonomía." In *Pensar las autonomías: Alternativas de emancipación al capital y el Estado*, edited by Jóvenes en Resistencia Alternativa, 49–65. México D.F.: Bajo Tierra.

aliwen and Lucy Quezada. 2021. *Yeguada Latinoamericana de Cheril Linett: Acciones, archivo y escrituras críticas (2017-2020).* Valparaíso: Trío Editorial.

Álvarez Velasco, Soledad. 2020. "(In)movilidad en las Américas y COVID-19." In *(Trans)Fronteriza: (In)movilidades en las Américas y COVID-19*, edited by Mariela Paula Díaz, 9–16. Buenos Aires: CLACSO.

Anderson, Benedict. 2006. *Imagined Communities: Reflections on the Origin and Spread of Nationalism*. New York: Verso.

Añiñir Guilitraro, David. 2009. *Mapurbe: venganza a raíz*. Santiago: Pehuén.

Antileo, Enrique. 2006. "La lucha de los mapuches urbanos en Chile". In *Movimiento indígena en América Latina: resistencia y proyecto alternativo, vol. 2*, edited by Raquel Gutiérrez and Fabiola Escárzaga, 324–328. Mexico: Juan Pablos.

Antileo, Enrique. 2011 "Diáspora mapuche y multiculturalismo en Santiago." *Revista Kütral* 2: 75–96.

Apfelbaum, Erika. 2010. "Halbwachs and the Social Properties of Memory." In *Memory: Histories, Theories, Debates*, edited by Susannah Radstone and Bill Schwarz, 77–92. New York: Fordham University Press.

Aravena Reyes, Andrea. 2008. *Mapuches en Santiago: Memorias de inmigrantes y residentes*. Santiago: Ediciones Escaparate.

Arditi, Benjamin. 2007. "Post-hegemony: Politics Outside the Usual Post-Marxist Paradigm." *Contemporary Politics* 13, no. 3: 205–226.

Arena, John. 2012. *Driven from New Orleans: How Nonprofits Betray Public Housing and Promote Privatization*. Minneapolis: University of Minnesota Press.

Arzola, María Paz and Catalina Larraín. 2019. "Hacia una definición y caracterización de la clase media en Chile." *Serie Informe Social* 176: 1–24.

Ascari, Maurizio. 2014. "The Dangers of Distant Reading: Reassessing Moretti's Approach to Literary Genres." *Genre* 47, no. 1: 1–19.

Assmann, Jan. 2011. *Cultural Memory and Early Civilization: Writing, Remembrance, and Political Imagination*. New York: Cambridge University Press.

Austin, Joe. 2001. *Taking the Train: How Graffiti Art Became an Urban Crisis in New York City*. New York: Columbia University Press.

Ayala, Leslie. 2019a. "Big Data del Gobierno: Los detalles del informe por el estallido social que entregó a la Fiscalía." *La Tercera*, 21 December. https://www.latercera.com/la-tercera-domingo/noticia/big-data-del-gobierno-los-detalles-del-informe-estallido-social-entrego-la-fiscalia/947967/

Ayala, Leslie. 2019b. "Jueces que se constituyeron en estación Baquedano: 'No encontramos a personas detenidas, ni menos colgando del techo.'" *La Tercera*, 23 October. https://www.latercera.com/nacional/noticia/jueces-se-constituyeron-estacion-baquedano-no-encontramos-personas-detenidas-menos-colgando-del-techo/874175/

Babidge, Sally and Paola Bolados. 2018. "Neoextractivism and Indigenous Water Ritual in Salar de Atacama." *Latin American Perspectives* 45, no. 5: 170–185.

Badilla, Manuela. 2021. "Memory on Chile's Frontlines." *NACLA Report on the Americas* 53, no. 2: 127–132.

Balcazar, Sebastián. 2016. "Poisoned Lives: Five Decades of Pollution in Chile's Quintero Ventanas Bay." *Mongabay: News and Inspiration from Nature's Frontline*, 4 October. https://news.mongabay.com/2016/10/poisoned-lives-five-decades-of-pollution-in-chiles-quintero-ventanas-bay/.

Barnett, Claudia. 1994. "The Death of Graffiti: Postmodernism and the New York City Subway." *Studies in Popular Culture* 16, no. 2: 25–38.

Barozet, Emmanuelle. 2017a. "Es usted de clase media? Probablemente no." *Ciper*, 10 April. https://www.ciperchile.cl/2017/04/10/es-usted-de-clase-media-probablemente-no/

Barozet, Emmanuelle. 2017b. "Serie sobre la clase media chilena (2): Ese gran miedo a resbalar." *Ciper*, 13 April. https://www.ciperchile.cl/2017/04/13/66957/

Barozet, Emmanuelle. 2017c. "Serie sobre la clase media chilena (3): educación superior, la obsesión por un espejismo." *Ciper*, 4 May. https://www.ciperchile.cl/2017/05/04/serie-sobre-la-clase-media-chilena-3-educacion-superior-la-obsesion-por-un-espejismo/

Barozet, Emmanuelle. 2017d. "Serie sobre clase media (4): Entre la meritocracia y el pituto." *Ciper*, 17 May. https://www.ciperchile.cl/2017/05/17/serie-sobre-clase-media-4-entre-la-meritocracia-y-el-pituto/

Barozet, Emmanuelle. 2017e. "Elecciones 2017: ¿Quién representa major a la clase media?" *Ciper*, 9 June. https://www.ciperchile.cl/2017/06/09/elecciones-2017-quien-representa-mejor-a-la-clase-media/

Barozet, Emmanuelle and Vicente Espinoza. 2016. "Current Issues on the Political Representation of Middle Classes in Chile." *Journal of Politics in Latin America* 8, no. 3: 95–123.

Barthes, Roland. 2013. *Mythologies*, translated by Richard Howard and Annette Lavers. New York: Hill and Wang.

Bauer, Carl. 1997. "Bringing Water Markets Down to Earth: The Political Economy of Water Rights in Chile, 1976–95." *World Development* 25, no. 5: 639–656.

Bauer, Carl. 1998. *Against the Current: Privatization, Water Markets, and the State in Chile*. Boston, MA: Kluwer.

Bauer, Carl. 2004. *Siren Song: Chilean Water Law as a Model for International Reform*. New York: Routledge.

Bauer, Carl. 2005. "In the Image of the Market: The Chilean Model of Water Resources Management." *International Journal of Water* 3, no. 2: 146–165.

Bauer, Carl. 2015. "Water Conflicts and Entrenched Governance Problems in Chile's Market Model." *Water Alternative* 8, no. 2: 147–172.

Beasley-Murray, Jon. 2010. *Post-Hegemony: Political Theory and Latin America*. Minneapolis: University of Minnesota Press.

Bellange, Ebe. 1995. *El mural como reflejo de la realidad social en Chile*. Santiago: Ediciones Chile América (CESOC).

Benjamin, Walter. 1996a. "Critique of Violence." In *Selected Writings, vol. 1: 1913–1926*, edited by Marcus Bullock and Michael W. Jennings, 236–252. Cambridge: Harvard University Press.

Benjamin, Walter. 1996b. "The Author as Producer." In *Selected Writings: Volume 2, 1931–1934*, edited by Michael W. Jennings, Howard Eiland, and Gary Smith, translated by Edmund Jephcott, 768–782. Cambridge: Harvard University Press.

Bennett, Joshua. 2020. *Being Property Once Myself: Blackness and the End of Man*. Cambridge: Harvard University Press.

Bernedo, Patricio. 2013. *Historia de la libre competencia en Chile, 1959–2010*. Fiscalía Nacional Económica: Santiago de Chile.

Beverley, John. 1993. *Against Literature*. Minneapolis: University of Minnesota Press.

Beverley, John. 2011. *Latinamericanism after 9/11*. Durham, NC: Duke University Press.

Bey, Hakim. 1991. *T.A.Z.: The Temporary Autonomous Zone, Ontological Anarchy, Poetic Terrorism*. Brooklyn, NY: Automedia.

Bidegain, Germán. 2017. "From Cooperation to Confrontation: The Mapuche Movement and Its Political Impact, 1990–2014." In *Social Movements in Chile:*

Organization, Trajectories and Political Consequences, edited by Sofia Donoso and Marisa von Bülow, 99–130. New York: Palgrave.

Blanche, María Jesús. 2019. "Daniela Catrileo, poeta: 'Voy construyendo nuestra identidad a punta de esquirlas y memorias comunes.'" *Biblioteca Viva*, 13 March. https://bibliotecaviva.cl/daniela-catrileo-poeta-voy-construyendo-nuestra-identidad-a-punta-de-esquirlas-y-memorias-comunes/

Bloembergen, Marieke. 2011. "The Perfect Policeman: Colonial Policing, Modernity, and Conscience on Sumatra's West Coast in the Early 1930s." *Indonesia* 91: 165–191.

Bonnefoy, Michel and Celeste Merino. 2020. *El negro tenia su historia*. Santiago: LOM.

Bonnefoy, Pascale. 2019. "After Fare Hike Stirs Violent Unrest in Chile, President Suspends It." *New York Times*, 19 October. https://www.nytimes.com/2019/10/19/world/americas/chile-protests-emergency.html.

Bonnet, Alberto. 2011. "The Political Form at Last Discovered: Workers' Councils against the Capitalist State." In *Ours to Master and to Own: Workers' Control from the Commune to the Present*, edited by Immanuel Ness and Dario Azzellini, 66–81. Chicago, IL: Haymarket.

Boose, Lynda. 1991. "Scolding Brides and Bridling Scolds: Taming the Woman's Unruly Member." *Shakespeare Quarterly* 42, no. 2: 179–213.

Bouteldja, Houria. 2016. *Whites, Jews, and Us: Toward a Politics of Revolutionary Love*, translated by Rachel Valinsky. Pasadena: Semiotext(e).

Bragassi H., Juan. 2010. "El Muralismo en Chile: Una Experiencia Histórica para el Chile del Bicentenario." *Memoria chilena: Biblioteca Nacional de Chile*, 28 September. http://www.memoriachilena.cl/602/articles-123178_recurso_2.pdf

Bravo Vargas, Viviana. 2010. *¡Con la Razón y la Fuerza, Venceremos! La Rebelión popular y la Subjetividad Comunista en los '80*. Santiago: Ariadna.

Bravo Vargas, Viviana. 2017. *Piedras, Barricadas y Cacerolas: Las jornadas nacionales de protesta. Chile 1983–1986*. Santiago: Ediciones Universidad Alberto Hurtado.

Brecht, Bertolt. 1964. "Alienation Effects in Chinese Action." In *Brech on Theatre*, edited and translated by John Willett, 91–99. New York: Hill and Wang.

Briziarelli, Marco and Susana Martínez Guillem. 2016. *Reviving Gramsci: Crisis, Communication, and Change*. New York: Routledge.

Budds, Jessica. 2013. "Water, Power, and the Production of Neoliberalism in Chile, 1973–2005." *Environment and Planning D* 31: 301–318.

Budds, Jessica. 2020. "Securing the Market: Water Security and the Internal Contradictions of Chile's Water Code." *Geoforum* 113: 165–175.

Bürger, Peter. 1984. *Theory of the Avant-Garde*, translated by Michael Shaw. Minneapolis: University of Minnesota Press.

Butler, Judith. 1997. "Merely Cultural." *Social Text* 52–53: 265–277.

Butler, Judith. 2018. *Notes Toward a Performative Theory of Assembly*. Cambridge: Harvard University Press.

Butler, Judith. 2019. *The Force of Nonviolence: An Ethico-Political Bind*. New York: Verso.

Cabrera, Federico. 2017. "Pedro Lemebel, cartógrafo de la ciudad neoliberal." *Telar* 18: 162–178.

Cademortori, José. 2011. "Growing Disparities and the Extreme Concentration of Wealth in Chile." In *Neoliberalism's Fractured Showcase: Another Chile Is Possible*, edited by Ximena de la Barra, 113–134. Chicago, IL: Haymarket Books.

Caldeira, Teresa. 2001. *City of Walls: Crime, Segregation, and Citizenship in Sao Paulo*. Berkeley: University of California Press.

Calfio, Margarita. 2016. "Visibilizar lo invisible: Mujeres de pueblos originarios y Asamblea Constituyente en Chile." In *Nueva constitución y pueblos indígenas*, edited by Ana María Moraga, 163–176. Santiago: Pehuén.

Calhoun, Craig. 2001. "Putting Emotions in Their Place." In *Passionate Politics: Emotions and Social Movements*, edited by Jeff Goodwin, James Jasper, and Francesca Polletta, 45–57. Chicago: The University of Chicago Press.

Callahan, Manuel. 2016. "Rebel Dignity." *Kalfou* 3, no. 2: 259–277.

Campos Johnson, Adriana Michele. 2010 *Sentencing Canudos: Subalternity in the Backlands of Brazil*. Pittsburgh: University of Pittsburgh Press.

Caniuqueo, Sergio. 2006. "Siglo XX en *Gulumapu*: De la fragmentación del *Wallmapu* a la unidad nacional *mapuche*. 1880 a 1978." In *¡Escucha, winka!: Cuatro ensayos de historia nacional mapuche y en epílogo sobre el futuro*, edited by Pablo Marimán, Sergio Caniuqueo, José Millalén, and Rodrigo Levil, 129–217. Santiago: LOM.

Caputo, Orlando and Graciela Galarce. 2011. "Chile's Neoliberal Reversion of Salvador Allende's Copper Nationalization." In *Neoliberalism's Fractured Showcase: Another Chile Is Possible*, edited by Ximena de la Barra, 47–71. Chicago, IL: Haymarket Books.

@Carabdechile. 2019. "A esta hora Carabineros ayuda con la limpieza y remoción de escombros en Plaza Baquedano, para que la comunidad tenga un normal desplazamiento a sus lugares de trabajo." *Twitter*, 23 October, 3:37AM, https://twitter.com/Carabdechile/status/1186894275495321601

Carrasco, Iván. 2000. "Poesía Mapuche etnocultural." *Anales de literatura chilena* 1: 195–214.

Castro Neira, Yerko. 2020. "Migrantes frente a la refronterización y la hipervigilancia en el control migratorio durante COVID-19: Lecciones aprendidas del primer conversatorio 'Cierre de fronteras e hipervigilancia.'" In *(Trans)Fronteriza: (In) movilidades en las Américas y COVID-19*, edited by Mariela Paula Díaz, 54–61. Buenos Aires: CLACSO.

Castro Riaño, Luis Carlos. 2018. "La acción colectiva feminisa: ¿De la lucha de clases a la lucha de géneros? Aportes para la comprensión práctica de los movimientos sociales: el caso 'Ni Una Menos.'" *Revista Amauta* 31: 115–157.

Catrileo, Antonio Calibán. 2019. *Awkan epupillan mew: dos espíritus en divergencia*. Santiago: Pehuen.

Catrileo, Daniela. 2016. *Río herido*. Santiago: Edicola.

Catrileo, Daniela. 2018. "Awka/Domo kawellu: provocación bestia. Esbozos sobre Yegua de Cheril Linett." *Escáner Cultural*, 18 June. http://revista.escaner.cl/node/8245.

Catrileo, Daniela. 2019a. *Piñen*. Santiago: Libros de Pez.

Catrileo, Daniela. 2019b. "El nacimiento del río o poética del río: Iñche Daniela Catrileo Pingen." *Heterotopías* 2, no. 4: 1–9.

Centro de Estudios Públicos. 2020. "Estudio Nacional de Opinión Público No. 84, Diciembre 2019." *Encuesta CEP*, 16 January. https://www.cepchile.cl/cep/encuestas-cep/encuestas-2010-2019/estudio-nacional-de-opinion-publica-n-84-diciembre-2019

Chakrabarty, Dipesh. 2000. "*Subaltern Studies* and Postcolonial Historiography." *Nepantla: Views from the South* 1: 9–32.

Chapin III, F. Stuart and Anthony M. Starfield. 1997. "Time Lags and Novel Ecosystems in Response to Transient Climatic Change in Arctic Alaska." *Climatic Change* 35, no. 4: 449–461.
Chibber, Vivek. 2013. *Postcolonial Theory and the Specter of Capital.* New York: Verso.
Chodor, Tom. 2015. *Neoliberal Hegemony and the Pink Tide in Latin America: Breaking Up with TINA?* New York: Palgrave MacMillan.
Ciccariello-Maher, George. 2020. "Review of *Latin America's Pink Tide: Breakthroughs and Shortcomings.*" *NACLA Report on the Americas* 52, no. 3: 353–354.
Cisternas, Pablo, Paula Loncón, and Juan Pablo Klenner (eds.). 2020. *De manifiesto: expresiones ciudadanos a un año del estallido social.* Puerto Varas: Oso Liebre and Núcleo MIlenio Arte Performatividad y Activismo (NMAPA).
Clark, Timothy. 2018. "The Paradox of the Neoliberal Developmentalist State: Reconstructing the Capitalist Elite in Pinochet's Chile." In *Dominant Elites in Latin America: From Neo-Liberalism to the 'Pink Tide,'* edited by Liisa North and Timothy Clark, 23–56. New York: Palgrave MacMillan.
Clastres, Pierre. 1989. *Society Against the State: Essays in Political Anthropology.* Trans. Robert Hurley. New York: Zone Books.
CNNChile. 2020. "Realizan cacerolazo en Iquique contra la inmigración ilegal." *CNNChile,* 29 September. https://www.cnnchile.com/pais/cacerolazo-iquique-inmigracion-ilegal_20200929/
Cogollos Amaya, Silvia and Jaime Ramírez León. 2004. "La perspectiva histórica del cabildo abierto. Una forma de participación ciudadana." *Memoria y Sociedad* 8, no. 16: 41–59.
Colectivo de Memoria Histórica. 2005. *Tortura en poblaciones del Gran Santiago (1973–1990).* Santiago: Corporación José Domingo Cañas.
Colegio Médico de Chile. 2021. "Estrategia sociosanitaria COVID cero." *Colegiomedico.cl,* June. https://www.colegiomedico.cl/wp-content/uploads/2021/06/Estrategia-sociosanitaria-cero.pdf
Colegio Médico Iquique. 2019. "Declaración Pública." *Colegio Médico de Chile Regional Iquique,* 26 September. http://www.colegiomedicoiquique.cl/?p=5597
Collier, Simon and William Sater. 2004. *A History of Chile, 1808–2002.* New York: Cambridge University Press.
Collins, Cath and Boris Hau. 2016. "Chile: Incremental Truth, Late Justice." In *Transitional Justice in Latin America: The Uneven Road from Impunity Towards Accountability,* edited by Elin Skaar, Jemima García-Godos and Cath Collins. New York: Routledge.
Collins, Patricia. 2000. *Black Feminist Thought: Knowledge, Consciousness, and the Politics of Empowerment.* New York: Routledge.
Comisión Nacional sobre Prisión Política y Tortura (CNPPT). 2004. *Informe.* Santiago: Ministerio del Interior.
Comunidad Catrileo+Carrión. 2020. "Paleoduna: tamices y vestigios." *Bitácora: Residencias de arte colaborativo.* https://bitacoraresidencias.cultura.gob.cl/paleoduna-tamices-y-vestigios/
Comunidad Catrileo+Carrión, Colectivo Cuerpo Mumo, PAIM Cartagena, and Patio Ferreiro. *Poyewün Nütramkan: Pikunmapu/Qullasuyu.* Self-published.
Contreras Román, Raúl. 2016. "El pueblo creador representado: Margot Loyola y Violeta Parra en el encuentro de la izquierda y la música folclórica en Chile." *Cuicuilco* 23, no. 66: 197–221.

Coordinador Acción Cultural Valparaíso. 2019. "Declaración de Principios." *Coordinadora Acción Cultural Valparaíso*. https://coordinadoraaccionculturalvalpo.wordpress.com/principios/.

Coordinadora Acción Cultural Valparaíso. 2020a. "Cabildo." *Coordinadora Acción Cultural Valparaíso*. https://coordinadoraaccionculturalvalpo.wordpress.com/primercabildo/.

Coordinadora Acción Cultural Valparaíso. 2020b. "Y ¿a dónde se fue la lluvia?" *YouTube*, 1 October. https://www.youtube.com/watch?v=3gp3SZt42dg.

Coordinadora Feminista 8M. 2020. "Coordinadora Feminista 8M se retira de Unidad Social – Declaración." *Facebook*, 7 January. https://www.facebook.com/coordinadorafeminista8M/posts/2805823969644369/. Accessed 22 August 2020.

Cornejo, Rodrigo, Juan González, Rodrigo Sánchez, Mario Sobarzo, and the Opech Collective. 2011. In *Neoliberalism's Fractured Showcase: Another Chile Is Possible*, edited by Ximena de la Barra, 153–177. Chicago, IL: Haymarket Books.

Correa, Martín, Raúl Molina and Nancy Yáñez. 2005. *La Reforma Agraria y las tierras mapuches: Chile 1962–1975*. Santiago: LOM.

Cortés, Luis. 2016. "Pueblos indígenas y nueva constitución política: ¿Por qué es necesario que los pueblos participen del proceso constituyente?" In *Nueva constitución y pueblos indígenas*, edited by Ana María Moraga, 132–136. Santiago: Pehuén.

Cowling, Mark and James Martin. 2002. "Introduction." In *Marx's Eighteenth Brumaire: (Post)modern Interpretations*, edited by Mark Cowling and James Martin, 1–15. London: Pluto Press.

Creech, James. 1993. *Closet Writing/Gay Reading: The Case of Melville's* Pierre. Chicago: University of Chicago Press.

CrimethInc. 2001. *Days of War, Nights of Love*. Salem: CrimethInc.

crow, scott (ed.). 2018. *Setting Sights: Histories and Reflections on Community Armed Self-Defense*. Oakland: PM Press.

Cuadra, Álvaro. 2003. *De la ciudad letrada a la ciudad virtual*. Santiago: Unedited Manuscript. https://mediatecalibre.cl/wp-content/uploads/2018/06/Delaciudadletradaalaciudadvirtual.pdf

Daniyal, Shoaib. 2020. "'The Rapist Is You': Feminist Sing Bengali Version of Chilean Piece to Protest Modi's Kolkata Visit." *Scroll.in*, 12 January. https://scroll.in/video/949602/the-rapist-is-you-feminists-sing-bengali-version-of-chilean-piece-to-protest-modis-kolkata-visit

Danza Ruiz, Freddo. 2019. "Evasión Chile. Manifestacion Popular Cantando a Los PRISIONEROS." *YouTube*, 19 October. https://www.youtube.com/watch?v=ptWfNH8lkDI&t=7s.

Dattwyler, Rodrigo, Luis Rivas, and Felipe Link. 2019. "New Neoliberal Public Housing Policies: Between Centrality Discourse and Peripheralization Practices in Santiago, Chile." *Housing Studies* 32, no. 3: 489–518.

de la Barra, Ximena. 2011. "Introduction." In *Neoliberalism's Fractured Showcase: Another Chile Is Possible*, edited by Ximena de la Barra, 1–8. Chicago, IL: Haymarket Books.

De Mattos, Carlos. 1999. "Santiago de Chile, globalización y expansión metropolitana: lo que existía sigue existiendo." *Revista eure* 25, no. 77: 29–56.

Dean, Jodi. 2012. "Occupy Wall Street: After the Anarchist Moment." In *The Question of Strategy: Socialist Register 2013*, edited by Leo Panitch, Gregory Albo, and Vivek Chibber, 52–62. New York: Monthly Review Press.

Debes, Remy (ed.). 2017. *Dignity: A History.* New York: Oxford University Press.
del Solar, Felipe and Andrés Pérez. 2008. *Anarquistas: Presencia libertaria en Chile.* Santiago: RiL Editores.
Deutsch, Ana. 2007. "Secuelas de la tortura en el individuo, la familia y la sociedad." In *Atención integral a víctimas de tortura en procesos de litigio: Aportes Psicosociales*, edited by LInda Berrón and Gloriana Espinosa, 247–274. San José: IIDH, 2007.
Diario Uchile. 2021. "Por un torniquete: Fiscalía pide 8 años de cárcel para profesor acusado de destrozos en el Metro." *DiarioUChile*, 20 April. https://radio.uchile.cl/2021/04/20/por-un-torniquete-fiscalia-pide-8-anos-de-carcel-para-profesor-acusado-de-destrozos-en-el-metro/
Díaz, Guillermo, Andrés Gómez-Lobo, and Andrés Velasco. 2004. "Micros en Santiago: de enemigo público a servicio público." *Estudios Públicos* 96: 5–48.
Dickinson, Maggie. 2008. "The Making of Space, Race and Place: New York City's War on Graffiti, 1970-the Present." *Critique of Anthropology* 28, no. 1: 27–45.
Dinerstein, Ana Cecilia. 2015. *The Politics of Autonomy in Latin America: The Art of Organising Hope.* New York: Palgrave MacMillan.
Domenech, Eduardo. 2020. "Pandemia y control de fronteras en el espacio sudamericano." In *(Trans)Fronteriza: (In)movilidades en las Américas y COVID-19*, edited by Mariela Paula Díaz, 17–23. Buenos Aires: CLACSO.
Donoso, Sofia. 2017. "'Outsider' and 'Insider' Strategies: Chile's Student Movement, 1990–2014." In *Social Movements in Chile: Organization, Trajectories and Political Consequences*, edited by Sofia Donoso and Marisa von Bülow, 65–98. New York: Palgrave.
Donoso, Sofia and Marisa von Bülow (eds.). 2017. *Social Movements in Chile: Organization, Trajectories and Political Consequences.* New York: Palgrave.
Dorfman, Ariel. 1991. *Death and a Maiden.* New York: Penguin.
Dorfman, Ariel. 2020a. "Chile: Notes from a Revolt." *The New York Review of Books*, 13 March. https://www.nybooks.com/daily/2020/03/13/chile-notes-from-a-revolt/
Dorfman, Ariel. 2020b. "The Challenge for Chile and the World." *The New York Times*, 24 January. https://www.nytimes.com/2020/01/24/opinion/chile-protests.html
Dorfman, Ariel. 2020c. *Chile: Juventud Rebelde.* Santiago: Fondo de Cultura Económica Chile.
Dorfman, Ariel. 2020d. "Confronting the Pandemic in a Time of Revolt: Voices from Chile." *The Nation*, 6 April. https://www.thenation.com/article/society/chile-protest-literature-coronavirus/
Dorfman, Ariel. 2020e. "What the United States Can Learn from Chile." *The Nation*, 26 October. https://www.thenation.com/article/world/chile-constitution-referendum-democracy/
Droguett, Carlos. 1965. *Patas de perro.* Santiago: Zig-Zag.
Dunbar-Ortiz, Roxanne. 2014. *An Indigenous Peoples' History of the United States.* New York: Beacon.
Durán, Gonzalo and Marco Kremerman. 2017. "Los bajos salarios de Chile: Análisis de la Encuesta CASEN 2015." *Ideas para el Buen Vivir* 10: 1–7.
Durán, Gonzalo and Marco Kremerman. 2019. "Identificación de la pobreza monetaria usando los ingresos del trabajo y las pensiones contributivas. El caso de Chile." *Economía y Política* 6, no. 2: 63–100.

Durán, Gonzalo and Marco Kremerman. 2020. "Los Verdaderos Sueldos de Chile: Panorama Actual del Valor de la Fuerza del Trabajo Usando la ESI (2019)." *Estudios de la Fundación SOL.*

Duran, Rodrigo. 1999. "'Los Prisioneros le pusieron música y letra al proceso social.'" *La Nación*, 3 April, "Ergo Sum."

Duwell, Marcus, Jens Braarvig, Roger Brownsword, and Dietmar Mieth (eds.). 2014. *The Cambridge Handbook of Human Dignity: Interdisciplinary Perspectives.* New York: Cambridge University Press.

Earl, Jennifer, Katrina Kimport, Greg Prieto, Carly Rush, and Kimberly Reynoso. 2012. "Hanging the World One Webpage at a Time: Conceptualizing and Explaining Internet Activism." *Mobilization: An International Journal* 15, no. 4: 425–446.

Echeverría, Andrea. 2014. "David Aniñir: poesía y memoria *mapurbe*." *Contracorriente* 2014, no. 3: 68–89.

Echeverría, Andrea. 2019. "*Mapurbe* Identity and *Admapu* in David Aniñir's Poetry." *Bulletin of Latin American Research* 38, no. 2: 208–221.

Edelman, Lee. 2004. *No Future: Queer Theory and the Death Drive.* Durham, NC: Duke University Press.

Ehrenreich, Ben. 2019. "Welcome to the Global Rebellion Against Neoliberalism." *The Nation*, 25 November. https://www.thenation.com/article/archive/global-rebellions-inequality/

El Desconcierto. 2019. "La metodología de trabajo para cabildos y asambleas que el municipio de Valparaíso puso a disposición de la sociedad civil." *El Desconcierto*, 1 November. https://www.eldesconcierto.cl/2019/11/01/la-metodologia-de-trabajo-para-cabildos-y-asambleas-que-el-municipio-de-valparaiso-puso-a-disposicion-de-la-sociedad-civil/

El Mostrador. 2019. "Evidencias de torturas en subterráneo de estación Baquedano moviliza INDH a presentar acciones legales." *El Mostrador*, 23 October. https://www.elmostrador.cl/noticias/pais/2019/10/23/evidencias-de-torturas-en-subterraneo-de-estacion-baquedano-moviliza-indh-a-presentar-acciones-legales/

El Mostrador. 2020. "Justicia sobreseyó investigación por denuncias de crucifixiones de detenidos durante el estallido social en comisaría de Peñalolén." *El Mostrador*, 23 November. https://www.elmostrador.cl/dia/2020/11/23/justicia-sobreseyo-investigacion-por-denuncias-de-crucifixiones-de-detenidos-durante-el-estallido-social-en-comisaria-de-penalolen/

El Mostrador. 2021. "Inquietud ante la variante Delta: encuesta Data Influye revela que el 93% apoya cierre total de fronteras por 30 días." *El Mostrador*, 30 June. https://www.elmostrador.cl/dia/2021/06/30/inquietud-ante-la-variante-delta-encuesta-data-influye-revela-que-el-93-apoya-cierre-total-de-fronteras-por-30-dias/

"El que no salta es Paco." 2019. *Youtube.* 18 November. https://www.youtube.com/watch?reload=9&v=dW8kTWse0Oc.

Ellner, Steve. 2019. *Latin America's Pink Tide: Breakthroughs and Shortcomings.* New York: Rowman and Littlefield.

Eltit, Diamela. 2019. "La poética ciudadana es la única que nos lidera." *El mostrador*, 27 December. https://www.eldesconcierto.cl/2019/12/27/la-poetica-ciudadana-es-la-unica-que-nos-lidera/.

EMOL. 2021. "Gobierno busca impulsar 'ingreso seguro' de migrantes por falta de mano de obra en el agro." *EMOL*, 8 July. https://www.emol.com/noticias/Economia/2021/07/08/1026108/ingreso-seguro-de-migrantes-agro.html

En Marcha. 2013. "Documental Matapacos." *YouTube*, 23 December. https://www.youtube.com/watch?v=wiEFhAAWCiw&feature=youtu.be&has_verified=1.

Equipo El Siglo. 2019. "Criminal: Estudio encontró soda cáustica en agua del guanaco." *El Siglo*, 16 December. https://elsiglo.cl/2019/12/16/criminal-estudio-encontro-soda-caustica-en-agua-del-guanaco/

Erll, Astrid. 2012. *Memoria colectiva y culturas del recuerdo: estudio introductorio*, translated by Johanna Córdoba y Tatijana Louis. Bogotá: Universidad de Los Andes.

Erll, Astrid and Ansgar Nünning (eds.). 2008. *Cultural Memory Studies: An International and Interdisciplinary Handbook*. Berlin: Walter de Gruyter.

Evans, Elizabeth and Matthew Wilkens. 2016. "Quantifying Geography and Identity in Modern London." Paper presented at the conference, "Modernist Studies Association 18," Pasadena, 18 November.

Facuse, Marisol and Raíza Cavalcanti. 2019. "Museo y revuelta: repercusiones del estallido social en las instituciones de la cultura en Chile." In *Los Futuros Imaginados*, edited by Fernando Gaspar and Guillermo Jarpa, 144–150. Santiago: Universidad de Chile.

Fanon, Frantz. 1986. *Black Skin, White Masks*, translated by Charles Lam Markmann. London: Pluto Press.

Farris, Sara. 2019. "Social Reproduction and Racialized Surplus Populations." In *Capitalism: Concept Idea Image—Aspects of Marx's Capital Today*, edited by Peter Osborne, Éric Alliez, and Eric-John Russell, 121–134. Kingston Upon Thames: CRMEP Books.

Favi, Gloria. 2014. "Bobi y la utopía del cinturón verde." *ARQ*, no. 86: 17–25.

Federici, Silvia. 2004. *Caliban and the Witch*. Brooklyn, NY: Autonomedia.

Feldman, Allen. 1991. *Formations of Violence: The Narrative of the Body and Political Terror in Northern Ireland*. Chicago: The University of Chicago Press.

Fernández, Nona. 2006. *Mapocho*. Santiago: Uqbar.

Fernández, Oriana. 2020. "Sequía: comunas con decreto de escasez hídrica ascienden a 136." *La Tercera*, 11 March. https://www.latercera.com/nacional/noticia/sequia-comunas-con-decreto-de-escasez-hidrica-ascienden-a-136/MXXUNOSJAJBDDNNSZDFLEQRYVM/

Fernández Osco, Marcelo. 2000. *La ley del ayllu: Práctica de jach'a justicia y jisk'a justicia (justicia mayor y justicia menor) en comunidades aymaras*. La Parz: Programa de investigación estratégica en Bolivia.

Ferrer, Consuelo. 2021. "'Estamos instalando una manera de ser democráticos': El primer discurso de Loncon como presidenta de la Convención." *EMOL*, 4 July. https://www.emol.com/noticias/Nacional/2021/07/04/1025714/primer-discurso-loncon-presidenta-convencion.html

Figueroa Irarrázabal, Gricelda and Álvaro Calfucoy Gutierrez. 2020. "Sentipensarse joven indígena de ciudad. Las voces cosmoconscientes del podcast *¿Origi-Ke?*" *UChile*, 3 July. https://www.uchile.cl/noticias/164855/sentipensarse-joven-indigena-de-ciudad

Filigrana, Pastora. 2020. "Las jornaleras marroquíes de la fresa: Feminismo antirracista o barbarie." In *La Internacional Feminista: Luchas en los territoriso y contra el neoliberalismo*, edited by Verónica Gago, Marta Malo, and Luci Cavallero, 23–36. Madrid: Traficantes de sueños.

Finch, Jason. 2016a. *Deep Locational Criticism: Imaginative place in literary research and teaching*. Amsterdam: John Benjamins Publishing.

Finch, Jason. 2016b. "The Experienced Slum Meets the Digital Humanities: Mobile Insider Perspectives on City Lives in London Jewish and Caribbean Fiction (1935–1975)." Paper presented at the conference, "Modernist Studies Association 18," Pasadena, 18 November.

Finch, Jason. 2021. *Literary Urban Studies and How to Practice It*. New York: Routledge.

Fiol-Matta, Licia. 2002. *A Queer Mother for the Nation: The State and Gabriela Mistral*. Minneapolis: University of Minnesota Press.

Fontana, Benedotto. 2015. "Intellctuals and Masses: Agency and Knowledge in Gramsci." In *Antonio Gramsci*, edited by Mark McNally, 55–75. New York: Palgrave MacMillan.

Forstenzer, Nicole. 2017. "Feminism and Gender Policies in Post-Dictatorship Chile (1990–2010)." In *Social Movements in Chile: Organization, Trajectories and Political Consequences*, edited by Sofia Donoso and Marisa von Bülow, 161–190. New York: Palgrave.

Forstenzer, Nicole. 2019. "Feminismos en el Chile Post-Dictadura: Hegemonías y marginalidades." *Revista Punto Género* 11: 34–50.

Foucault, Michel. 1978a. *Discipline and Punish: The Birth of the Prison*, translated by Alan Sheridan. New York: Vintage Books.

Foucault, Michel. 1978b. *The History of Sexuality, vol. 1: An Introduction*, translated by Robert Hurley. New York: Pantheon.

Franceschet, Susan. 2005. *Women and Politics in Chile*. Boulder, CO: Lynne Rienner Publishers.

Fraser, Nancy. 2013. *Fortunes of Feminism: From State-Managed Capitalism to Neoliberal Crisis*. New York: Verso.

Fuguet, Alberto and Sergio Gómez. 1996. *McOndo*. Barcelona: Grijalbo-Mondadori.

Furnaro, Andrea. 2019. "Hegemony and Passivity in Mining Regions: Containing Dissent in North-Central Chile." *The Extractive Industries and Society* 6: 215–222.

@gabrielboric. 2019. "Y además en votación particular rechazamos artículos que penaliza barricadas (que se aprobó con votos transversales). Las barricadas en el contexto de la lucha social nos parecen legítimas expresiones de resistencia, y aunque para algunos sea impopular defenderlo lo haremos." *Twitter*, 4 December, 7:20PM, https://twitter.com/gabrielboric/status/1202351994226302984

Gago, Verónica. 2018. "Critical Times / The Earth Trembles." Translated by Ramsey McGlazer. *Critical Times* 1, no. 1: 158–164.

Gago, Verónica. 2019. *La potencia feminista: O el deseo de cambiarlo todo*. Madrid: Traficantes de Sueños.

Gago, Verónica, Marta Malo, and Luci Cavallero. 2020. *La Internacional Feminista: Luchas en los territorios y contra el neoliberalismo*. Madrid: Traficantes de Sueños.

Gago, Verónica, Raquel Gutiérrez Aguilar, Susan Draper, Mariana Menéndez Díaz, Marina Montanelli, and Suely Rolnik. 2018. *8M Constelación feminista: ¿Cuál es tu huelga? ¿Cuál es tu lucha?* Buenos Aires: Tinta Limón.

Gajardo, Juan. 2019. "Unidad Social: Unidad Política." *El Siglo*, 28 July. https://elsiglo.cl/2019/07/28/unidad-social-unidad-politica/

Galaz Ulloa, Isabella and Ozzo Ukumari. 2019. "Newen Kimün: La fuerza de la sabiduría. Entrevista a Ozzo Ukumari." *Artishock: Revista de Arte Contemporáneo*, 10 December. https://artishockrevista.com/2019/12/10/entrevista-boliviano-ozzo-ukumari-tsonami/

Gamba. 2019. "Metro Baquedano como Centro de Tortura: Video muestra a Carabineros 'limpiándolo' a las 3 de la mañana." *Gamba*.cl. http://www.gamba.cl/2019/10/metro-baquedano-como-centro-de-tortura-video-muestra-a-carabineros-limpiandolo-a-las-3-de-la-manana/.

Gandy, Matthew. 2002. *Concrete and Clay: Reworking Nature in New York City.* Cambridge: MIT Press.

Garcés, Mario. 2020. "October 2019: Social Uprising in Neoliberal Chile." *Journal of Latin American Cultural Studies* 28, no. 3: 483–491.

García, Mabel. 2012. "El proceso de retradicionalización cultural en la poesía Mapuche actual: *Üi* de Adriana Paredes Pinda." *Revista chilena de literatura*, no. 81: 51–68.

García-Corrales, Guillermo. 2005. "La Figura de Pedro Lemebel en el Contexto de la Nueva Narrative Chilena." *Chasqui* 34, no. 1: 25–31.

Garrido, Felipe. 2019. "¿Cuánto ha subido el precio del Metro de Santiago desde 2007 a la actualidad." *FayerWayer*, 18 October. https://www.fayerwayer.com/2019/10/aumento-tarifa-metro-2007/

Gaspar, Fernando and Guillermo Jarpa. 2019. "Los futuros del arte." In *Los Futuros Imaginados*, edited by Fernando Gaspar and Guillermo Jarpa, 14–23. Santiago: Universidad de Chile.

Gaviola, Edda, Ximena Bedregal, and Rosa Rojas. 2009. "Feminismos Cómplices, Más Gestos para una Construcción Radicalmente Antiamnésica." In *Feminismos Cómplices 16 Años Después*, 6–24. Mexico: Feminismos Cómplices/Taller Editorial La Corea Feminista/CICAM.

Gelbard, Sarah. 2018. "Ask a Punk: From Informality to Anti-formality and Anti-authority and When to Say Fuck." Paper presented at the conference, "Curating Resistance," Los Angeles, February.

Geraghty, Niall H.D. and Adriana Laura Massidda. 2019. "Introduction." In *Creative Spaces: Urban culture and marginality in Latin America*, edited by Niall H.D. Geraghty and Adriana Laura Massidda, 1–28. London: Institute of Latin American Studies.

Glasrud, Bruce A. and Michael N. Searles (eds.). 2016. *Black Cowboys in the American West: On the Range, on the Stage, Behind the Badge.* Norman: University of Oklahoma Press.

Glissant, Édouard. 1997. *Poetics of Relation*, translated by Betsy Wing. Ann Arbor: The University of Michigan Press.

Gluckstein, Donny. 2011. "Workers' Councils in Europe: A Century of Experience." In *Ours to Master and to Own: Workers' Control from the Commune to the Present*, edited by Immanuel Ness and Dario Azzellini, 32–47. Chicago, IL: Haymarket.

Godoy Ramos, Carmen Gloria. 2016. "'No somos feministas.' Género, igualdad y neoliberalismo en Chile." *Estudos Feministas* 24, no. 3: 871–890.

Godoy Sepúlveda, Eduardo. 2016. "Historia e historiografía del anarquismo en Chile." *Cuadernos de historia* 44: 101–137.

Goldman Environmental Foundation. 2019. "Alberto Curamil." *The Goldman Environmental Foundation*. https://www.goldmanprize.org/recipient/alberto-curamil/.

Gómez-Barris, Macarena. 2018. *Beyond the Pink Tide: Art and Political Undercurrents in the Americas.* Berkeley: University of California Press.

Gonzalez, Mike. 2019. *The Ebb of the Pink Tide: The Decline of the Left in Latin America.* London: Pluto.

Gonzalez, Ricardo and Carmen Le Foulon Morán. 2020. "The 2019–2020 Chilean Protests: A First Look at Their Causes and Participants." *International Journal of Sociology* 50, no. 3: 227–235.

González, Tomás. 2020. "El mito de la 'Clase Media': ¿De quiénes están hablando el Gobierno y las fuerzas políticas?" *diarioUChile*, 1 July. https://radio.uchile.cl/2020/07/01/el-mito-de-la-clase-media-de-quienes-estan-hablando-el-gobierno-y-las-fuerzas-politicas/

Goodwin, Jeff, James Jasper, and Francesca Polletta. 2001. "Introduction: Why Emotions Matter." In *Passionate Politics: Emotions and Social Movements*, edited by Jeff Goodwin, James Jasper, and Francesca Polletta, 1–24. Chicago: The University of Chicago Press.

Gopal, Priyamvada. 2019. *Insurgent Empire: Anticolonial Resistance and British Dissent*. New York: Verso.

Graeber, David. 2004. *Fragments of an Anarchist Anthropology*. Chicago, IL: Prickly Paradigm Press.

Graeber, David. 2009. *Direct Action: An Ethnography*. Oakland: AK Press.

Graham, Elspeth. 2021. "The Training Relationship: Horses, Hawks, Dogs, Bears, and Humans." In *The Routledge Handbook of Shakespeare and Animals*, edited by Karen Raber and Holly Dugan, 177–189. New York: Routledge, 2021.

Gramsci, Antonio. 1979. *Letters from Prison*, translated by Lynne Lawner. London: Quartet.

Gramsci, Antonio. 1992a. *Prison Notebooks, vol. 1*, translated by Joseph A. Buttigieg and Antonio Callari, edited by Joseph A. Buttigieg. New York: Columbia University Press.

Gramsci, Antonio. 1992b. *Selections from the Prison Notebooks*, translated and edited by Quintin Hoare and Geoffrey Nowell Smith. New York: International Publishers.

Green, Marcus E. 2015. "Gramsci and Subaltern Struggles Today: Spontaneity, Political Organization and Occupy Wall Street." In *Antonio Gramsci*, edited by Mark McNally, 156–178. New York: Palgrave MacMillan.

Grez Toso, Sergio. 2007. *Los anarquistas y el movimiento obrero: La alborada de 'la Idea' en Chile, 1893–1915*. Santiago: LOM Ediciones.

Grossman, Jonathan. 2012. *Charles Dickens's Networks: Public Transport and the Novel*. New York: Oxford.

Guerra, Lucía. 2000. "Ciudad neoliberal y los devenires de la homosexualidad en las crónicas urbanas de Pedro Lemebel." *Revista Chilena de Literatura* 56: 71–92.

Guha, Ranajit. 1983 *Elementary Aspects of Peasant Insurgency in Colonial India*. New York: Oxford University Press.

Guha, Ranajit. 1988. "Preface: On Some Aspects of the Historiography of Colonial India." In *Selected Subaltern Studies*, edited by Ranajit Guha, 35–44. New York: Oxford University Press.

Guha, Ranajit. 1998. *Dominance without Hegemony: History and Power in Colonial India*. New York: Oxford University Press.

Gutiérrez, Maria Laura and Camila Arbuet Osuna. 2020. "Resistencias feministas en Chile: subjetivaciones y acciones estético-políticas ante las violencias neoliberales." *Gênero*, vol. 20, no. 2: 178–200.

Gutiérrez Aguilar, Raquel. 2008. *Los ritmos de Pachakuti: movilización y levantamiento indígena popular en Bolivia (2000–2005)*. Buenos Aires: Tinta Limón.

Gutiérrez Aguilar, Raquel. 2018. "La lucha de las mujeres contra todas las violencias en México: reunir fragmentos para hallar sentido." In *8M Constelación feminista: ¿Cuál es tu huelga? ¿Cuál es tu lucha?*, 25–48. Buenos Aires: Tinta Limón.
Halbwachs, Maurice. 1980. *The Collective Memory*, translated by F. Ditter and V. Yazdi. New York: Harper Colophon.
Hall, Stuart. 1986. "Gramsci's Relevance for the Study of Race and Ethnicity." *Journal of Communication Inquiry* 10, no. 5: 5–27.
Halvorsen, Sam. 2015. "Taking Space: Moments of Rupture and Everyday Life in Occupy London." *Antipode* 47, no. 2: 401–417.
Handerson, Joseph. 2020. "Cierre de fronteras, deportaciones y retorno en el caribe." In *(Trans)Fronteriza: (In)movilidades en las Américas y COVID-19*, edited by Mariela Paula Díaz, 30–37. Buenos Aires: CLACSO.
Hansen, Natalie Corinne. 2017. "Dressage: Training the Equine Body." In *Foucault and Animals*, edited by Matthew Chrulew and Dinesh Joseph Wadiwel, 132–160. Boston: Brill.
Hardt, Michael and Antonio Negri. 2000. *Empire*. Cambridge: Harvard University Press.
Hardt, Michael and Antonio Negri. 2004. *Multitude: War and Democracy in the Age of Empire*. New York: Penguin.
Hardt, Michael and Antonio Negri. 2017. *Assembly*. New York: OUP.
Harnecker, Marta. 2011. "Where Was the Chile I had Left Behind?" In *Neoliberalism's Fractured Showcase: Another Chile Is Possible*, edited by Ximena de la Barra, 93–109. Chicago, IL: Haymarket Books.
Harrison, Oliver. 2018. "From 'Dignity' to 'Self-Realisation': Rethinking Holloway's Emancipatory Theory." *Capitalism Nature Socialism* 30, no. 3: 52–69.
Hartwig, Joan. 1982. "Horses and Women in *The Taming of the Shrew*." *Huntington Library Quarterly* 45, no. 4: 285–294.
Harvey, David. 1990. *The Condition of Postmodernity: An Enquiry into the Origins of Cultural Change*. Cambridge: Blackwell.
Harvey, David. 2000. *Spaces of Hope*. Edinburgh: Edinburgh University Press.
Harvey, David. 2005. *A Brief History of Neoliberalism*. Oxford: Oxford University Press.
Henríquez Salgado, Marta. 2015. *Afrochilenos: Una historia oculta*. Arica: Krom.
Hererra, Polet. 2021. "Entrevistas: David Arboleda." *PuroPeriodismo*, 2 August. http://www.puroperiodismo.cl/david-arboleda-periodista-e-integrante-de-la-red-de-periodistas-migrantes-faltan-mas-voces-migrantes-en-todo-el-pluralismo-es-importante-porque-es-la-base-de-todo-2/
Hernández, Isabel. 2003. *Autonomía o ciudadanía incompleta. El pueblo Mapuche en Chile y Argentina*. Santiago: Pehuén.
Herrera, Mauricio, Cristian Candia, Diego Rivera, Douglas Aitken, Daniel Brieba, Camila Boettiger, Guillermo Donoso, and Alex Godoy-Faúndez. 2019. "Understanding Water Disputes in Chile with Text and Data Mining Tools." *Water International* 44, no. 3: 302–320.
Hidalgo, Rodrigo, Voltaire Alvarado, and Daniel Santana. 2016. "Los expulsados de la metrópoli: expolio y esquilmo en la locación de la vivienda social en la ciudad neoliberal. Una perspectiva de Santiago y Valparaíso." *Estudios socioterritoriales* 20: 41–55.
Hietanen, Anna-Emilia. 2007. "Comisión Valech y cambios en las políticas de la memoria en Chile." Paper presented at XXVI Congreso de la Asociación Latinoamericana de Sociología, Guadalajara.

Hite, Katherine, and Cath Collins. 2009. "Memorial Fragments, Monumental Silences and Reawakenings in 21st-Century Chile." *Millenium Journal of International Studies* 38, no. 2: 379–400.

Hite, Katherine, Cath Collins, and Alfredo Joignant. 2013a. "The Politics of Memory in Chile." In *The Politics of Memory in Chile: From Pinochet to Bachelet*, edited by Cath Collins, Katherine Hite, and Alfredo Joignant, 1–29. Boulder, CO: Lynne Rienner.

Hite, Katherine, Cath Collins, and Alfredo Joignant. 2013b. "Afterword." In *The Politics of Memory in Chile: From Pinochet to Bachelet*, edited by Cath Collins, Katherine Hite, and Alfredo Joignant, 239–250. Boulder, CO: Lynne Rienner.

Hobbs, Richard J., Eric Higgs, and James A. Harris. 2009. "Novel Ecosystems: Implications for Conservation and Restoration." *Trends in Ecology and Evolution* 24, no. 11: 599–605.

Hobbs, Richard J., Eric S. Higgs, and James A. Harris. 2014. "Novel Ecosystems: Concept or Inconvenient Reality? A Response to Murcia *et al.*" *Trends in Ecology and Evolution* 29: 645–646.

Holloway, John. 1998. "Dignity's Revolt." In *Zapatista! Reinventing Revolution in Mexico*, edited by John Holloway and Eloína Peláez, 159–198. London: Pluto Press.

Holloway, John. 2005. *Change the World Without Taking Power.* Ann Arbor, MI: Pluto Press.

Howell, Philip and Ilanah Taves. 2021. "Black Protest and the Man on Horseback: Race, Animality, and Equestrian Counter-Conduct." *GeoHumanities*, Advanced online publication.

Huenchumil, Paula. 2021. "Daniela Catrileo, poeta mapuche: 'Algunos feminismos no luchan contra el racismo ni el colonialismo.'" *Interferencia*, 8 March. https://interferencia.cl/articulos/daniela-catrileo-poeta-mapuche-algunos-feminismos-no-luchan-contra-el-racismo-ni-el

Hughes, Glenn. 2011. "The Concept of Dignity in the Universal Declaration of Human Rights." *Journal of Religious Ethics* 39: 1–24.

Hugo, Victor. 1992. *Les Misérables*, translated by Charles E. Wilbour. New York: The Modern Library.

Huidobro, Vicente. 2000. *Vicente Huidobro a la Intemperie: Entrevistas (1915–1946)*, edited by Cecilia García-Huidobro. Santiago de Chile: Editorial Sudamericana.

Hurston, Zora Neale. 1990. *Their Eyes Were Watching God.* New York: Perennial.

Iglesias, Margarita and Ximena Valdés. 2019. "Calle, asambleas y cabildos." *Le Monde Diplomatique*, October. https://www.lemondediplomatique.cl/2019/12/calle-asambleas-y-cabildos.html

Ikotun, Omotomilola, Allwell Akhigbe, and Samuel Okunade. 2021. "Sustainability of Borders in a Post-COVID-19 World." *Politikon* 48, no. 2: 297–311.

Iles Johnston, Sarah. 2018. *The Story of Myth.* Cambridge: Harvard University Press.

INDH (Instituto Nacional de Derechos Humanos). 2014. *Informe de observación provincia de Petorca.* Approved by the Council of the INDH on 10 December. https://bibliotecadigital.indh.cl/bitstream/handle/123456789/774/Informe.pdf?sequence=1

Jackson, Zakiyyah. 2020. *Becoming Human: Matter and Meaning in an Antiblack World.* New York: NYU Press.

Jacobs, Isidora. 2019. "Con desayuno vecinos de Cerros Monjas y Mariposas cortaron la calle en Valparaíso." *Soy Chile*, 12 November. https://www.soychile.cl/

Valparaiso/Sociedad/2019/11/12/624737/Con-desayuno-comunitario-vecinos-de-Cerros-Monjas-y-Mariposas-cortaron-la-calle-en-Valparaiso.aspx

Jadue, Daniel. 2019. "Building a New Chile Requires a New Social Contract." *Jacobin*, 31 October. https://jacobinmag.com/2019/10/chile-uprising-neoliberalism-social-contract. Accessed 6 May 2020.

Jameson, Fredric. 1991. *Postmodernism: Or, the Cultural Logic of Late Capitalism.* Durham, NC: Duke University Press.

@JaimeCuyanao. 2020. "Una lamngen (hermana) me pregunto con respect al #TRAUCO y de que en las MARCHAS FEMINISTAS se le apunta como un ser mitológico #VIOLADOR (abro hilo)." *Twitter*, 9 March, 7:00PM. https://twitter.com/JaimeCuyanao/status/1237136317542260737

Jasper, James. 1999. *The Art of Moral Protest: Culture, Biography, and Creativity in Social Movements.* Chicago: University of Chicago Press.

Jessop, Bob. 2002. "The Political Scene and the Politics of Representation: Periodising Class Struggle and the State in the *Eighteenth Brumaire*." In *Marx's Eighteenth Brumaire: (Post)modern Interpretations*, edited by Mark Cowling and James Martin, 179–194. London: Pluto Press.

Jessop, Bob. 2013. "Putting Neoliberalism in Its Time and Place: A Response to the Debate." *Social Anthropology* 21, no. 1: 65–74.

Jessop, Bob. 2016. *The State: Past, Present, Future.* Malden: Polity.

Jessop, Bob. 2019. "Authoritarian Neoliberalism: Periodization and Critique." *South Atlantic Quarterly* 118, no. 2: 343–361.

Jones, Reece. 2016. *Violent Borders: Refugees and the Right to Move.* New York: Verso.

Jones-Rogers, Stephanie. 2019. *They Were Her Property: White Women as Slave Owners in the American South.* New Haven, CT: Yale University Press.

Kalb, Don. 2012. "Thinking About Neoliberalism as if the Crisis Was Actually Happening." *Social Anthropology* 20: 318–330.

Kautzer, Chad. 2018. "Notes for a Critical Theory of Community Self-Defense." In *Setting Sights: Histories and Reflections on Community Armed Self-Defense*, edited by scott crow, 35–48. Oakland: PM Press.

Kemmer, Laura. 2020. "Free Riding Rio: Protest, Public Transport, and the Politics of a Footboard." *City and Society* 32, no. 1: 157–181.

Kemmer, Laura. Forthcoming. *Bonding: Infrastructure, Affect, and the Emergence of Urban Collectivity.* Oxford: Berghahn Books.

Kemmer, Laura and AbdouMaliq Simone. 2021. "Standing by the Promise: Acts of Anticipation in Rio and Jakarta." *Environment and Planning D: Society and Space* 39, no. 4: 573–589.

Kemmer, Laura, Wladimir Sgibnev, Tonio Weicker, and Maxwell Woods. Forthcoming. "Spaces of Exposure: Re-thinking 'publicness' through public transport." *Cultural Geographies*

Klein, Kerwin Lee. 2000. "On the Emergence of Memory in Historical Discourse." *Representations* 69: 127–150.

Klein, Naomi. 2007. *The Shock Doctrine: The Rise of Disaster Capitalism.* Verso: New York.

Klein, Naomi. 2014. *This Changes Everything: Capitalism vs. The Climate.* New York: Simon and Schuster.

Knudson, Cory Austin. 2020. "Beyond the Periphery of the Skin: Silvia Federici." *Full Stop*, 28 May. https://www.full-stop.net/2020/05/28/reviews/cory-austin-knudson/beyond-the-periphery-of-the-skin-silvia-federici/

Krastev, Ivan and Stephen Holmes. 2019. *The Light that Failed: A Reckoning.* New York: Penguin.

Kremerman, Marco. 2004. "Distribución del ingreso en Chile: Una bomba de tiempo." *Análisis de Políticas Públicas* 29: 1–4.

La lista del pueblo. "Somos la lista del Pueblo." *Lalistadelpueblo.com.* https://www.lalistadelpueblo.cl/somos/

Laclau, Ernesto. 1990. *New Reflections on the Revolution of Our Time.* New York: Verso.

Lamadrid Alvarez, Silvia and Alexandra Benitt Navarrete. 2019. "Cronología del movimiento feminista en Chile 2006–2016." *Revista de Estudos Feministas* 27, no. 3.

Lambert, David. 2015. "Master-Horse-Slave: Mobility, Race and Power in the British West Indies, c. 1780–1838." *Slavery and Abolition* 36, no. 4: 618–641.

Larraín, Sara. 2012. "Human Rights and Market Rules in Chile's Water Conflicts: A Call for Structural Changes in Water Policy." *Environmental Justice* 5, no. 2: 82–88.

Larraín, Sara, Pamela Poo, and Programa Chile Sustentable (eds.). 2010. *Conflicto por el agua en Chile: Entre los Derechos Humanos y las Reglas del Mercado.* Santiago: Fundación Heinrich Böll.

LASTESIS. 2021a. *Antología Feminista.* Santiago: Debate.

LASTESIS. 2021b. *Quemar el miedo: un manifiesto.* Ciudad de México: Editorial Planeta.

LASTESIS. 2021c. "Hemos esperado tanto tiempo: Reflexiones en torno a la convención asamblea constituyente." *Le Monde Diplomatique*, August. https://www.lemondediplomatique.cl/2021/08/reflexiones-en-torno-a-la-convencion-asamblea-constituyente.html

Latorre, Guisela. 2017. "Indigenous Images of Democracy on City Streets: Native Representations in Contemporary Chilean Graffiti and Muralism." In *Street Art of Resistance*, edited by B. Wagoner, 87–112. New York: Palgrave.

Latorre, Guisela. 2019. *Democracy on the Wall: Street Art of the Post-Dictatorship Era in Chile.* Columbus: The Ohio State University Press.

Lazzara, Michael. 2006. *Chile in Transition: The Poetics and Politics of Memory.* Gainesville: University Press of Florida.

Lea, John. 2002. *Crime and Modernity: Continuities in Left Realist Criminology.* London: Sage.

Lemebel, Pedro. 1997. *Loco afán: Crónicas de sidario.* Santiago: LOM Ediciones.

Lemebel, Pedro. 2001. *La esquina es mi corazón.* Chile: Seix Barral.

Lemebel, Pedro. 2006. "Juan Dávila (La silicona del libertador)." 6 March. http://lemebel.blogspot.com/2006/03/juan-dvila-la-silicona-del-libertador.html

Lemebel, Pedro. 2010. *De perlas y cicatrices.* Santiago: Seix Barral, 2010.

Lemgruber, Luisa. 2019. "Nuevos Ecosistemas // Tsonami Festival." *Vimeo.* https://vimeo.com/user36909441

Lennon, John F. 2016. "Trains, Railroad Workers and Illegal Riders: The Subcultural World of Hobo Graffiti." In *The Routledge Handbook of Graffiti and Street Art*, edited by Jeffrey Ian Ross, 27–35. New York: Routledge.

Lewis, Vek. 2010. *Crossing Sex and Gender in Latin America.* New York: Palgrave MacMillan.

Li, Victor. 1992. "Policing the City: Modernism, Autonomy and Authority." *Criticism* 34, no. 2: 261–279.

Liguori, Guido. 2015a. "Conceptions of Subalternity in Gramsci." In *Antonio Gramsci*, edited by Mark McNally, 118–133. New York: Palgrave MacMillan.

Liguori, Guido. 2015b. *Gramsci's Pathways*, translated by David Broder. Boston, MA: Brill.

Lincoln, Bruce. 1999. *Theorizing Myth: Narrative Ideology and Scholarship*. Chicago: University of Chicago Press.

Linett, Cheril (dir.). 2019. "Comunicado." *Artishock*, 10 December. https://artishockrevista.com/2019/12/10/comunicado-yeguada-latinoamericana/

Linett, Cheril. 2020. "Proyecto Yeguada Latinoamericana." *Cuadernos de Teoría Social* 6, no. 12: 86–106.

Linett, Cheril, Jennifer Concha, and Lorna Remmele. 2018. "Banda de Guerra (manifiesto." *Vitrina Dystópica*, 7 February. https://dystopica.org/2018/02/07/yeguada-latinoamericana-banda-de-guerra-manifiesto/

Link, Felipe, Felipe Valenzuela, and Luis Fuentes. 2015. "Segregación, estructura y composición social del territorio metropolitano en Santiago de Chile: Complejidades metodológicas en el análisis de la diferenciación social en el espacio." *Revista de Geografía Norte Grande* 62: 151–168.

Loftus, Alex and Jessica Budds. 2016. "Neoliberalizing Water." In *The Handbook of Neoliberalism*, edited by Simon Springer, Kean Birch, and Julie MacLeavy, 503–513. New York: Routledge.

Loncon, Elisa. 2021. "Otra forma de ser plural: Hacia una democracia plurinacional." *Le monde diplomatique*, August, p. 6.

López y Rivas, Gilberto. 2011. "Autonomías indígenas, poder y transformaciones sociales en México." In *Pensar las autonomías: Alternativas de emancipación al capital y el Estado*, edited by Jóvenes en Resistencia Alternativa, 103–115. México D.F.: Bajo Tierra.

Lugones, María. 2010. "Toward a Decolonial Feminism." *Hypatia* 25, no. 4: 742–759.

Mack, Mehammed Amadeus. 2017. *Sexagon: Muslims, France and the Sexualization of National Culture*. New York: Fordham University Press.

Mamani, Ariel. 2018. "Arte callejero, militancia política y reinterpretación del pasado: La Brigada Ramona Parra y los murales a orillas del Mapocho, Chile 1971–72." *Revista Hablemos de Historia* 9.

Mansilla Quiñones, Pablo and Miguel Melin Pehuen. 2019. "Una lucha por territorio, una lucha en contra de la frontera." *NACLA*, 30 April. https://nacla.org/news/2019/05/02/una-lucha-por-territorio-una-lucha-en-contra-de-la-frontera

Marimán, Pablo, Sergio Caniuqueo, José Millalén, and Rodrigo Levil. 2006. "Introducción." In *¡Escucha, winka!: Cuatro ensayos de historia nacional mapuche y en epílogo sobre el futuro*, edited by Pablo Marimán, Sergio Caniuqueo, José Millalén, and Rodrigo Levil, 11–16. Santiago: LOM.

Marín, Gladys. 1999a. *Regreso a la esperanza. Derrota de la Operación Cóndor*. Santiago: Ediciones ICAL.

Marín, Gladys. 1999b. *Entrevista de Claudia Korol*. Santiago: Ediciones América Libre.

Marín, Gladys. 2002. *La vida es hoy*. Santiago: Salesiana.

Marquand, Robert. 2011. "At the Heart of the Arab Revolts: A Search for Dignity." *Christian Science Monitor*, 3 March. http://www.csmonitor.com/World/Middle-East/2011/0303/At-the-heart-of-the-Arab-revolts-a-search-for-dignity

Martin, James. 2002. "Performing Politics: Class, Ideology and Discourse in Marx's *Eighteenth Brumaire*." In *Marx's Eighteenth Brumaire: (Post)modern Interpretations*, edited by Mark Cowling and James Martin, 129–142. London: Pluto Press.

Marx, Karl. 2002. "The Eighteenth Brumaire of Louis Napoleon." In *Marx's Eighteenth Brumaire: (Post)modern Interpretations*, edited by Mark Cowling and James Martin, translated by Terrell Carver, 19–109. London: Pluto Press.

Marx, Karl and Frederick Engels. 1974. *The German Ideology, Part One*, edited by C.J. Arthur, translated by W. Lough, C. Dutt, C.P. Magill, and C.J. Arthur. London: Lawrence and Wishart.

Marx, Karl and Frederick Engels. 2010. *Manifesto of the Communist Party*, translated by Samuel Moore. Marxists Internet Archive. https://www.marxists.org/archive/marx/works/download/pdf/Manifesto.pdf

Masiello, Francine. 2001. *The Art of Transition: Latin American Culture and Neoliberal Crisis*. Durham, NC: Duke University Press.

Mbembe, Achille. 2003. "Necropolitics." Translated by Libby Meintjes. *Public Culture* 15, no. 1: 11–40.

McCann, Eamonn. 2018. *War and an Irish Town, 3rd Edition*. Chicago, IL: Haymarket Books.

McClure, Tess. 2021. "New Zealand to Cut 'Low-Skill' Immigration and Refocus on Wealthy." *The Guardian*, 17 May. https://www.theguardian.com/world/2021/may/17/new-zealand-to-cut-low-skill-immigration-and-refocus-on-wealthy

McCormick, John. 1998. "The Dilemmas of Dictatorship: Carl Schmitt and Constitutional Emergency Powers." In *Law as Politics: Carl Schmitt's Critique of Liberalism,* edited by David Dyzenhaus, 217–251. Durham, NC: Duke University Press.

McCutcheon, Russell. 2000. "Myth." *Guide to the Study of Religion*, edited by Willi Braun and Russell McCutcheon, 190–208. Sheffield: Continuum.

McMillan, Kate and Matthew Gibbons. 2020. "Immigration and Populism in the New Zealand 2017 Election." In *A Populist Exception?: The 2017 New Zealand General Election*, edited by Jack Vowles and Jennifer Curtin. Canberra: Australian National University Press, 2020.

McNally, Mark. 2015. "Introduction: The Life of a Reflective Revolutionary." In *Antonio Gramsci*, edited by Mark McNally, 1–8. New York: Palgrave MacMillan.

McNaughton, Colm. 2008. "A critique of John Holloway's *Change the World Without Taking Power*." *Capital and Class* 32, no. 2: 3–28.

McWhorter, Ladelle. 2010. "Enemies of the Species." In *Queer Ecologies*, edited by Catriona Mortimer-Sandilands and Bruce Erickson, 73–101. Bloomington: Indiana University Press.

Medel, Rodrigo and Nicolás Somma. 2016. "Demonstrations, Occupations or Roadblocks?: Exploring the Determinants of Protest Tactics in Chile." *Política y gobierno* 23, no. 1: 159–194.

Merrifield, Andy. 2013. *The Politics of the Encounter: Urban Theory and Protest Under Planetary Urbanization*. Athens: The University of Georgia Press.

Micropolis: Memoria histórica del transporte público de Chile. [Online]. http://www.micropolis.cl.

Mignolo, Walter. 2002. "The Zapatista's Theoretical Revolution: Its Historical, Ethical, and Political Consequences." *Review* 25, no. 3: 245–275.

Mignolo, Walter. 2005. "On Subalterns and Other Agencies." *Postcolonial Studies* 8, no. 4: 381–407.

Mignolo, Walter. 2009. "The Communal and the Decolonial." *Turbulence* 5. http://www.turbulence.org.uk/index.html@p=391.html

Mignolo, Walter. 2011. *The Darker Side of Western Modernity: Global Futures, Decolonial Options*. Durham, NC: Duke University Press.

Millalén Paillal, José. 2006. "La sociedad mapuche prehispánica: Kimün, arqueología y etnohistoria." In *¡Escucha, winka!: Cuatro ensayos de historia nacional mapuche y en epílogo sobre el futuro*, edited by Pablo Marimán, Sergio Caniuqueo, José Millalén, and Rodrigo Levil, 17–52. Santiago: LOM.

Mistral, Gabriela. 2013. *Poema de Chile*. Chile: Libros la Calabaza del Diablo.

Modonesi, Massimo. 2011. "El concepto de la autonomía en el marxismo contemporáneo." In *Pensar las autonomías: Alternativas de emancipación al capital y el Estado*, edited by Jóvenes en Resistencia Alternativa, 19–47. México D.F.: Bajo Tierra.

Mohanty, Chandra. 2003. *Feminism Without Borders: Decolonizing Theory, Practicing Solidarity*. Durham: Duke University Press.

Mondaca, Eduardo. 2013. "La re-existencia Mapuche frente al extractivismo forestal en un contexto de neoliberalismo armado." In *Ecología política del extractivismo en América Latina: casos de resistencia y justicia socioambiental*, edited by Gian Carlo Delgado Ramos, 19–42. Buenos Aires: CLACSO.

Montanelli, Marina. 2018. "El sujeto imprevisto de la huelga feminista." In *8M Constelación feminista: ¿Cuál es tu huelga? ¿Cuál es tu lucha?*, 85–106. Buenos Aires: Tinta Limón.

Montesinos, Elisa and Eduardo Gálvez. 2020. "Daniela Catrileo, escritora: 'Hay una mapuchización de la ciudad de Santiago, más que nosotros nos hayamos awinkado." *El Desconcierto*, 20 August. https://www.eldesconcierto.cl/tipos-moviles/2020/08/20/daniela-catrileo-escritora-hay-una-mapuchizacion-de-la-ciudad-de-santiago-mas-que-nosotros-nos-hayamos-awinkado.html

Moraga, Ana María (ed.). 2016. *Nueva constitución y pueblos indígenas*. Santiago: Pehuén.

Morandé, Felipe and Esteban Doña, Juan. 2007. "Transantiago: el remedio que está matando al paciente." *Trabajos de Investigación en Políticas Públicas* 5: 1–17.

Moreiras, Alberto. 2001. *The Exhaustion of Difference: The Politics of Latin American Cultural Studies*. Durham, NC: Duke University Press.

Moreiras, Alberto. 2016. *Marranismo e inscripción, o el abandono de la conciencia desdichada*. Madrid: Escolar y Mayo Editores.

Moreno Brid, Juan Carlos and René Antonio Hernández. 2004. "Chile: The Lonely Success Story." *ReVista: Harvard Review of Latin America*. https://revista.drclas.harvard.edu/book/chile-lonely-success-story

Moretti, Franco. 2000. "Conjectures on World Literature." *New Left Review* 1: 54–67.

Moretti, Franco. 2005. *Graphs, Maps, Trees: Abstract Models for a Literary History*. New York: Verso.

Mosca, Lorenzo. 2008. "A double-faced medium? The challenges and opportunities of the Internet for social movements." In *Net Working/Networking: Citizen Initiated Internet Politics*, edited by Tapio Häyhtiö and Jarmo Rinne, 41–73. Tampere: Tampere University Press.

Mouffe, Chantal. 1993. *The Return of the Political*. New York: Verso.

Mouffe, Chantal. 2005. *On the Political*. New York: Routledge.

Moulian, Tomás. 1997. *Chile actual: anatomía de un mito*. Santiago: LOM Ediciones.

Muñoz, Ariel, et al. 2020. "Water Crisis in Petorca Basic, Chile: The Combined Effects of a Mega-Drought and Water Management." *Water* 12: 1–17.

Munoz, Betilde. 1999. "WHERE ARE THE WOMEN? The Case of Chilean Women: 1973–1989." *International Social Science Review* 74, no. 1–2: 3–19.

Muñoz, Juan Carlos and Antonio Gschwender. 2008. "Transantiago: A tale of two cities." *Research in Transportation Economics* 22, no. 1: 45–53.

Muñoz Cortés, Víctor. 2013. *Sin dios ni patrones: Historia, diversidad y conflictos del anarquismo en la región chilena (1890–1990)*. Valparaíso: Mar y Tierra Ediciones.

Murcia, C, J Aronson, GH Karan, D Moreno-Mateosa, K Dixon, D Simberloff. 2014. "A Critique of the 'Novel Ecosystem' Concept." *Trends in Ecology & Evolution* 29: 548–553.

Nahuelpan Moreno, Héctor Javier and Jaime Antimil Caniupán. 2019. "Colonialismo republicano, violencia y subordinación racial mapuche en Chile durante el siglo XX." *HiSTOReLo: Revista de Historia Regional y Local* 11, no. 21: 213–247.

Namuncura, Domingo. 2016. "Pueblos indígenas, reformas constitucionales en América Latina y derechos indígenas en una nueva constitución." In *Nueva constitución y pueblos indígenas*, edited by Ana María Moraga, 19–63. Santiago: Pehuén.

Nancy, Jean-Luc. 1991. *The Inoperative Community*, translated by Peter Connor, Lisa Garbus, Michael Holland, and Simona Sawhney. Minneapolis: University of Minnesota Press.

Nancy, Jean-Luc and Philippe Lacoue-Labarthe. 1990. "The Nazi Myth." *Critical Inquiry* 16, no. 2: 291–312.

Navarro, Federico and Carlos Tromben. 2019. "'Estamos en guerra contra un enemigo poderoso, implacable': los discursos en Sebastián Piñera y la reveulta popular en Chile." *Literatura y lingüística* 40: 295–324.

Navarro, Marcelo. 2017. "Profesores, médicos y policías. El monstruo abyecto y la crisis del Régimen Biopolítico en *Patas de perro*, de Carlos Droguett." *Isla Flotante* 7.Neruda, Pablo. 1989. *Canto General*. Barcelona: Planeta.

Ness, Immanuel and Dario Azzellini (eds.). 2011a. *Ours to Master and to Own: Workers' Control from the Commune to the Present*. Chicago, IL: Haymarket Books.

Ness, Immanuel and Dario Azzellini. 2011b. "Introduction." In *Ours to Master and to Own: Workers' Control from the Commune to the Present*, edited by Immanuel Ness and Dario Azzellini, 1–7. Chicago, IL: Haymarket.

NODAL. 2019. "Chile: cómo funcionan los Cabildos Abiertos que buscan organizar el descontento social." *NODAL: Noticias de America Latina y el Caribe*, 1 November. https://www.nodal.am/2019/11/chile-como-funcionan-los-cabildos-abiertos-que-buscan-organizar-el-descontento-social/

Nora, Pierre. 1989. "Between Memory and History: Les Lieux de Mémoire." *Representations* 26: 7–24.

Nora, Pierre. 1996–1998. *Realms of Memory: Construction the French Past vol. 1–3*, edited by Pierre Nora and Lawrence D. Krtizman, translated by Arthur Goldhammer. New York: Columbia University Press.

North, Liisa and Timothy Clark (eds.). 2018. *Dominant Elites in Latin America: From Neo-Liberalism to the 'Pink Tide.'* New York: Palgrave MacMillan

Notes from Nowhere. 2003. *We Are Everywhere: The Irresistible Rise of Global Anticapitalism*. New York: Verso.

Nott, Josiah. 1854. *Types of Mankind*. Philadelphia, PA: Lippincott. https://archive.org/details/typesmankindore01pattgoog/

Núcleo de Sociología Contingente. 2020. *Informe resultados oficial: Encuesta Zona Cero*. https://nudesoc.cl/wp-content/uploads/2020/03/Informe-Resultados-OFICIAL.pdf

Ocejo, Richard and Stéphane Tonnelat. 2014. "Subway Diaries: How People Experience and Practice Riding the Train." *Ethnography* 15, no. 4: 493–515.
Olick, Jeffrey, Vered Vinitzky-Seroussi, and Daniel Levy (eds.). 2011. *Collective Memory Reader*. New York: Oxford University Press.
Olvarría-Gambi, Mauricio. 2020. "Policy Failure Revisited: Conceptual Implications from the Chilean Case of Transantiago." *Administration and Society* 52, no. 5: 690–717.
Opazo, Cristián. 2004. "*Mapocho*, de Nona Fernández: la inversión del romance nacional." *Revista Chilena de Literatura* 64: 29–45.
Oviedo, Enrique. 2007. "Modernización policial: el caso de Carabineros de Chile." *URVIO: Revista Latinoamericana de Estudios de Seguridad* 2: 71–84.
Páez-Sandoval, Claudia. 2015. "El proceso de trabajo de las brigadas muralistas de los '80: hacia una contribución del concepto de 'arte político' en Chile, Colectivo Muralista La Garrapata, Unidades Muralistas Camilo Torres, Brigada Pedro Mariqueo." *Contenido: Arte, Cultura y Ciencias Sociales* 5: 65–78.
Pairicán, Fernando. 2012. "Sembrando ideología: el *Aukiñ Wallmapu Ngulam* en la transición de Aylwin (1990–1994)." *SudHistoria* 4: 12–42.
Pairicán, Fernando. 2014. *Malón: La rebelión del movimiento mapuche*. Santiago: Pehuén.
Pairicán, Fernando. 2016. "Resquebrajando la república homogénea: la lucha por derechos civiles indígenas." In *Nueva constitución y pueblos indígenas*, edited by Ana María Moraga, 105–113. Santiago: Pehuén.
Pairicán, Fernando. 2019. "Algunos apuntes sobre *Awkan Epupillan Mew* de Antonio Calibán Catrileo." In *Awkan epupillan mew: dos espíritus en divergencia*, by Antonio Calibán Catrileo, 9–10. Santiago: Pehuen.
Pairicán, Fernando (ed.). 2020. *Wallmapu: Ensayos sobre plurnacionalidad y nueva constitución*. Santiago: Pehuén.
Pairicán, Fernando (ed.). 2021. *Küme Mongen, Suma Qamaña, Mo Ora Riva Riva: Ensayos y propuestas para una constitución plurinacional*. Santiago: Pehuén.
Palaversich, Diane. 2005. *De MacOndo a McOndo: Senderos de la postmodernidad latinoamericana*. Barcelona: Plaza y Valdés.
Palaversich, D. and Allatson, Paul. 2002. "The Wounded Body of Proletarian Homosexuality in Pedro Lemebel's Loco Afán." *Latin American Perspectives* 29: 99–118.
Palmer, Rodney. 2011. *Arte Callejero en Chile*. Santiago de Chile: Ocho Libros.
Palmer, Rodney. 2015. *Murallas del Cono Sur*. Santiago de Chile: Ocho Libros.
Palmer, Rodney. 2016. "The Battle for Public Space along the Mapocho River, Santiago de Chile, 1964–2014." In *Routledge Handbook for Graffiti and Street Art*, edited by Jeffrey Ian Ross, 258–269. New York: Routledge.
Panez-Pinto, Alexander, Rodrigo Faúndez-Vergara, and Camilo Mansilla-Quiñones. 2017. "Politización de la crisis hídrica en Chile: Análisis del conflicto por el agua en la provincia de Petorca." *Agua y Territorio* 10: 131–148.
Panotto, Nicolás. 2019. "Estado de excepción: sobre las revueltas en Chile." *Bordes: Revista de Política, Derecho, y Sociedad* 14: 187–190.
Parvelescu, Anca. 2017. "Reproduction and Queer Theory: Between Lee Edelman's *No Future* and J.M. Coetzee's *Slow Man*," *PMLA* 132, no. 1: 86–100.
Pastén, Agustín. 2009. ""Ni grobalizado ni glocalizado: ¿la metrópolis de Fuguet o la metrópolis de Lemebel?" *Revista Electrónica DU&P* 6, no. 17: 2–36.

Patton, Stacey. 2011. "Mules of the World." *Women's Review of Books*. https://www.wcwonline.org/WRB-Issues/the-mules-of-the-world

Patzi Paco, Félix. 2009. *Sistema Comunal: Una propuesta alternativa al sistema liberal*. Bolivia: Editorial Vicuña.

Peña, Carlos. 2019. "Trouble in Paradise: Chile's Inequality Explodes." *New York Times*, 26 October. https://www.nytimes.com/2019/10/25/opinion/25chile-pinera-crisis.html?searchResultPosition=8

Pendleton-Jullian, Ann M. 1996. *The Road That Is Not a Road and the Open City, Ritoque, Chile*. Cambridge: MIT Press.

Pereira, Andrés. 2010. "Teatralidad Mapuche Urbana (o Estética *Mapunky*): Tentativas Teoréticas sobre Estrategias Performativas de Identidad Cultural." *Aisthesis* 48: 257–277.

Pico, Giovanni and Giannozzo Manetti. 2017. "Dignity, Vile Bodies, and Nakedness." In *Dignity: A History*, edited by Remy Debes, 127–174. New York: Oxford University Press.

Pino-Ojeda, Walescka. 2006. "Gay Proletarian Memory: the Chronicles of Pedro Lemebel." *Continuum* 20, no. 3: 395–406.

Pisano, Margarita. 1996. *Un cierto desparpajo*. Santiago: Ediciones número crítico.

Pizarnik, Alejandra. 2016. *Prosa completa*. Barcelona: Lumen.

PNUD. 2017. *Desiguales: orígenes, cambios y desafíos de la brecha social en Chile*. Santiago: Uqbar Editores.

@Portadasonada. 2020. "Reopening of Baquedano Subway Station." *Instagram*, 4 May. https://www.instagram.com/p/B_w9GkolP5H/?utm_source=ig_web_copy_link

Pratt, Mary Louise. 1994. "Women, Literature, and National Brotherhood." *Nineteenth-Century Contexts* 18, no. 1: 27–47.

Price, Roger. 2002. "Louis-Napoleon Bonaparte: 'Hero' or 'Grotesque Mediocrity'?" In *Marx's Eighteenth Brumaire: (Post)modern Interpretations*, edited by Mark Cowling and James Martin, 145–162. London: Pluto Press.

Provoste, Yasna. 2016. "Pueblos indígenas y constitución: La palabra en las luchas del reconocimiento." In *Nueva constitución y pueblos indígenas*, edited by Ana María Moraga, 137–142. Santiago: Pehuén.

Puchner, Martin. 2005. *Poetry of the Revolution: Marx, Manifestos, and the Avant-Gardes*. Princeton: Princeton University Press.

PUTSPACE. 2019. *Public Transport as Public Space in European Cities: Narrating, Experiencing, Contesting*. https://putspace.eu/

Rabasa, José. 2001. "Beyond Representation? The Impossibility of the Local (Notes on Subaltern Studies in Light of a Rebellion in Tepoztlán, Morelos)." In *The Latin American Subaltern Studies Reader*, edited by Ileana Rodríguez, 191–210. Durham, NC: Duke University Press.

Rabasa, Magalí. 2019. *The Book in Movement: Autonomous Politics and the Lettered City Underground*. Pittsburgh: University of Pittsburgh Press.

Radil, Steven, Jaume Castan Pinos, and Thomas Ptak. 2021. "Borders Resurgent: Towards a Post-Covid-19 Global Border Regime?" *Space and Polity* 25, no. 1: 132–140.

Radstone, Susannah and Bill Schwarz (eds.). 2010. *Memory: Histories, Theories, Debates*. New York: Fordham University Press.

Rajaram, Prem. 2018. "Refugees as Surplus Population: Race, Migration and Capitalist Value Regimes." *New Political Economy* 23, no. 5: 627–639.

Rancière, Jacques. 2010. *Dissensus: On Politics and Aesthetics*, edited and translated by Steven Corcoran. New York: Continuum.

Rankine, Patrice. 2017. "Dignity in Homer and Classical Greece." In *Dignity: A History*, edited by Remy Debes, 19–46. New York: Oxford University Press.

Reiner, Robert. 1992. "Policing a Postmodern Society." *The Modern Law Review* 55, no. 6: 761–781.

Resumen TV. 2019. "Aquí se respira lucha." *YouTube*, 12 February. https://www.youtube.com/watch?v=O8yCjN1KDsM&fbclid=IwAR0lOfk8hdi2R1SgNhuc-JApXOPsZkRjUTJCOu9D3FAR_y4to-mMyYr_4_Hg.

Revolución Demócrata. 2019. "Forma tu cabildo: El pueblo de Chile decide sobre su futuro." *Revolución Demócrata*, 25 October. https://revoluciondemocratica.cl/forma-tu-cabildo-el-pueblo-de-chile-decide-sobre-su-futuro/

Reyes, Romina. 2019. "Organización directa desde los territorios: Cabildos autoconvocados." *The Clinic*, 30 October. https://www.theclinic.cl/2019/10/30/organizacion-directa-desde-los-territorios-cabildos-autoconvocados/

Richard, Nelly. 1994. *La insuburdinación de los signos: cambio político, transformaciones culturales y poéticas de la crisis*. Santiago de Chile: Editorial cuarto propio.

Richard, Nelly. 2021. *Zona de tumultos: Memoria, arte y feminism*. Buenos Aires: CLACSO.

Richner, Andrew and Abigail Gutmann-Gonzalez. 2019. "Chile Awakens." *Jacobin*, 26 October. https://www.jacobinmag.com/2019/10/chile-protests-sebastian-pinera-frente-amplio

Ricoeur, Paul. 2004. *Memory, History, Forgetting*, translated by Kathleen Blamey and David Pellauer. Chicago, IL: University of Chicago Press.

Riesco, Manuel. 2011. "Neoliberalism, a Counter-revolution in Chile." In *Neoliberalism's Fractured Showcase: Another Chile Is Possible*, edited by Ximena de la Barra, 13–45. Chicago, IL: Haymarket Books.

Rios Tobar, Marcela, Lorena Godoy Catalán, and Elizabeth Guerrero Caviedes. 2003. *¿Un nuevo silencio feminista?: La transformación de un movimiento social en el Chile posdictadura*. Santiago: Editorial Cuarto Propio.

Rivera Cusicanqui, Silvia. 1987. "El potencial epistemológico y teórico de la historia oral: de la lógica instrumental a la descolonización de la historia." *Temas Sociales* 11: 49–67.

Rivera Cusicanqui, Silvia. 2010a. *Violencias (re)encubiertas en Bolivia*. La Paz: Editorial Piedra Roja.

Rivera Cusicanqui, Silvia. 2010b. *Oprimidos pero no vencidos: Luchas del campesinado aymara y qhechwa 1900–1980*. La Paz: La mirada salvaje.

Rivera Cusicanqui, Silvia. 2012. "Mito, olvido y trauma colonial. Formas elementales de resistencia cultural en la región andina de Bolivia." *La Biblioteca: Mitológicas* 12: 308–401.

Rivera Cusicanqui, Silvia. 2018. *Un mundo ch'ixi es posible: Ensayos desde un presente en crisis*. Buenos Aires: Tinta Limón.

Robinson, Jason, Barbara Cosens, Sue Jackson, Kelsey Leonard, and Daniel McCool. 2018. "Indigenous Water Justice." *Lewis & Clark Law Review* 22: 841–921.

Rodríguez Ferrer, Rocío. 2011. "Sobre reescritura y vigencia de la picaresca en la narrative hispanoamericana: *Patas de perro* de Carlos Droguett." *Acta literaria* 43: 9–25.

Rojas, René. 2019. "We Don't Fuck Shit Up, We Don't Exist to Them." *Jacobin*, 22 October. https://www.jacobinmag.com/2019/10/chile-protests-public-transit-austerity-democracy

Rojas, Sergio. 2015. "Profunda superficie: memoria de lo cotidiano en la literatura chilena." *Revista chilena de literatura* 89: 231–256.

Rolston, Bill. 2011. "Hasta La Victoria!: Murals and Resistance in Santiago, Chile." *Identities: Global Studies in Culture and Power* 18: 113–137.

Rosen, Michael. 2012. *Dignity: Its History and Meaning.* Cambridge: Harvard University Press.

Ross, Kristin. 2015. *The Communal Luxury: The Political Imaginary of the Paris Commune.* Verso: New York.

Rossi, Federico. 2015. "Conceptualizing Strategy Making in a Historical and Collective Perspective." In *Social Movements Dynamics: New Perspectives on Theory and Research from Latin America,* edited by Federico Rossi and Marissa von Bülow, 15–41. New York: Routledge.

Routledge, Paul. 2017. *Space Invaders: Radical Geographies of Protest.* London: Pluto Press.

Rovira Sancho, Guiomar. 2016. *Activismo en red y multitudes conectadas: comunicación y acción en la era de internet.* Mexico City: Universidad Autónoma Metropolitana.

Rozas Bugueño, Joaquín and Antoine Maillet. 2019. "Entre marchas, plebiscitos e iniciativas de ley: innovación en el repertorio de estrategias del movimiento No Más AFP en Chile (2014–2018)." *Izquierdas* 48: 1–21

Rubenstein, Michael. 2010. *Public Works: Infrastructure, Irish Modernism, and the Postcolonial.* Notre Dame: University of Notre Dame Press.

Rubilar Barahona, Karla. 2019. "Una y otra vez en estación #Baquedano de @metrodesantiago y alrededores, jóvenes colaboran aseando los sectores en los que se ha destruido el mobiliario público que nos pertenece a todos. Sigamos sumando más manos para levantar la #RMdeTodos. Miren como quedó #ArribaStgo." *Twitter.* 25 October. https://mobile.twitter.com/KarlaEnAccion/status/1187739595376644098.

Ruiz, Agustín. 2006. "Margot Loyola y Violeta Parra: Convergencias y divergencias en el paradigma interpretativo de la Nueva Canción chilena." *Cátedra de Artes* 3: 41–58.

Ruiz Encina, Carlos and Camila Miranda Medina. 2016. "El neoliberalismo y su promesa incumplida de emancipación: bases del malestar y de la ola feminista." *Revista Anales* 14: 191–201.

Rumié Rojo, Sebastián Andrés. 2019. "Chicago Boys en Chile: neoliberalismo, saber experto y el auge de una nueva tecnocracia." *Revista Mexicana de Ciencias Políticas y Sociales* 64, no. 235: 139–164.

Sáez, Benjamín. 2019. "¿Es Chile un país de clase media?" *Fundación Sol,* 8 December. https://fundacionsol.cl/blog/presentaciones-4/post/es-chile-un-pais-de-clase-media-6668

Said, Edward. 1983. *The World, the Text, and the Critic.* Cambridge: Harvard University Press.

Salah, Trish. 2014. "Subaltern." *TSQ* 1, no. 1–2: 200–204.

Salas Zúñiga, Fabio. 2003. *La primavera terrestre: cartografías del rock chileno y la nueva canción chilena.* Santiago: Editorial Cuarto Propio.

Sandoval, Chela. 2000. *Methodology of the Oppressed.* Minneapolis: University of Minnesota Press.

Sanfuentes Vio, Manuel. 2019a. "Pareman," *Malecón,* no. 1.

Sanfuentes Vio, Manuel. 2019b. *Noli me tangere.* Santiago: Al Fragor.

Schild, Verónica. "Feminismo y neoliberalismo en América Latina." *Nueva Sociedad* 265: 32–49.

Schmitt, Carl. 2005. *Political Theology: Four Chapters on the Concept of Sovereignty*, translated by George Schwab. Chicago: University of Chicago Press.
Schmucki, Barbara. 2002. "On the Trams: Women, Men and Urban Transport in Germany." *Journal of Transport History* 23, no. 1: 60–72.
Schmucki, Barbara. 2012. "The Machine in the City: Public Appropriation of the Tramway in Britain and Germany, 1870–1915." *Journal of Urban History* 38, no. 6: 1060–1093.
Schroeder, Doris and Abol-Hassan Bani-Sadr. 2017. *Dignity in the 21st Century: Middle East and West*. New York: Springer Open.
Sciortino, Silvana. 2018. "Consideraciones sobre el movimiento amplio de mujeres a partir del 'ni una menos': continuidad histórica, diversidad y trayectorias locales." *Publicar* 16, no. 24: 27–47.
SCOOP. 2021. "Immigration System Reset—Setting the Scene." *Scoop: Parliament*, 17 May. https://www.scoop.co.nz/stories/PA2105/S00140/immigration-system-reset-setting-the-scene.htm
Segal, Robert. 2004. *Myth: A Very Short Introduction*. New York: Oxford University Press.
Sepúlveda, Bastien y Paulina Zúñiga. 2015. "Geografías indígenas urbanas: el caso mapuche en La Pintana, Santiago de Chile." *Revista de Geografía Norte Grande* 62: 127–149.
Serratos, Francisco. 2019. "Monstruosidad, animalidad, humanidad: hacia una condición posthumana en *Patas de perro* de Carlos Droguett." *Revista latinoamericana de estudios críticos animales* 5, no. 2: 35–57.
Shakespeare, William. 2003. *The Taming of the Shrew*, edited by Ann Thomson. New York: Cambridge University Press.
Shantz, Jeffrey. 2000. "A Post-Sorelian Theory of Social Movement Unity: Social Myth Reconfigured in the Work of Laclau and Mouffe." *Dialectical Anthropology* 25, no. 1: 89–108.
Sheller, Mimi. 2018. *Mobility Justice: The Politics of Movement in an Age of Extremes*. New York: Verso.
Silverblatt, Irene. 1987. *Moon, Sun, and Witches: Gender Ideologies and Class in Inca and Colonial Peru*. Princeton: Princeton University Press.
Simone, AbdouMaliq. 2016. *Always Something Else: Urban Asia and Africa As Experiment*. Basel: Basler Afrika Bibliographien.
Sitrin, Marina and Dario Azzellini. 2014. *They Can't Represent Us!: Reinventing Democracy from Greece to Occupy*. New York: Verso.
Skewes, Juan Carlos. 2005. "De invasor a deudor: el éxodo, desde los campamentos a las viviendas sociales en Chile." In *Los con techo: Un desafío para la política de vivienda social*, edited by Alfredo Rodríguez and Ana Sugranyes, 101–122. Santiago: Ediciones SUR.
Smith, Nicola. 2020. *Capitalism's Sexual History*. New York: Oxford.
Soja, Edward W. 1996. *Thirdspace: Journeys to Los Angeles and Other Real-and-Imagined Places*. Cambridge, MA: Blackwell.
Somma, Nicolás M. and Rodrigo Medel. 2017. "Shifting Relationships Between Social Movements and Institutional Politics." In *Social Movements in Chile: Organization, Trajectories and Political Consequences*, edited by Sofia Donoso and Marisa von Bülow, 29–62. New York: Palgrave.
Somma, Nicolás M., Matías Bargsted, Rodolfo Disi Pavlic, and Rodrigo M. Medel. 2021. "No Water in the Oasis: The Chilean Spring of 2019–2020." *Social Movement Studies* 20, no. 4: 495–502.

Sorel, Georges. 1999. *Reflections on Violence*, edited by Jeremy Jennings. New York: Cambridge University Press.

Sorell, Tom. 2015. "Human Rights and Hacktivism: The cases of Wikileaks and Anonymous." *Journal of Human Rights Practice* 7, no. 3: 391–410.

Spivak, Gayatri Chakravorty. 1999. *A Critique of Postcolonial Reason: Toward a History of the Vanishing Present*. Cambridge: Harvard University Press.

Spivak, Gayatri Chakravorty. 2003. *Death of a Discipline*. New York: Columbia University Press.

Spivak, Gayatri Chakravorty. 2005. "Scattered Speculations on the Subaltern and the Popular." *Postcolonial Studies* 8, no. 4: 475–486.

Spivak, Gayatri Charkavorty. 2006. "World Systems and the Creole." *Narrative* 14, no. 1: 102–112.

Spivak, Gayatri Chakravorty. 2012. *An Aesthetic Education in the Era of Globalization*. Cambridge: Harvard University Press.

Spivak, Gayatri Chakravorty. 2014. "Review of *Postcolonial theory and the specter of capital*." *Cambridge Review of International Affairs* 27, no. 1: 184–203.

Stern, Steve. 2010. *Reckoning with Pinochet: The Memory Question in Democratic Chile, 1989–2006*. Durham, NC: Duke University Press.

Stryker, Susan. 2006. "My Words to Victor Frankenstein above the Village of Chamounix: Performing Transgender Rage." In *Transgender Studies Reader*, edited by Susan Stryker and Stephen Whittle, 244–256. New York: Routledge.

Subercaseaux, Bernardo. 2007. "Literatura, nación y nacionalismo." *Revista chilena de literatura* 70: 5–37.

Sultana, Farhana. 2018. "Waterjustice: Why It Matters and How to Achieve It." *Water International* 43, no. 4: 483–493.

Sultana, Farhana and Alex Loftus (eds.). 2019. *Water Politics: Governance, Justice and the Right to Water*. New York: Routledge.

Swyngedouw, Erik. 1999. "Modernity and Hybridity: Nature, *Regeneracionismo*, and the Production of the Spanish Waterscape, 1890–1930." *Annals of the Association of American Geographers* 89, no. 3: 443–465.

Swyngedouw, Erik. 2015. *Liquid Power: Contested Hydro-Modernities in Twentieth-Century Spain*. Cambridge: MIT Press.

Taub, Amanda. 2019. "'Chile Woke Up': Dictatorship's Legacy of Inequality Triggers Mass Protests." *New York Times*, 18 November. https://www.nytimes.com/2019/11/03/world/americas/chile-protests.html

Taylor, Marcus. 2006. *From Pinochet to the 'Third Way': Neoliberalism and Social Transformation in Chile*. Ann Arbor, MI: Pluto Press.

Thayer, Luis Eduardo. 2021. "Nueva ley de migraciones: por qué precariza el trabajo y la residencia de los migrantes y puede promover más ingresos clandestinos." *CIPER*, 27 April. https://www.ciperchile.cl/2021/04/27/nueva-ley-de-migraciones-por-que-precariza-el-trabajo-y-la-residencia-de-los-migrantes-y-puede-promover-mas-ingresos-clandestinos/

Thomas, Peter D. 2015. "Gramsci's Marxism: The 'Philosophy of Praxis.'" In *Antonio Gramsci*, edited by Mark McNally, 97–117. New York: Palgrave MacMillan.

Thomas, Peter D. 2020. "After (post)hegemony." *Contemporary Political Theory* 20: 318–340.

Thwaites Rey, Mabel. 2011. "La autonomía: entre el mito y la potencia emancipadora." In *Pensar las autonomías: Alternativas de emancipación al capital y el Estado*, edited by Jóvenes en Resistencia Alternativa, 145–207. México D.F.: Bajo Tierra.

Tironi, Eugenio. 1990. *Autoritarismo, modernización y marginalidad: el caso de Chile 1973–1989*. Santiago de Chile: Ediciones SUR.

Tironi, Manuel and Javiera Barandiarán. 2015. "Neoliberalism as Political Technology: Expertise, Energy, and Democracy in Chile." In *Beyond Imported Magic: Essays on Science, Technology, and Society in Latin America*, edited by Eden Medina, Ivan da Costa Marques, and Christina Holmes, 305–329. Cambridge: MIT Press.

@tmbravo.scl. 2019. "Por un habitar digno!" *Instagram*, 30 October. https://www.instagram.com/p/B4QA8VPn3kv/?utm_source=ig_web_copy_link

Tombs, Robert. 1999. *The Paris Commune 1871*. New York: Longman.

Torres, Rodrigo. 2004. "Cantar la diferencia: Violeta Parra y la canción chilena." *Revista Musical Chilena* 58, no. 201: 53–73.

Tricot, Tito. 2013. *Autonomía: El movimiento Mapuche de resistencia*. Santiago: CEIBO.

Trotsky, Leon. 2008. *The History of the Russian Revolution*. Chicago, IL: Haymarket Books.

Trumper, Camilo D. 2016. *Ephemeral Histories: Public Art, Politics, and the Struggle for the Streets in Chile*. Berkeley: University of California Press.

Tsonami. "Encuentro Tsonami 2019: Prácticas sonoras en contextos de crisis, 02 al 07 de diciembre – Valparaíso." *Tsonami*. https://www.tsonami.cl/ver-archivo/2019/.

Tuck, Eve and K. Wayne Yang. 2012. "Decolonization Is Not a Metaphor." *Decolonization: Indigeneity, Education & Society* 1, no. 1: 1–40.

Tyner, James. 2012. *Space, Place, and Violence: Violence and the Embodied Geographies of Race, Sex, and Gender*. New York: Routledge.

Ukumari, Ozzo. "Statement." *Ozzo Ukumari*. https://www.ozzoukumari.com/about.

Ulin, Julieann. 2011. "'Famished Ghosts': Famine Memory in James Joyce's *Ulysses*." *Joyce Studies Annual*: 20–63.

Ureta, Cariola. 2020. *La Ciudad como Texto*. https://laciudadcomotexto.cl/.

Ureta, Sebastián. 2015. *Assembling Policy: Transantiago, Human Devices, and the Dream of a World-Class Society*. Cambridge: MIT Press.

Uribe Ugalde, Julio. 2018. "'Los pobres no son ni grises ni café': La marginalidad urbana como eje narrativo en las crónicas de Pedro Lemebel." *Revista Laboratorio* 19.

Urzúa Martínez, Sergio. 2019. "Aportes a una etnografía de los movimientos feministas: recursos expresivos en las marchas #Ni una menos y #8M en Santiago de Chile." *Antípoda: Revista de Antropología y Arqueología* 35: 115–124.

Valdés, Teresa. 2000. *De lo social a lo político: La acción de las mujeres latinoamericanas*. Santiago: LOM.

Valdivia Ortiz de Zárate, Verónica. 2003. *El Golpe después del Golpe: Leigh vs Pinochet, Chile, 1960–1980*. Santiago de Chile: LOM Ediciones.

Valenzuela Pérez, Leonardo. 2016. "Coppered Lives: The Chilean Sacrifice Zone of Quintero Bay." PhD dissertation. Sydney: University of Sydney.

Valenzuela Prado, Luis. 2018. "Formas residuales en la narrativa de Nona Fernández." *Mitologías hoy* 17: 181–197.

Vallejos Muñoz, Camilo. 2019. "Carabineros de Chile y la seguridad nacional: una mirada a las representaciones policiales del orden público durante la dictadura, 1973–1990." *Revista Historia y Justicia* 13.

Vamos hacia la vida (eds.). 2021. *Marx y Bakunin están de vuelta: Documentos y panfletos del entorno comunista radical sobre la revuelta de octubre de 2019 en la región chilena*. Santiago: Editorial Pensamiento y Batalla.

van der Linden, Marcel. 2004. "On Council Communism." *Historical Materialism* 12, no. 4: 27–50.

Villablanca Canales, Iván and Karen Oyola Espinoza. 2011. "El arte muralista como instrumento político: transformaciones coyunturales de Chile (1960–2000)." *Revista f@ro* 14.

Villarroel, María José. 2019. "Carabineros investigados por torturas en Peñalolén habrían 'crucificado' a detenidos." *Bíobío*, 24 October. https://www.biobiochile.cl/noticias/nacional/region-metropolitana/2019/10/24/carabineros-investigados-por-torturas-en-penalolen-maniatado-y-colgado-a-detenidos.shtml

Wallis, Victor. 2011. "Workers' Control and Revolution." In *Ours to Master and to Own: Workers' Control from the Commune to the Present*, edited by Immanuel Ness and Dario Azzellini, 10–31. Chicago, IL: Haymarket.

Walsh, Catherine and Walter Mignolo. 2018. *On Decoloniality: Concepts, Analytics, Praxis*. Durham, NC: Duke University Press.

Walters, Ian. 2007. "Policing, Modernity and Postmodernity." *Policing and Society* 17, no. 3: 257–278.

Warhol, Andy. 1975. *The Philosophy of Andy Warhol (From A to B and Back Again)*. New York: Harvest.

Weicker, Tonio. 2020. "Marshrutka (In)Formality in Southern Russian Cities and Its Role in Contentious Transport Policies." *Geoforum*, Advanced Online Publication.

White, Micah. n/d. "To the Barricades!: A Tactical History of Activism." https://www.micahmwhite.com/adbusters-articles/to-the-barricades

Wieviorka, Michel. 2009. *Violence: A New Approach*, translated by David Macey. New York: Sage.

Winn, Peter, Steve J. Stern, Federico Lorenz, and Aldo Marchesi. 2014. *No hay mañana sin ayer: Batallas por la memoria en el Cono Sur*. Santiago: LOM.

Wong, Pearly. 2018. "Water Justice vs. Western Development in Nepal." *EdgeEffects*, 18 October, https://edgeeffects.net/water-justice/.

Wood, Elisabeth Jean. 2001. "The Emotional Benefits of Insurgency in El Salvador." In *Passionate Politics: Emotions and Social Movements*, edited by Jeff Goodwin, James Jasper, and Francesca Polletta, 267–281. Chicago: The University of Chicago Press.

Woods, Clyde. 2017. *Development Drowned and Reborn: The Blues and Bourbon Restoration in Post-Katrina New Orleans*, edited by Jordan Camp and Laura Pulido. Athens: University of Georgia Press.

Woods, Maxwell. 2019. "Hospitality; or a Critique of Un/Inhabitability." *Cultural Politics* 15, no. 1: 202–222.

Woods, Maxwell. 2020a. "Communality, Decoloniality, and Antisemitism." *Cultural Dynamics* 32, no. 4: 241–260.

Woods, Maxwell. 2020b. *Politics of the Dunes: Poetry, Architecture, and Coloniality at the Open City*. New York: Berghahn Books, 2020.

Woods, Maxwell. 2021a. "Buried Dublin: Registering and Redeeming Urban History in James Joyce's *Ulysses*." *Literary Geographies* 7, no. 1: 23–39.

Woods, Maxwell. 2021b. "Punk Urbanism: Insurgency, Crisis, and Cultural Geography." *Social and Cultural Geography* 22, no. 5: 666–685.

Woods, Maxwell. 2021c. "Review of *The Book in Movement: Autonomous Politics and the Lettered City Underground* by Magalí Rabasa," *A contracorriente* 19, no. 1: 260–269.

Woods, Maxwell. Forthcoming a. "Modernity, Hegemony, and Public Transport as Public Space: A Reading of Alfred Döblin's *Berlin Alexanderplatz*." *Cultural Critique*.

Woods, Maxwell. Forthcoming b. "Narrative, the Chilean Social Explosion, and Affective Geography: On the Catharsis of the 'Artistic Candlelight Vigil' of Valparaíso." *Cultural Geographies*.

Woods, Peter. 2019. "Mapping Critical Anthropocene Discourses in Musical Artefacts: Whiteness, Absence, and the Intersecting '-Cenes' in Prurient's *The HIstory of Aids*." *Open Cultural Studies* 3: 541–552.

Wright, Erik Olin. 1985. *Classes*. New York: Verso.

Wright, Erik Olin. 1997. *Class Counts*. New York: Cambridge University Press.

Wright, Erik Olin. 2015. *Understanding Class*. New York: Verso.

Wu Ming (Roberto Bui). 2002. "Tute Bianche: The Practical Side of Myth-Making (in Catastrophic Times)." *Autonomedia*, 15 August. http://dev.autonomedia.org/node/1160

Wynter, Sylvia. 2003. "Unsettling the Coloniality of Being/Power/Truth/Freedom: Towards the Human, After Man, Its Overrepresentation—An Argument." *CR: The New Centennial Review* 3, no. 3: 257–337.

Yampara Huarachi, Simón. 2011. "Cosmovivencia Andina: Vivir y convivir en armonía integral—*Suma Qamaña*." *Revista de estudios bolivianos* 18: 1–22.

Zamorano Pérez, Pedro Emilio and Claudio Cortés López. 2007. "Muralismo en Chile: Texto y Contexto de su Discurso Estético." *Universum: Revista de Humanidades y Ciencias Sociales* 2, no. 22: 264–284.

Zibechi, Raúl. 2010. *Dispersing Power: Social Movements as Anti-State Forces*, translated by Ramor Ryan. Oakland: AK Press.

Zibechi, Raúl. 2012. *Territories in Resistance: A Cartography of Latin American Social Movements*, translated by Ramor Ryan. Oakland: AK Press.

Žižek, Slavoj. 2007. "Robespierre, or, the Divine Violence of Terror." In *Virtue and Terror* by Maximilien Robespierre, edited by Jean Ducange, vii–xxxix. New York: Verso.

Zurlatente Producciones. 2014. "Territorio Sagrado, por la defensa Kintuante, Documental." *YouTube*, 19 August. https://www.youtube.com/watch?v=C__IxvJW2Bs

Zwarteveen, Margreet and Rutgert Boelens. 2014. "Defining, Researching and Struggling for Water Justice: Some Conceptual Building Blocks for Research and Action." *Water International* 39, no. 2: 143–158.

Index